Focus on Urban and Regional Economics

FOCUS ON URBAN AND REGIONAL ECONOMICS

LAWRENCE YEE
EDITOR

Nova Science Publishers, Inc.
New York

For permission to use material from this book please contact us:
Telephone 631-231-7269; Fax 631-231-8175
Web Site: http://www.novapublishers.com

LIBRARY OF CONGRESS CATALOGING-IN-PUBLICATION DATA
Available upon request

ISBN 1-59454-740-8

Published by Nova Science Publishers, Inc. ✣ New York

As reported in Chapter 3, this study analyzes the effect of wages on the job tenure in the Finnish manufacturing industry using microeconomic data. The alternative channels out from a company to other industrial jobs or outside the industry are explicitly accounted for. Semi-parametric models of job tenure were estimated in a competing risk framework allowing for piece-wise linear hazards for the predefined intervals of job tenure. According to the results the relative wage of the worker is negatively related to the exit rate for the persons who leave industry. On average there are no remarkable wage gains at job changes within industry, but a closer analysis indicates that low-paid workers are able to gain higher wages whereas the high-wage workers incur wage decreases.

Chapter 4 focuses on specially-designed questionnaires, published in major newspapers of five Siberian cities - *Novosobirsk, Kasnoyarsk, Barnaul, Norilsk*, and *Lesosibirsk,* - were used to rank residential neighborhoods in these cities according to their attractiveness for residence and business activity. The newspaper polls were supplemented by expert surveys, designed to investigate differences between environmental priorities of ordinary city-dwellers and local decision-makers. The factors affecting the environmental assessments of city-residents and city-officials were then investigated using multivariate statistical techniques. As the study indicates, social evaluations of the urban physical environment (UPE) do not appear to reflect genuine qualities of this environment. Instead they reflect a range of local conditions, such as the average level of urban development achieved in a particular city; the variation of environmental conditions across individual neighborhoods, and the socio-demographic composition of the local population. It was also revealed that priorities and assessments of ordinary city residents and of city officials (e.g., urban planners, designers, and city-engineers) differ prominently. While the specialists tend to put an emphasis on the spatial qualities of the UPE (e.g., access to the city center, and access to recreational areas), ordinary city-dwellers pay more attention to functional issues, such as the availability of services and facilities in residential neighborhoods, structural conditions of the housing stock, etc. A system of evaluation indices (the *Index of Prestige*, the *Residents' Evaluation Index*, and the *Business Attractiveness Index*) is proposed for use during the period of transition from a planned to market-oriented economy, for both long-term physical planning and urban land appraisal.

Stability has been an essential topic in economic theory, particularly in the analysis of general equilibrium. A recent mainstream research area of urban and regional economics, called "New Economic Geography" (NEG), sets up a general equilibrium framework to explain how regional economic activities agglomerates or disperses. A dynamic approach plays an important role in describing the migration behavior of this study, and we need to know whether an equilibrium is stable. Since the literature of traditional stability research in the general equilibrium theory does not provide us enough results, Chapter 5 aims to fill this gap and summarize some recent stability results that might help us to enrich the study of NEG, for example, from two regions to multiple regions and from a specific dynamic system to a class of dynamic systems. Furthermore, the evolutionary stability of game theory and the potential function approach are investigated. Surprisingly, we show that they are closely related to the asymptotical stability.

Singapore's regionalization stratagem led to the establishment of industrial parks in China, India and several South-East Asian countries. The strategic intent behind these overseas projects was two-fold: exporting Singapore's competencies such as management know-how, technological capabilities and corrupt-free administration to regions where such

PREFACE

If all politics are local, then all economics are regional and local. Globalization, for all its mystery and so-called inevitability, has its foundations and bloodlines in urban and regional economics. The economic impacts of poverty, housing, transportation, education, and crime are included. This new book includes within its scope: multiplier and impact analysis, input-output models, growth theory, migration, urban and regional labor markets, urban and regional public policy, regional devolution, small firms policy, and foreign direct investment.

Chapter 1 analyzes the existing relationship between the armed conflict and the different manifestations of violence and criminal activity. For this purpose, a historical review on the internal conflicts and civil wars in Colombia since the XIX Century is presented, with emphasis on the Violence Period (1926-1962), followed by the analysis of the origin and evolution of the illegally armed groups in Colombia (FARC-EP, ELN and paramilitary groups). Likewise, the document describes the trends of violence and criminal activity indicators, and analyzes, by using spatial analysis techniques, the existing dynamics between conflict and violent crimes. Finally and using spatial econometric tools, the determinants of violent crimes (homicides, kidnapping, crimes against property and robbery) are shown. The results suggest that persistence and spatial diffusion are present in all crimes. The efficiency of justice, the narcotraffic, and, to a great extent, the activity of the illegally armed groups, are the variables that mostly explain violence (homicides). Furthermore, kidnapping is basically explained by the activity of those groups. Therefore, the results of this paper show that the conflict dynamics determines the *global* violence dynamics in the country and not only the deaths directly associated with the conflict.

Chapter 2 examines the process of provincial convergence that has taken place in Spain between 1985 and 2002. By taking labour productivity as its variable of analysis, the paper estimates the so-called "classical" models of convergence, concluding that, contrary to what has been suggested by previous work, convergence has not stagnated. After stressing the limitations of this type of approach, the paper attempts to overcome them, by, on the one hand, estimating the density function and the degree of internal mobility in the provincial productivity distribution; and on the other, by considering the influence of possible spatial effects on the aforementioned distribution. The conclusion arrived at is three-fold: we confirm the existence of provincial convergence of productivity; we reveal the low level of intradistributional mobility; and we do indeed find spatial effects, although they do not seem to be too relevant for the convergence process.

CONTENTS

positive factors were lacking and secondly, exploiting comparative advantages that each region had to offer. Chapter 6 revisits Singapore's flagship projects in Indonesia and India. Evidence from on-site surveys and interviews are presented. This chapter contends that progress in these privileged investment zones remains stymied by particular dependencies and challenges in the host environments.

Chapter 7 uses comparative statics to derive the effects of a median preserving increase in wage inequality on the welfare of households. It assumes that the commuting cost is a function of distance and income and that two income classes are living in a city. An increase in income of the wealthy living in the suburban area can either improve or hurt the welfare of the poor depending on the relative magnitudes of operating cost and time cost. If technology development, driving wage inequality, reduces time cost of commuting of the rich, it may increase the welfare of the poor.

In Chapter 8, agent-based models, an instance of the wider class of connectionist models, allow bottom-up simulations of organizations constituted by a large number of interacting parts. Thus, geographical clusters of competing or complementary firms constitute an obvious field of application. This contribution explains what agent-based models are, reviews applications in the field of industrial clusters and focuses on a simulator of infra- and inter-firm communications.

In: Focus on Urban and Regional Economics
Editor: Lawrence Yee, pp. 1-38
ISBN 1-59454-740-8

Chapter 1

THE RELATIONSHIP BETWEEN CONFLICT, HOMICIDAL VIOLENCE AND CRIME IN COLOMBIA: A SPATIAL ANALYSIS[1]

Fabio Sanchez* and Ana María Díaz#
*University of Los Andes, Bogotá, Colombia
#Universidad de Los Andes, Bogotá, Colombia

ABSTRACT

This document analyzes the existing relationship between the armed conflict and the different manifestations of violence and criminal activity. For this purpose, a historical review on the internal conflicts and civil wars in Colombia since the XIX Century is presented, with emphasis on the Violence Period (1926-1962), followed by the analysis of the origin and evolution of the illegally armed groups in Colombia (FARC-EP, ELN and paramilitary groups). Likewise, the document describes the trends of violence and criminal activity indicators, and analyzes, by using spatial analysis techniques, the existing dynamics between conflict and violent crimes. Finally and using spatial econometric tools, the determinants of violent crimes (homicides, kidnapping, crimes against property and robbery) are shown. The results suggest that persistence and spatial diffusion are present in all crimes. The efficiency of justice, the narcotraffic, and, to a great extent, the activity of the illegally armed groups, are the variables that mostly explain violence (homicides). Furthermore, kidnapping is basically explained by the activity of those groups. Therefore, the results of this paper show that the conflict dynamics determines the *global* violence dynamics in the country and not only the deaths directly associated with the conflict.

[1] We thank the dedicated work of Michael Formisano and Silvia Espinosa who did a great job with the editing of the text. The comments of the participants in the Yale seminar were very helpful particularly Norman Loayza's.

INTRODUCTION

The objective of this paper is to analyze the relationship that exists between armed conflict and the diverse demonstrations of violence and criminal activity. Nowadays, Colombia combines a group of factors that intertwine and feedback each other - drug trafficking, the rise of criminal activities such as kidnapping and extortion - which perpetuate conflict and make its solution very difficult. International comparisons show that Colombia's domestic conflict is the fourth longest conflict since 1950, not considering that it still persists (Echeverry et al, 2001). An investigation such as this one that contributes to understand the connections between conflict, violence and criminal activity can also help to design policies aim at decreasing the intensity of armed conflict and its consequences.

The present paper is divided into six sections. The first section briefly describes the history of the domestic conflicts and civil wars in Colombia since the 19th Century, emphasizing on the period of La Violencia (1946-1962). The second section presents the origins and consolidation of the FARC-EP and ELN guerrillas and illegal self-defense groups. The third section describes the evolution of the violence and criminal activity indicators, in particular homicide, kidnapping and drug trafficking. The fourth section analyzes the dynamics of the relationship between conflict and violent crime from a theoretical and empirical point of view. Spatial analysis techniques will be used, in particular to examine clusters and the diffusion dynamics of criminal activity. The fifth section uses spatial econometric tools to analyze the determinants of the different crimes on a municipal and a departmental level. The sixth and last section is dedicated to the conclusions.

CONFLICT IN COLOMBIA

Nineteenth Century Civil Wars

Colombian history is often perceived as a constant succession of national civil wars and regional and local conflicts[2]. Under this perception, the current conflict is not but the continuation of that long historical chain of violence, which started in 1839. Colombia's first civil war began few years after the definitive liberation from Spain in 1819 when those in favor of Simon Bolivar -El Libertador- attempted a *coup d'etat* against the *santanderistas* (those in favor of Francisco de Paula Santander, one of the leaders of Colombian Independence). This war, known in Colombian history as the War of the Supremes (*Guerra de los Supremos*) ended 1841. After the war, the Liberal and Conservative political parties were born and since then dominated national politics until the end of the 20th century.

The civil wars continued as wars between political parties. Thus, the 1851 armed confrontation originated in the disputes towards slave emancipation. After the Conservative's defeat, the Liberal party imposed a Federalist Constitution in 1963, that divides the country into 9 autonomous states. The experiment's results were disastrous since the struggle for regional hegemony brought about numerous armed confrontations within the states.

---

[2] The definition of civil war and the classification of the Colombian conflict has been debated by several authors. About this debate see Ramirez (2002), Pizarro (2002) and Posada (2001).

(Delpar,1994). Some historians (Alape, 1985) counted 54 civil wars in 20 years within the different sates, which included both confrontations between and within parties.[3]

From "La Violencia" to the Current Conflict

Between 1902 and 1948 the country experience relative calm. A slow process of industrial and financial modernization began, along with the initiation of agrarian movements in the 1920s and 1930s. The land tenants demanded better conditions in their contracts and the right to cultivate coffee in their land, whereas the Native Indians demanded the restitution of their communal land. Meanwhile, thousands of peasants in the frontier regions invaded the newly-formed land properties (*haciendas*) reclaiming the public land they had lost (LeGrand, 1986). On the other hand, the Liberal Party regained power in 1930 after almost half a century, whereas the Conservative Party recovered it in the 1940s. The assassination of the liberal leader Jorge Eliécer Gaitán in April 1948, represents the beginning of the period known as La Violencia.

As a consequence, and after accusing the Conservative government of the murder, Liberal and Communist followers hid in the mountains. In November 1949 the Communist Party proclaimed the self-defense of the population, which was the origin of peasant self-defense organizations. Popular discontent was on the rise with the violence, and the government of Ospina Perez (1946-1950) imposed the state of siege in November 1949. The military offensive against Liberal and Communist followers hidden in Colombia's mountains, along with the intensification of violence, forced the Liberal Party to abstain from participating in the elections and to promote a civil strike on November 27th. The armed resistance extended countrywide and small guerrilla groups were formed in the Eastern Plains (*Llanos Orientales*), Antioquia's south-west, the south of Córdoba and in Tolima. Without the participation of the Liberal Party in the elections, Laureano Gómez became president, continuing the repression against the liberal forces (Molina, 1973; Henderson, 1984).

In June 1953 a military *coup d'etat* took place, lead by the General Rojas Pinilla. This military government brought a momentary truce, after promising to cease confrontations and to grant amnesty to combatants that put down arms. Nevertheless, many refused to give up their guns, opening a new period of military actions, which reached momentum in 1955 with the declaration of the regions of Sumapaz and eastern Tolima as "regions of military operations".

The escalation of violence and the fall of the military regime lead to the birth of the *Frente Nacional* in 1958. The new political regime was based in the alternation of power between the Liberal and Conservative Parties. This Frente Nacional agreement stopped the armed confrontation, reducing violent deaths and bringing to an end the years of La Violencia. However, it failed to eradicate the guerrilla groups as a result the exclusion of all other political movements (like the Communist Party) from any possible electoral access to power.

---

[3] Out of these 54 wars, 14 were initiated by Liberals and against Conservatives, 2 by Conservatives and against Liberals, and 38 were between Liberals.

RISE AND CONSOLIDATION OF ILLEGAL ARMED GROUPS

Rise and Evolution of FARC

During the years following La Violencia, and after the signature of the agreements that established the *Frente Nacional*, the number of confrontations and of violent deaths decreased drastically, although they never reached the levels experienced before La Violencia. However, some guerrilla and peasant self-defense groups emerged in different regions like Marquetalia (in the south of Tolima), the region of Aríari in the Eastern Plains (*Llanos Orientales*) and Sumapaz in the center of the country. These regions began to be called "Independent Republics", and were strongly attacked by the army and air force in 1963, particularly in Marquetalia. After the retreat of the military, the peasant resistance groups reorganized under the name of Southern Block (*Bloque Sur*) with the support of the Communist Party. A year later they name themselves Revolutionary Armed Forces of Colombia (FARC)[4]. Thus, the peasant self-defense groups of southern Tolima, with support from the Communist Party, c called the First Guerrilla Conference in 1965. In this Conference, they set as their main objectives the subsistence of the movement and the definitive transformation into moving guerrillas.

The rise of the FARC peasant guerrilla groups in the 1960s has its remote origin in the so-called Peasant Leagues, which also experienced State repression. This explains in part the rise of guerrilla in those regions where the agrarian movement was stronger (Pizarro, 1991) and where the frustration because of the failure of the agrarian reform was stronger. In addition, political party confrontation motivated the fighting and rebellion of those groups. Thus, according to Pizarro (1991), the deepest roots of the conflict are not found in the fight for the land, but in the confrontation between political parties. According to Gilhodés (1985), the political factors that explain the years of La Violencia also explain the later formation of guerrilla groups. No short-term economic conditions, such as high inflation or poor economic performance could explain conflict. In contrast, structural causes such as the crisis of minifundio (small property of land) or unequal land distribution, did explain in part the mid-20th century violence. The FARC rose as an organization that, according to themselves, "gathered the tradition of Colombian agrarian struggle that started in the 1920s"[5].

The Second Guerrilla Conference was held on April 1966 in the region of the Duda River. In this meeting the FARC pledge to expand guerilla activities nationwide and to transform guerrilla operations from defensive to offensive. During this period the guerrilla maintained a dynamics of moderate expansion, creating new fronts very slowly. The FARC did not have a national presence in the 1970s; they rather grew by locating themselves in

---

[4] In a biographical book that reconstructs the life of the FARC-EP's current leader (Pedro Antonio Marín, otherwise known as Manuel Marulanda Vélez or Tirofijo), Alape (1989) states that the rise of the first peasant self-defense groups follows the Liberals' response (among them Pedro Antonio Marín) to Conservative violence. According to this author, at first these liberal self-defense groups did not consider themselves guerrilla groups, they had a political defensive character and only killed Conservatives in an urge for revenge. However, in the midst of party confrontations, an alliance between Liberal armed groups and Communists took place, which permeated Pedro Antonio Marín's political inclination. The Liberals rejected the proposal to overthrow the Conservative regime. Nonetheless, Marín did not agree with his party's position, and on the contrary, started its turning towards the Communist Party. In this context, the Communist guerrilla were born, with Pedro Antonio Marín as one of the leaders, having as the the main objective the overthrowing of the regime.

[5] FARC-EP: 30 Years of Struggle for Peace, Democracy and Sovereignty, in www.farc-ep.org

particular focal points. So they concentrated their actions in the departments of Tolima, Cauca, Meta, Huila, Caquetá, Cundinamarca, the Urabá region and the Mid-Magdalena River (*Magdalena Medio*). By 1978, the FARC had already 1000 men, adopting the strategy of front multiplication by breaking out existing fronts having the goal as a front by each department.

The 1980s marked an historical turn in the growth and consolidation of the FARC. In May 1982, after the Seventh Guerrilla Conference, this guerrilla group named itself the People's Army (FARC-EP), revisiting their modus operandi and objectives. Thus, they decide to urbanize the conflict and search for greater financing sources in the cities (by means of kidnapping and intimidation). They also decide to duplicate the number of men and fronts until reaching 40 fronts. They pledged to expand their influence area to the east covering the region between the Eastern Mountain Range and the Venezuelan border. They also established the Central Mountain Range as their strategic axis of expansion to the West. Graph 1 shows the progressive growth of the FARC over the time. The guerrilla group grew from 7 fronts and 850 men in 1978, to more than 16,000 men in 2000 distributed in 66 fronts.

Map 1. FARC Presence 1980 Map 2. FARC Presence 2000

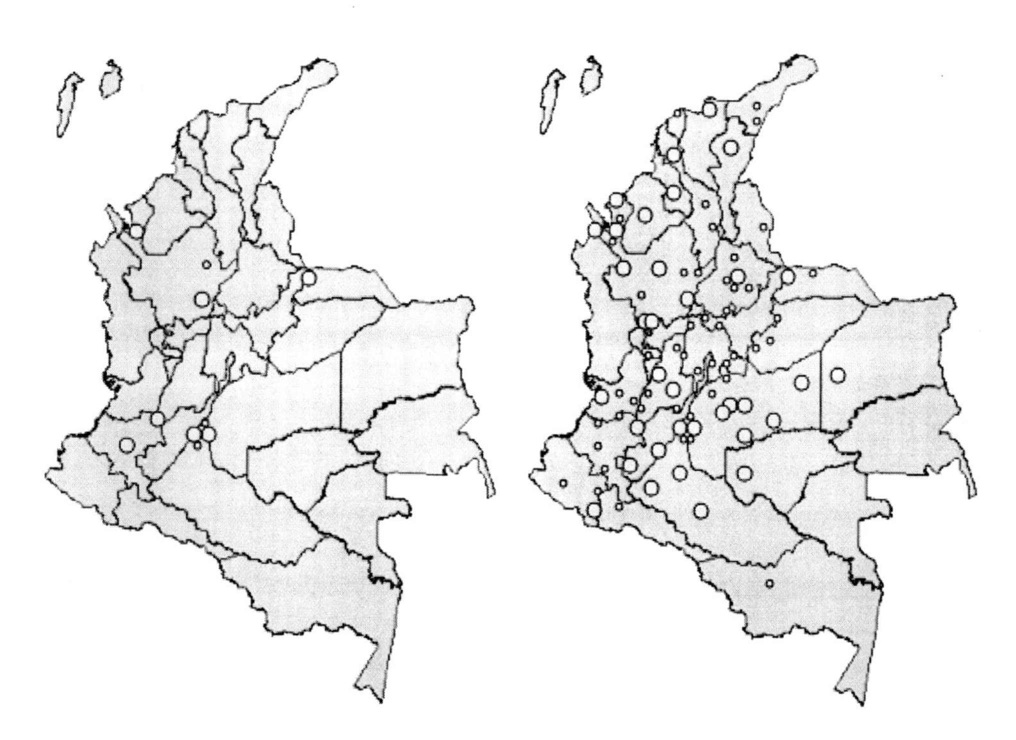

The geographic dynamics of FARC's o since the 1980s is depicted in maps 1 to 2. The number of fronts grew from10 in 5 regions of the country in 1980 (map 1), to more than 35 fronts in 1987 scattered throughout almost all of the country's departments. Nowadays, the FARC have 66 fronts, having presence even in urban zones like Bogotá, Medellín and Barrancabermeja (map 2).

Graph 1. Number of Men and Fronts – FARC

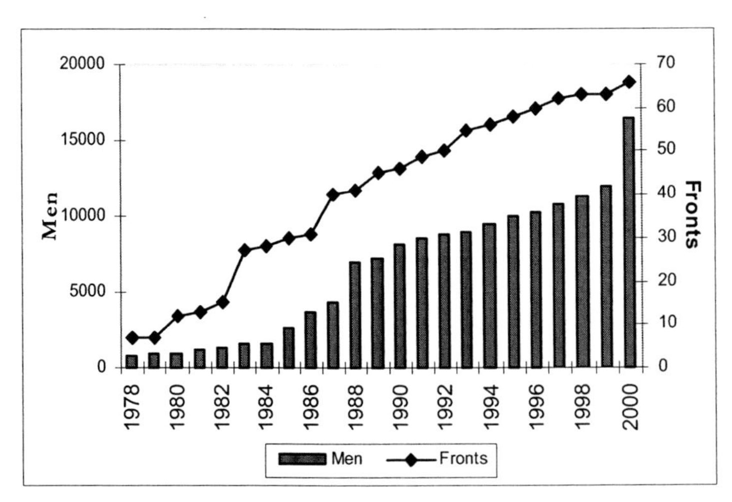

Source: National Department of Security

Although the FARC was born as peasant self-defense organization, under the guidance of the Communist Party fighting for the equal land ownership, its actions and expansion dynamics changed drastically since 1980s, due to the adoption of new military and economic strategies. The systematic failures of the several peace processes, and the successful sources of financing based on extortion, kidnapping and the alliance with drug trafficking cartels, are factors that have influenced the expansion and strengthening of the FARC[6]. (Gómez, 1991).

Rise and Evolution of the ELN

The National Liberation Army (ELN) was created under the influence of the Cuban revolution. The initial core was formed by 16 men who started to operate in 1962. In 1965 under the name of Army of National Liberation (ELN) they launched their first attack against the police post in the town of Simacota,. Their strategic objectives were the taking over of power by the poor, the defeat of the national oligarchy, of the Armed Forces that preserve it, and of North America's imperialist economic, political and military interests. (Medina, 2001). Their commitment towards armed confrontations granted this group a large amount of publicity in the idealistic, student and university circles. Thus by the end of 1965, 30 men were enrolled in the group[7].

Between 1966 and 1973 the ELN had its first military momentum: by 1973, 270 men were enrolled. However, the retaliation for the attack of the police post of Anorí, in

---

[6] The guerrilla's financial sources go far beyond the depredation of primary goods (Collier, 2001) and are based on illegal activities such as coca cultivation. In fact, the expansion dynamics of the FARC are determined by their search for sources of finance. (Bottía, 2002)

[7] Among its members it is found the priest Camilo Torres, who would perish during his first combat. Unexpectedly, his death would make him and his group very famous among leftist European circles. With this recognition, ELN started attacking towns, robbed the local bank (*Caja Agraria*) in order to finance its actions and defined their area of operations in Santander, Antioquia and southern Cesar.

Antioquia, almost lead it to its extinction[8]. Between 1974 and 1978 the number of ELN members decreases significantly, and the group went through a periods of internal crisis and slow recoveries, changing leaders constantly and revising their objectives. Since the 1980s, and after recovering from the disaster experienced in Anorí, this guerrilla group grew significantly in men and fronts, extending its actions to other regions of Colombia. Graph 2 shows the growth of the ELN throughout the 1980s and 1990s: while in 1984 there were 350 members, by 2000 the number of men had grown to 4500, distributed in 41 fronts. Along with the increase in number of fronts and men, the presence of the ELN extended to a vast part of the country[9] (maps 3 and 4). The recovery and expansion of the ELN are the result partly from a change in strategy (an imitation of the activities that had resulted successful for the FARC), and to the economic strengthening that followed the extortions carried out by the Domingo Laín front. These extortions were undertaken in the oil region of Sarare, against the foreign companies in charge of the construction of the Caño Limón-Coveñas pipe line (Offstein, 2002).

Map 3. ELN Presence 1983 **Map 4. ELN Presence 2000**

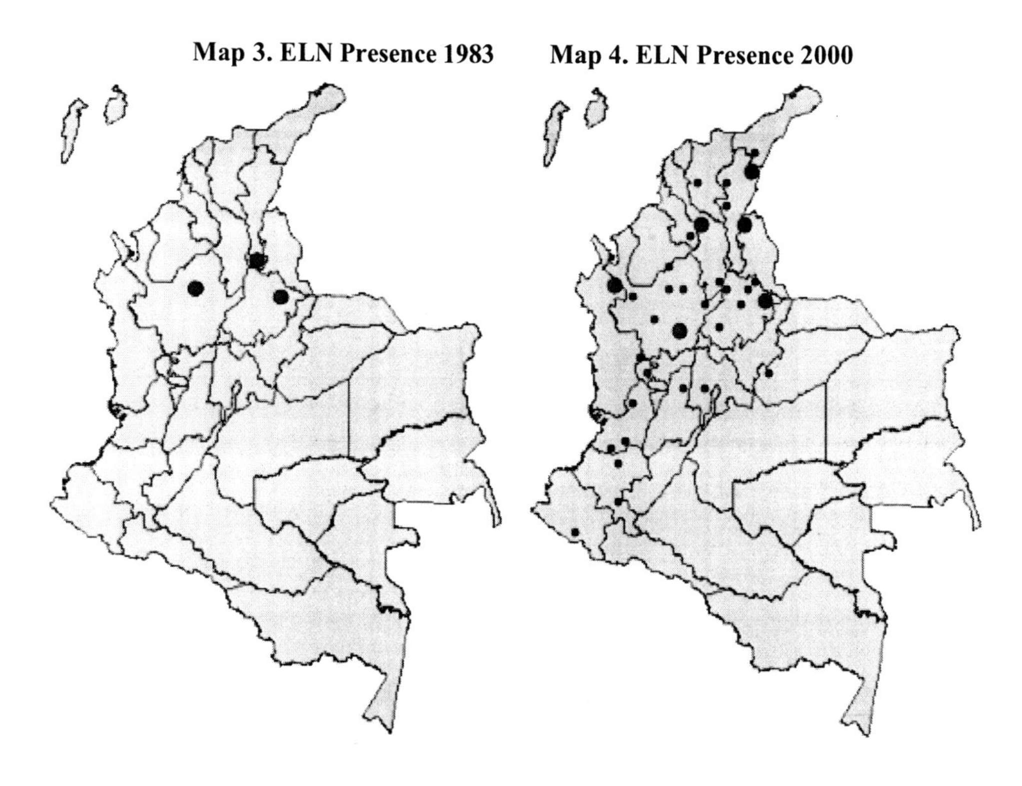

[8] As a result of this attack, 90 ELN men perished, triggering a widespread persecution against this group, which almost caused its definite defeat. ELN men decreased to 70 in only a year.

[9] In 1983 this guerrilla group had only 3 fronts that acted in Antioquia, Santander, the Mid-Magdalena River (*Magdalena Medio*), southern Cesar and in the Sarare region. From then on, the ELN's main zones of influence grew gradually from northern Cesar to the country's south-west. At the same time, this group began attacking urban areas.

Graph 2. Number of Men and Fronts – ELN

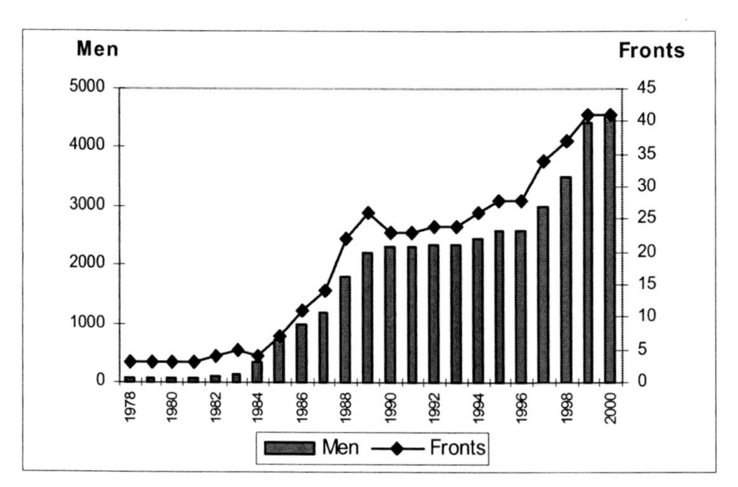

Source: National Department of Security

Nowadays, the ELN is the second largest guerrilla group in the country after the FARC, both in terms of enrolled men as of number of perpetrated attacks. Just like the FARC, the finances of the ELN depend on extortion, alliances with drug trafficking cartels and kidnapping. Despite having only half of the men that FARC has, the ELN is apparently responsible for the same amount of kidnappings and acts of sabotage. Furthermore, the actions of the ELN have extended in the cities as much as in the rural areas.

Illegal Self-Defense Groups (Paramilitary)

These armed groups were born in the 1980s during the government of Belisario Betancur, after the failure of the peace process.. At the beginning they were groups of self-defense sponsored and financed by land owners, making an army of not more than 1000 men. However, they quickly changed their defensive character to an offensive strategy, started attributing themselves certain functions of the State, fighting against the guerrilla and murdering leftist leaders and the so-called "friends of the guerrilla" (Cubides, 1999). After grouping themselves under a single leadership, the paramilitary start calling themselves United Self-defense of Colombia (AUC), they consolidated as a counterinsurgency organization and began to make presence in regions traditionally dominated by the guerrilla, such as Urabá in Antioquia, Cordoba to the north of the country, and Meta and Putumayo to the south of the country, aiming at creating one paramilitary front wherever there was a guerrilla front, both in rural and urban areas (Presidency, 2002)

In the 1990s these groups grew exponentially and nowadays have more than 10,000 men enrolled, scattered throughout almost all of the country (map 5) playing a fundamental role Colombian conflict. These groups have an intense activity in different regions, expelling or disputing territories with the guerrilla. They perpetrated selective murders and massacres in order to intimidate or to displace the population, undermining the guerrilla's support. They have become the armed group to which people attribute most of the massacres taking place in the country. Between 1997 and 2001 more than 70 massacres were attributed to these groups.

Map 5. Paramilitary Presence 2000

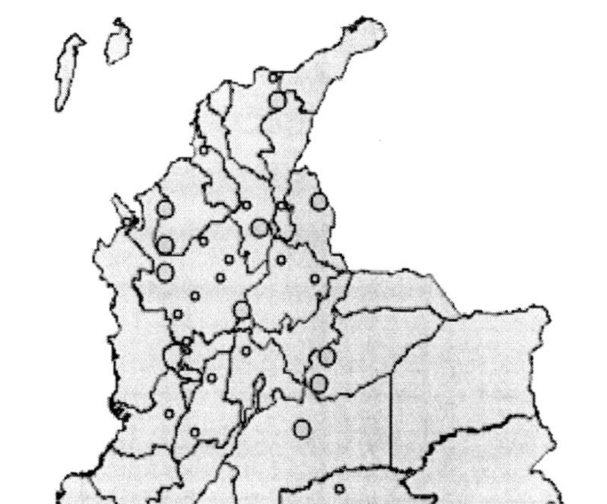

The AUC finance their activities with contributions from landowners, cattle dealers and even urban business people they protect. Just like guerrilla groups, they got most of their financing from drug traffickers by means of offering protection for illicit crops. There is recent evidence that the paramilitary also choose kidnapping as a source of finance.

HOMICIDAL VIOLENCE, CRIME AND DRUG TRAFFICKING IN COLOMBIA

Homicidal Violence

There is a high correlation between conflict in Colombia and the evolution of the homicide rate. The first period of intensification of homicidal violence takes place between 1950 and the beginnings of the 1960s, period that matches the beginning and end of La Violencia, as observed in graph 3. At that time, homicidal violence skyrocketed, growing from 10 homicides per hundred thousand inhabitants (hphti) in 1946 to 40 hphti in 1952. The military coup in 1953 managed to diminish the number of violent deaths only momentarily, but soon the homicide rate increased again, reaching a record level of 50 hphti in 1957. Soon after the *Frente Nacional* political agreement was signed, the homicide rate began to decrease slowly and progressively, reaching approximately 20 hphti by the end of the 1960s.

Graph 3. Homicide Rate (1945 -2000)

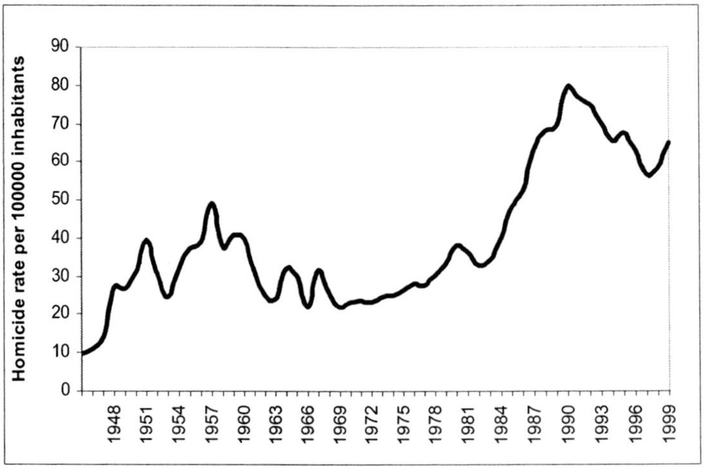

Source: National Department of Statistics and National Police

The years of relative low violence lasted very little. The second cycle of intense homicidal violence began in the 1980s and up to date still persists. At first, this increase in Colombia's homicide rate corresponded with the strong growth of cocaine trade and the consolidation of the so-called drug cartels, and later with the strengthening of the guerrilla groups. The homicide rate escalated, reaching its highest level of 81 hphti in 1992; from then on, the homicide rate decreased slightly although the trend was reverse in last years coinciding with the intensification of the armed conflict and the fortification of the guerrilla and paramilitary groups.

Although Colombia has had high homicide rates during long periods of time, these differ strongly between regions and throughout time. As table 1 shows, the 1990s is the period with the highest homicide rate in the last 50 years. On the other hand, the homicide rate differs in level between regions. While the Caribbean region has been historically characterized as having lower homicide rates than the rest of the country, the Andean and Eastern regions have had the highest homicide rates since the mid-1940s. Nevertheless, all regions share the same tendencies: the homicide rate decreases and increases simultaneously in all regions, although they have different levels.

The casualties related directly to the armed conflict are included in the homicide rate. According to the existing data, we can say that the deaths attributed to the illegal armed actors are in average 15% of the total reported homicides[10]. These numbers can be misleading for several reasons. First there can be homicides that are not included in such figures, but are committed by members of different illegal groups. Second, as we will show later on, these numbers hide the connections that exist between the deaths related to the conflict and the homicide rate. Base on the false separation between conflict and general violence some researchers have wrongly concluded that violence in Colombia is a "cultural problem".

[10] Of the total deaths related to the illegal armed actors for the period 1995-2000 (according to the Administrative Department of Security DAS), in average 26% are attributed to the FARC-EP, 13% to the ELN and 52% to the urban militias and illegal self-defense groups.

Table 1. Municipal Estimations of Homicides and Kidnappings

Dependent Variables:	Homicide Rate 1990-2000	Homicide Rate 1995-2000	Kidnapping Rate 1995-2000	Kidnapping Rate 1998-2000
Variables	Coefficient	Coefficient	Coefficient	Coefficient
Constant	20.61 ***	16.81 ***	-1.32 ***	-1.01 ***
Spatial and Temporal Dynamic				
Neighbor Homicide Rate	0.21 ***	0.12 ***		
One year Lagged Homicide Rate	0.68 ***	0.56 ***		
Neighbor one year lagged Homicide rate	-0.03 *	0.05 **		
Neighbor Kidnapping Rate			0.21 ***	0.29 ***
One year Lagged Kidnapping Rate			1.01 ***	0.92 ***
Neighbor one year lagged kidnapping rate			-0.09	-0.07
Armed Actors				
ELN presence	2.06 ***	2.64 ***	0.01	-0.09
Neighbor ELN presence	0.05	0.54	-0.01	-0.28
FARC presence	1.63 ***	4.13 ***	0.10 **	0.16 **
Neighbor FARC presence	2.65 ***	3.15 ***	0.10	-0.19
Delinquency presence		10.70 ***	0.01 *	0.01
Neighbor Delinquency presence		4.64	0.05 ***	0.08 ***
ELN and Delinquency Interaction		-1.21 *		
FARC and ELN Interaction		0.04		
FARC and Delinquency Interaction		-0.07 ***		
Justice and Drug Trafficking				
Justice efficiency	-14.35 ***	-15.56 ***		
Drug trafficking incomes	2.19 ***	4.29 ***	0.07	0.11
Neighbor drug trafficking incomes			0.12 **	0.08
Social				
Poverty rate	-0.11 ***	-0.15 ***	0.00 **	0.00
Neighbor poverty rate			0.01 ***	0.01 ***
Education coverage	-0.08	-0.08	0.02 *	0.01
Neighbor Education coverage			-0.01	-0.02
GINI of Property Value	1.50	5.09	0.27	0.00
Neighbors GINI of Property Value	-12.13 **	-6.96	-0.43 *	-0.50

Estimation Method:	Autoregressive ax. Likelihood pc	Autoregressi Likelihood	Autoregressiv Probit pool	Autoregressiv Probit pool
R^2	0.6017	0.4617		
No of observations	9850	5910		
log-likelihood	-89494.918	-52437.39	5910	2955
Sigma ^2			1.067	1.0787
No of 0			4125	2153
No of 1			1785	802

*** significant at 99%
** significant at 95%
* significant at 90%

Kidnapping

In addition to homicides, kidnapping is the main criminal activity related to Colombian conflict. At the end of the 1980s, this type of crime increases dramatically, and as depicted in graph 4, it has evolved pari passu with the intensity of conflict and the expansion of illegal armed groups, especially the guerrilla. At the beginning of the 1960s there were very few cases of kidnapping. However during the 1980s and 90s, this crime grew exponentially, increasing from 258 cases in 1985, to 3706 in 2000 and, making Colombia the country with the highest number of kidnappings in the world.

Graph 4. Kidnappings and Guerrilla Attacks

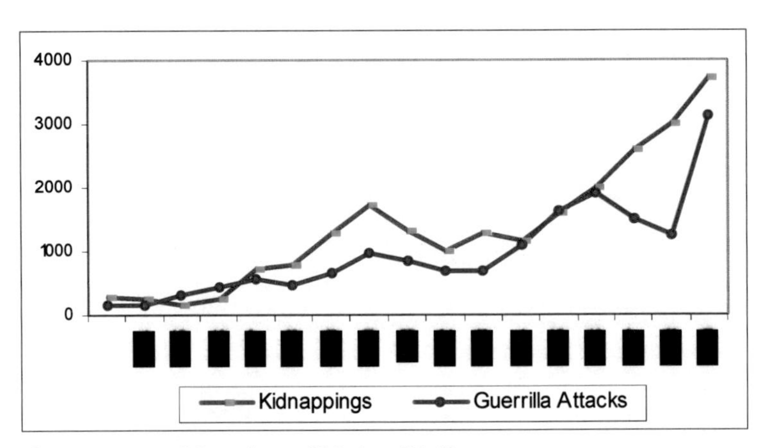

Source: National Department of Security and National Police

Kidnappings also expanded spatially as shown in maps 6 to 7. In 1985, only the least inhabited departments had no kidnappings. Moreover, no department had more than 35 kidnappings a year, and in most departments only few cases were registered every year (map 6). However, in 1990 the situation became critical: there were kidnappings in most of the country's departments, and there were some departments where kidnappings exceeded 100 per year. In the year 2000 kidnappings continued growing and only the three least inhabited departments registered had no, whereas other regions experienced almost one case per day (map 7).

Map 6. Kidnappings 1985 **Map 7. Kidnappings 2000**

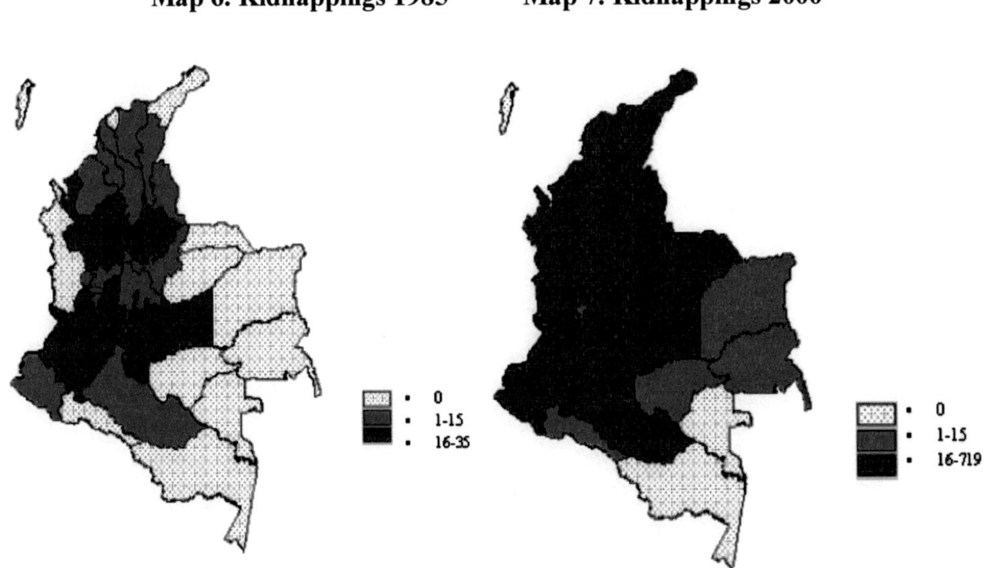

Kidnapping has grown along with conflict and has become one of the most important sources of finance for illegal groups, particularly for the guerrilla. The data from the organization *Pais Libre* for 1999-2000 indicate that between 1999 and 2000, 50% of kidnappings can be attributed to the FARC and the ELN guerrillas, showing an average of 1430 kidnappings per year between both guerrilla groups. During this same period, 6% of the cases were attributed to the paramilitary, and 10% to groups of common criminals.

Drug Trafficking

One of the factors that is most closely related to the persistence and intensification of Colombian conflict is drug trafficking. Still, the importance of drug trafficking within the conflict has not been the same throughout time. In the 1980s, Colombia became the most important cocaine exporter in the world, turning this activity into the main source of illegal income for the Medellín, Cali and Caribbean Coast cartels. Since drug trafficking was so profitable, and given the financial needs, the Colombian guerrilla began to charge taxes on illicit crops, cocaine laboratories located in the jungle and to intermediaries, in exchange for protection from governmental actions against this business, and the limitation of the size of the market (Thoumi, 2002; Molano, 1999). During the 1980s the cocaine business decreased steadily (Graph 5), although on average the income derived from such activity has been around US$ 2.0 billion dollars per year (Steiner, 1998; Rocha 2000). The illegal profits generated by this business resulted in violent fights within the different cartels, between the cartels and the guerrilla, and between the cartels and the Government, causing an important increase in the number of homicides during the 1980s. Additionally, the money from drug trafficking filtrated into governmental institutions, causing intimidation, corruption and a weakening of the judicial system, which in turn facilitated criminal activities (Sanchez and Nuñez, 2000; Gaviria, 2000).

Graph 5. Drug Trafficking Income as a Percentage of GDP

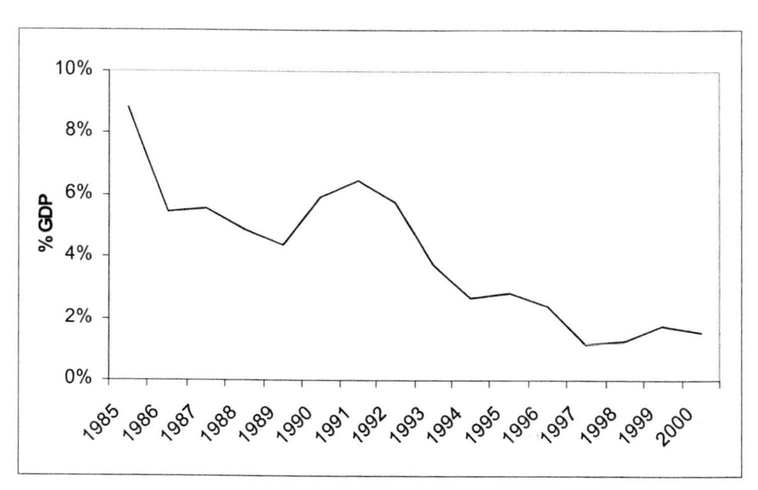

Source: Rocha(2000) and Steiner (1998).

Following the eradication of illegal crops carried out in Peru and Bolivia at the beginning of the 1990s, cocaine crops moved to Colombia, more precisely to the regions of frontier colonization in southern Colombia, mainly appearing in the territories controlled by the FARC. From then on, the number of hectares cultivated with cocaine grew from 20,000 in 1990 to 160,000 in 2000, while the number of laboratories that produced cocaine paste scattered in the jungle increased. The dismantling of the Medellín and Cali cartels in the first half of the 1990s, along with the boom of the Mexican cartels, allowed the FARC and the AUC to increase their importance in the business of drug trafficking. Graph 6 shows the correlation between the increase of the number of hectares cultivated with cocaine and the number of FARC men. Due to their increase in participation in the drug business, the guerrilla was able to take over additional resources that have allowed them to expand their military capacity, and therefore to intensify the Colombian conflict (Echandía, 1999; Rangel, 1999; Cubides, 1999). Nowadays, both the guerrilla and the AUC finance great part of their activity with resources provided by the drug business, and at the same time exchange drugs for armaments in the black market.

Graph 6. FARC Men and Cocaine Crops

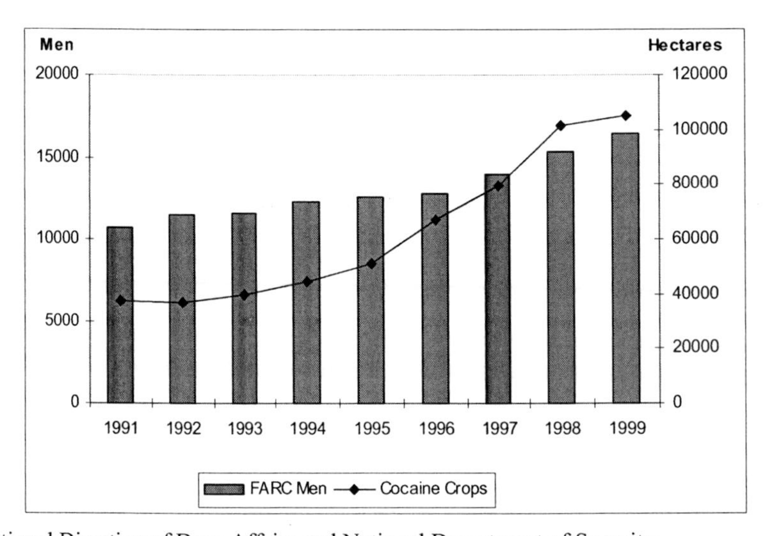

Source: National Direction of Drug Affairs and National Department of Security.

Property Crimes and Road Piracy

The evolution of property crimes has fluctuated around 250 per hundred thousand inhabitants; this rate fell from 300 to 200 between 1985 and 1993, increased to 290 in 1997 and once again decreased to 240 in 2000 (graph 7). This pattern is quite different from the one for homicides and kidnapping, which grew during the period under analysis. The department with the highest rate is Bogotá, where there has been an average of over 600 phti crimes during the same period, although the rate has decreased in the last years (Appendix 1). The departments with the lowest rates are isolated departments such as Putumayo, Vichada or Vaupés[11].

Graph 7. Property Crime Rate and Road Piracy Rate

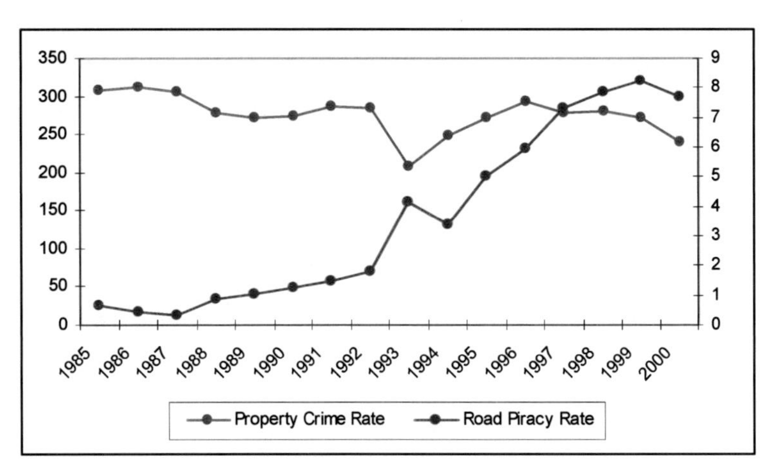

Source: National Police

Road piracy has increased significant in the last years. While in 1985 there were 206 cases, in 1993 there were 1557, and in 2000 this figure grew to 3260. Therefore, the rate per hundred thousand inhabitants increased from 0.64 in 1985 to 4.2 in 1993, and nearly 8.0 in 2000. The most important increases took place in Antioquia, Bogotá and Santander, although all departments experienced significant increases in the incidence of this crime (Appendix 1). There is not a very precise explanation of the causes of the increase in road piracy, although this crime is associated to guerrilla activities, mainly ELN and to groups of common criminals.

RELATIONSHIP BETWEEN CONFLICT AND HOMICIDAL VIOLENCE IN COLOMBIA

Conflict and Violence in the Literature

In the literature on Colombian conflict it is found a great deal of research and papers on the determinants of the origins of conflict, but few study its dynamics[12]. Particularly, the violence and the strategy of terror exerted by the illegal armed groups help us a great deal to understand the dynamics of Colombian conflict. It is through violence and terror that these illegal groups extend their control and establish their hegemony. To this respect, Kalyvas (2000) states that one of the most important and less studied aspects in the development of

---

[11] These departments may have some underreporting problems, especially in the information of property crimes.

[12] To this respect, Bejarano (1995) asks "would it not be a bit naive to try to find an explanation for the causes of conflict without even trying to understand what these illegal armed and unarmed actors involved in the conflict are really searching for?"

civil wars is the violence oriented towards the civil population[13]. However, Kalyvas (2000) insists that this type of violence, "is not an aim in itself, it is an instrument, a resource, not the final product". It is the mechanism that allows the armed participants of the conflict to obtain their objectives, may this be territorial control or the development of illegal activities. Therefore, the support or control of population is a matter of survival, and it is through violence how such control o support is gained. For the Colombian case, Salazar and Castillo (2001) claim that both terror and violence have been applied upon the civil population methodically. The authors argue that illegal armed groups uses a terror strategy, to intimidate the population, in order to gain the people support and loyalty (toward whoever exerts this intimidation). Consequently, Salazar and Castillo (2001) conclude that there exist an apparent relation between the presence of drug trafficking, the guerrilla, the paramilitary and the conflict in general, with homicidal violence in Colombia.

Other analysts have pointed out the geographical relationship between homicide rates, the influence of armed groups and drug trafficking activities (Rubio, 1998, Echandía, 2000; Sanchez and Nuñez, 2000). According to Rubio (1998), in 1995, in 9 of the 10 regions with higher homicide rates there was active presence of guerrilla groups, compared to a national presence of 54%. In 7 of these 10 regions drug trafficking activities had been detected, compared to a national level of 23%; in the same manner, paramilitary presence exceeds the national average. The effect of the conflict on homicidal violence is so large that almost all homicides in Colombia in 1995 (93%) occurred in municipalities where presence of at least one of the three illegal armed groups had been detected. The municipalities without presence of illegal actors account for 36% of the country's municipalities, comprised only 14.9% of the population, and their homicide rate (39 hphti) was much lower than the national average, although it was still high for international standards.

The transmission mechanisms of this relationship occur through the terror and intimidation generated by these groups. The absence of the coercion function of the State in turn allows the spontaneous development of parallel organizations that try to replace it by means of force and terror provoking a blast of violent crime. Such increase reproduces itself as a result of its own diffusion and spillover dynamics. Such dynamics will be analyzed below. The drug trafficking activities and the dispute for illegal profits are factors of additional violence. As the data show that there is a geographic correspondence between the presence of illegal armed groups, high homicide rates and the existence of illegal crops (Thoumi, 2002).

Another factor of that has affected the expansion of violence is the change in strategy of illegal armed groups. These groups used to play a central role in the regions of frontier colonization, distant from the main cities and lacking governmental presence. Now those groups have made presence in inhabited regions and urban areas, given their potential for extortion and depredation. This geographical shift of Colombian conflict coincides with the shift in the intensity of homicidal violence, which has moved from the Eastern region of the country (regions of colonization) towards the Andean region (region of urban metropolitan areas) and towards cocaine cultivation regions in the south of the country. The eastern

[13] In fact, in most civil wars the population becomes the deliberate target of violence, mainly with the objective of gaining, through intimidation, support or at least indifference. Kalyvas (2000) states that unlike in conventional wars, in civil wars there is an interaction between not only two (or more) armed actors, but also with the civil population. In civil wars, there are few military confrontations between armed actors but many military and non-military actions against civilians.

departments that had the highest rates of violent in 1985 with homicide rates of more than 65 hphti (map 8) became the second most violent in the 1990s having a homicide rate inferior to 35 hphti in 2000 (map 9). In contrast, the departments of the Andean region register the highest homicide rates nowadays. In fact, violence in departments such as Antioquia has risen considerably due to the expansion of the conflict but now it is located in rural areas. Antioquia had extremely high rates of homicide mostly explained by metropolitan Medellin where drug trafficking was a very important activity.

Map 8. Homicide Rate 1985 **Map 9. Homicide Rate 2000**

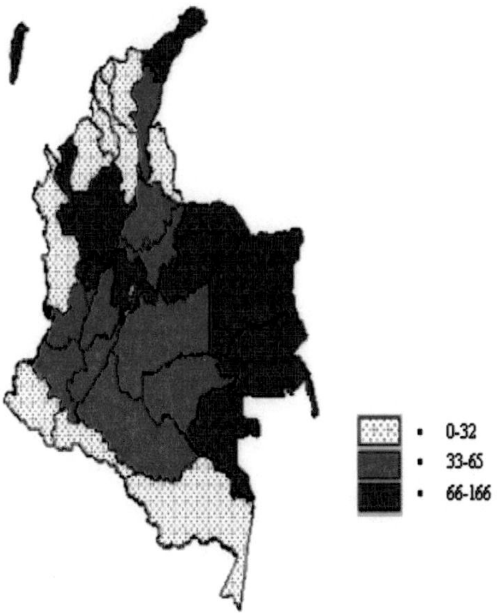

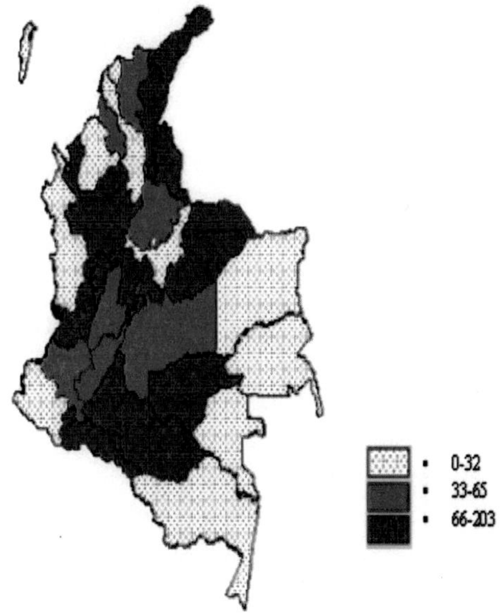

Diffusion of Conflict to Homicidal Violence

The dynamics of expansion and diffusion is one of the most important aspects to take into account when studying phenomena such as the guerrilla, its activities or the homicide rates. Spatial analysis techniques can be used to determine the patterns of diffusion of criminal activities and of illegal armed groups (Cohen and Tita 1999). Thus, higher violence or greater presence of illegal groups in certain spatial units (regions, municipalities) spreads to neighboring units, creating an increase and expansion of violence. Therefore, by means of contagion, a space unit can spread violence to neighboring space units; even though the latter may or mat not have factors that create violence. In the case of homicides, it is not probable that the contagious diffusion of violence involves a single criminal acting by himself. On the contrary, this type of diffusion tends to involve criminal organizations that perpetrate or instigate homicides following the objectives of the organization, which in turn generates more homicides. For example, an illegal organization competing for the control of a certain territory can trigger attacks and retaliations from other organizations fighting for the same territory. The attacks and retaliations can involve non-participant individuals or towns, causing a generalized increase of violence.

The patterns of contagious diffusion of violence and criminal activity can be divided into two groups: a) *relocation*, when violence moves from one region to another. This means that there is a shift of criminal activities because of an increase in law enforcement presence or because illegal profits have been exhausted; and b) *diffusion*, when violence and criminal activities spread out from the center towards neighboring spatial units, but the center continues having high crime rates. Another mechanism of criminal activity dissemination is so-called *hierarchic diffusion*, which consists of criminal activity dissemination that does not require spatial contact, and takes place through imitation or innovation (Cohen and Tita, 1999). For example, groups of common criminals learn and imitate the guerrilla's or paramilitary's criminal techniques (homicide, kidnapping, extortion, etc), leading to an increase in the crime rate of other regions.

Spatial Indicators of Conflict and Homicidal Violence

This section presents a group of indicators that show the relationship between conflict (measured using an index of presence of illegal armed groups) and violence and crime indicators. Graphs 8 to 11 show the relationship between standardized local homicide rate[14] with homicide rates in neighboring municipalities, and between illegal armed group presence in neighboring municipalities and local and neighboring homicide rates. The correlation between local and neighbor indicators shows the different patterns of space association between the units that are being studied. Graph 8 shows the existing relationship between the local homicide rate and the average homicide rate of neighboring municipalities[15]. Each point is located on the Euclidian space (L,N), where L denotes the local standardized homicide rate and N the standardized homicide rate of the neighbors. Each point in the space is either low (L) or high (H) relative to the other local or neighbor observations. Consequently, the space is formed by four quadrants with points where both local and neighbor homicide rates are high (quadrant H,H), one of them is high and the other one low (H,L), low and high (L,H) or low and low (L,L). Graph 8 shows that the spatial relationship for homicide rates between local and neighboring municipalities is positive with a correlation coefficient of 0.5. In addition, the points located in the (H,H) quadrant, outside the circle denoting two standard deviations, are groups of municipalities with very high homicide rates. These are groups or clusters of municipalities, called "hot spots."

Graphs 9 to 11 show the relationship between groups neighboring municipalities with illegal armed actor presence, and homicide rates in groups neighboring municipalities. The graphs clearly show that a grouping pattern between these two variables exists. Hence, groups of municipalities with low homicide rates coincide spatially with municipalities with low presence of illegal armed actors, while groups with high homicide rates coincide with a high presence of illegal groups. The correlation is positive and significant for the FARC (0.18), the ELN (0.29) and the groups of common criminals (0.30) (this includes the Paramilitary). In addition, in all cases we detect groups of municipalities that are "hot spots," i.e. high presence

---

[14] Standardized means (Xi-Xmean)/STD, where Xi is the value of observation i of variable X, Xmean is the mean value and STD is the standard deviation.

[15] The average neighbor homicide rate is constructed as the sum of the other municipalities' homicide rate, weighed by the inverse of the distance between the local municipality and the other municipalities.

of illegal armed groups with groups of municipalities with high homicide rates. Appendix 2 shows other groups of relationships between neighboring and local municipalities. Thus, the relationship between the presence of illegal armed groups in neighboring municipalities and the homicide rate in the local municipality is also positive. This means that regional presence of illegal armed groups is associated with local violence, even if there are no factors that generate violence in the local municipality.

Graph 8. Local and Neighbor Homicide Rate

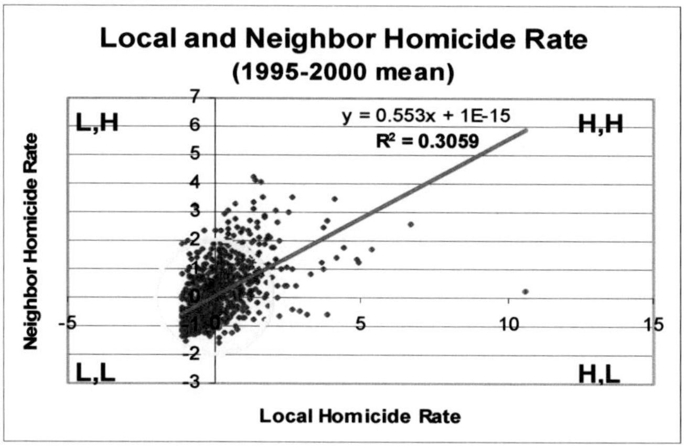

Local and Neighbor Homicide Rate
(1995-2000 mean)
y = 0.553x + 1E-15
$R^2 = 0.3059$
L,H
H,H
L,L
H,L
Neighbor Homicide Rate
Local Homicide Rate

Source: Calculations of the Authors

Graph 9. Neighbor Farc vs. Neighbor Homicide Rate

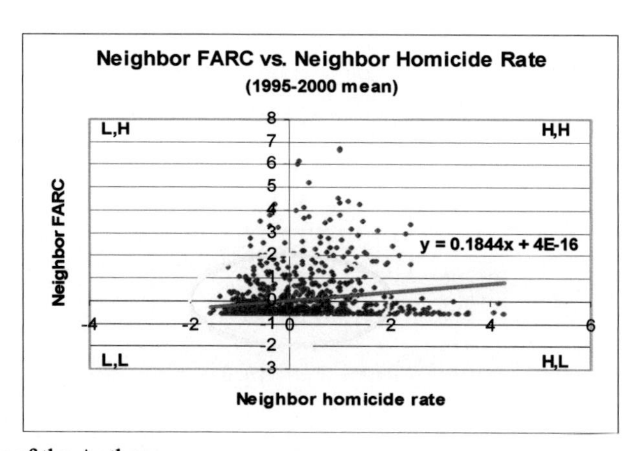

Source: Calculations of the Authors

Graph 10. Neighbor ELN vs. Neighbor Homicide Rate

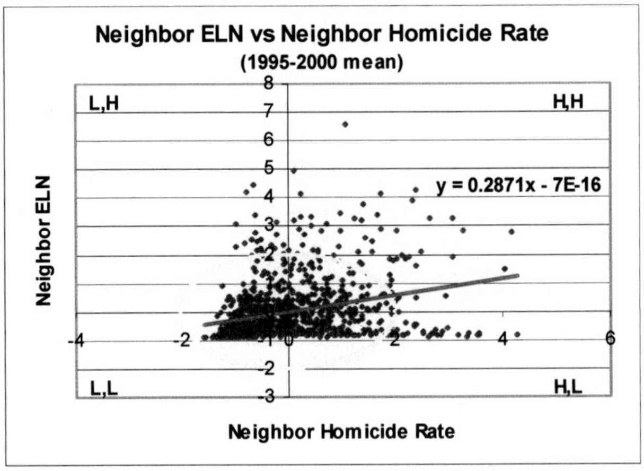

Source: Calculations of the Authors

Graph 11. Neighbor Common Criminals – Neighbor Homicide Rate

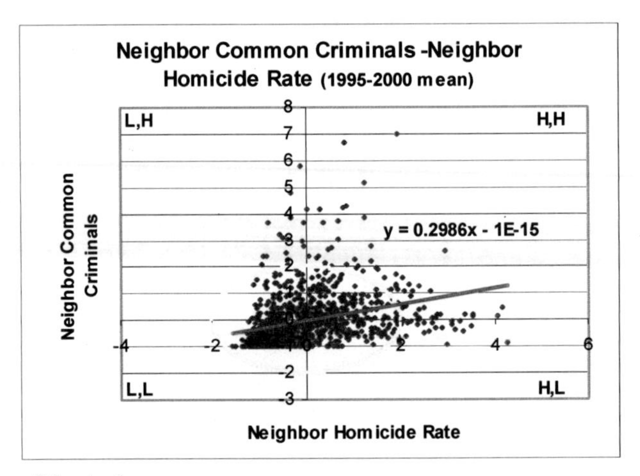

Source: Calculations of the Authors

The Spatial Dynamics of Conflict and Homicidal Violence

In the previous section we analyzed the behavior of the local-neighbor combinations and used it as a tool to identify clusters of violent crime (homicides) and clusters of presence of illegal armed groups and violence. However, in order to determine the diffusion *dynamics* we must analyze how the local-neighbor combinations of violent crime and local-neighbor combinations of conflict and violent crime, change throughout time. The dissemination can take place between neighboring municipalities or between municipalities that are not close geographically to one another.

There are several combinations of changes throughout time. For example, the share of local municipalities with high homicide rates can increase. This can happen simultaneously both with an increase or a decrease of the homicide rate of the neighbors. The same occurs with the relationship between the changes in local or neighbor homicide rates and changes in the presence of illegal armed groups in the neighbors. There are two types of contagious diffusion (graph 12): a) expansion between neighbors, when the violence rate is low in the local municipality and high in the neighbor, and changes to high in the local municipality and to high in the neighbor, i.e. a group of municipalities changes from quadrant (L,H) to quadrant (H,H). The opposite case can also occur, where a groups of municipalities can change from quadrant (H,L) to quadrant (L,L); b) relocation between neighbors, when the violence rate changes from low in the local municipality and high in the neighbor, to high in the local municipality and low in the neighbors, i.e. a group of municipalities changes from quadrant (L,H) to quadrant (H,L). The opposite case is also possible, in which a group of municipalities changes from quadrant (H,L) to quadrant (L,H).

Graph 12. Contagious Diffusion Patterns of Changes

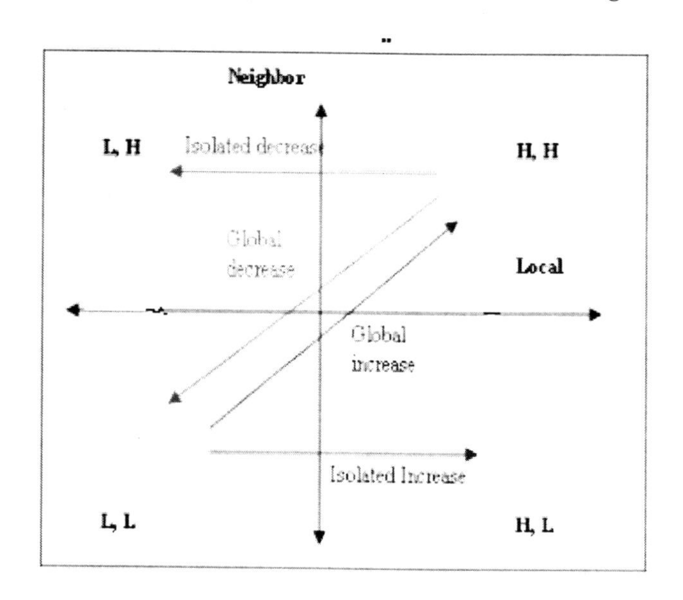

The dynamics of hierarchical expansion can be classified in the following way (graph 13): a) Isolated increase or decrease, which is present when the violence rate in the local municipality increases (decreases) without the neighbor's rate being high (low) or decreases (increases) without the neighbor's rate being low (high). Local municipalities move from quadrant (L,L) to quadrant (H,L) in the case of an increase, and from quadrant (H,H) to quadrant (L,H) in the case of a decrease; b) Global increase or decrease, which takes place when both the local municipality and its neighbor move together from low violence rates to high ones, or from high ones to low ones. In the first case of a global increase they move from quadrant (L,L) to quadrant (H,H) and in the case of the global decrease they change from quadrant (H,H) to (L,L).

Graphs 14 to 17 show evidence of contagious and hierarchical expansion between the 1995-97/1998-00 periods, for the combinations of: a) local homicide – neighbor homicide; b) neighbor homicide – neighbor FARC; c) neighbor homicide – neighbor ELN and d) neighbor homicide – neighbor paramilitary. The combination of local homicide - neighbor homicide (graph 14) shows that 56 municipalities presented contagious diffusion of expansion and relocation, and 46 of them presented contagious diffusion of contraction and relocation. On the other hand, 55 municipalities had increasing hierarchical diffusion, both isolated and global, while decreasing hierarchical diffusion, both isolated and global, appeared only in 26 municipalities.

Graph 13. Hierarchical Diffusion

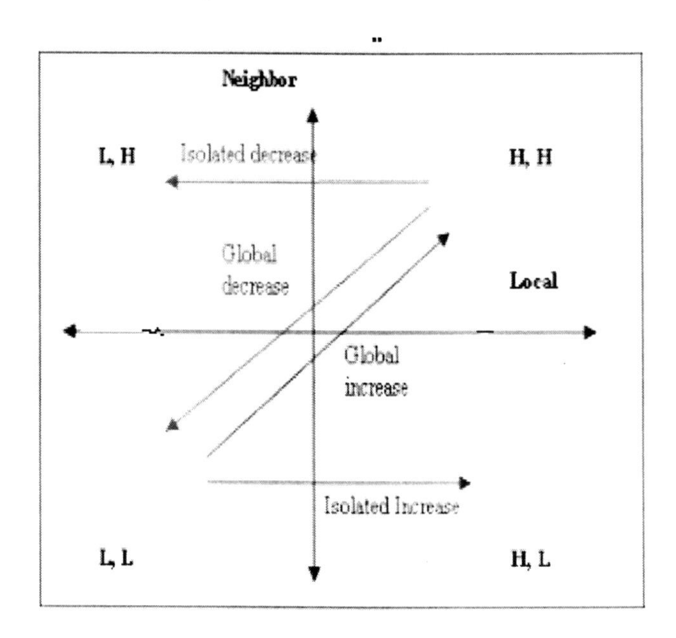

Graph 15 shows the results for combinations of neighbor homicide – neighbor FARC, which illustrates how regional FARC expansion is translated into regional increases of violence. For the 95-97, 98-00 period, the exercise shows that 94 groups of neighboring municipalities experienced contagious diffusion of expansion or relocation, whereas 56 groups experienced contagious diffusion of contraction or relocation. On the other hand, 55 groups of municipalities had increasing hierarchical diffusion, while 26 groups of municipalities experienced decreasing hierarchical diffusion. This means that regional increases in the homicide rates were preceded by high previous regional presence of FARC in 75% of the cases. The other 25% are caused by increasing hierarchical diffusion. In addition, the number of groups of neighboring municipalities that had increases in violence rates (either of contagious or hierarchical diffusion) was greater than the number of groups with decreases.

The combinations of neighbor homicides – neighbor ELN is shown in graph 16. As can be seen, 59 groups of neighboring municipalities presented increasing contagious diffusion or relocation in their violence rates, while 28 groups of neighbors experienced decreasing contagious diffusion or relocation. On the other hand, 20 groups of neighboring municipalities had decreasing hierarchical contagious diffusion, while 32 had decreasing hierarchical diffusion. Again, 75% of the groups of neighboring municipalities (within the neighbor homicides – neighbor ELN combinations) that had increases in their standardized violence rates had a high previous presence of ELN.

Graph 17 shows the same diagram for neighbor homicide rates – neighbor paramilitary. The results show that 103 municipalities within the analyzed combination experienced increasing contagious diffusion or relocation, and 32 had increasing hierarchical diffusion. Additionally, during the period under analysis 75 municipalities experienced decreasing contagious diffusion, and 75 had decreasing hierarchical diffusion. Therefore, during the analyzed period the largest increase of illegal self-defense groups was experienced, which was reflected in an increase of violence in those municipalities where their presence increased. Accordingly, in 78% of the groups of neighboring municipalities where standardized homicide rates increased, there was a high previous presence index of illegal self-defense groups.

Graph 14. Local and Neighbor Homicide Rate (Number of Municipalities that Experienced Change Between 1995-98/1998-00)

Contagious Diffusion *Hierarchical diffusion*

L, H
Neighbor homicide
H, H
Expansion
Relocation increases
56
Local homicide
46
Relocation decreases
Contraction
L, L
H, L

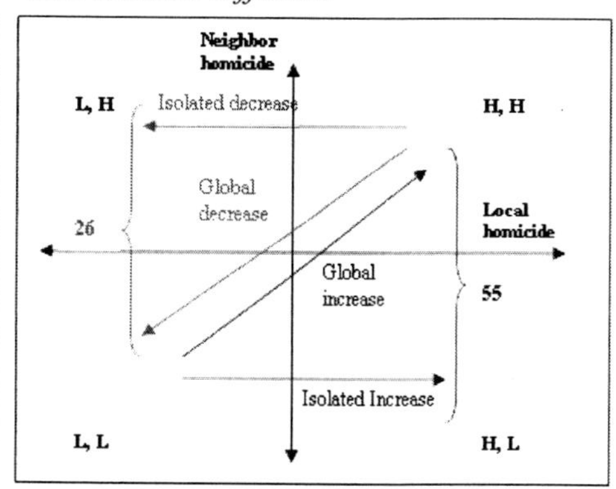

Graph 15. Neighbor Homicide Rate - Neighbor FARC (Number of Groups that Experienced Change Between 1995-98/1998-00)

Contagious Diffusion *Hierarchical diffusion*

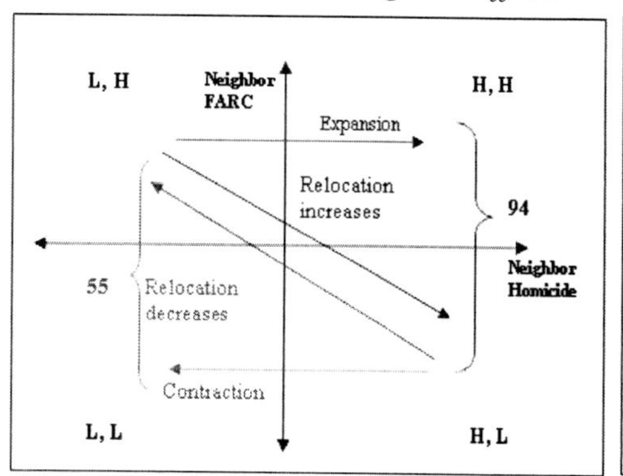

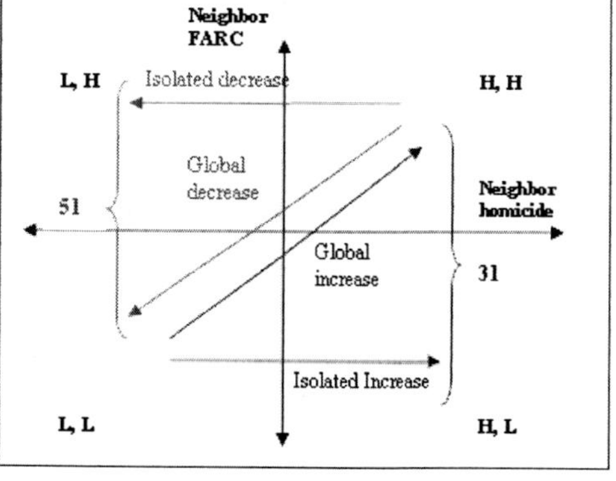

Graph 16. Neighbor Homicide Rate - Neighbor ELN (Number of Groups that Experienced Change Between 1995-98/1998-00)

Contagious Diffusion *Hierarchical diffusion*

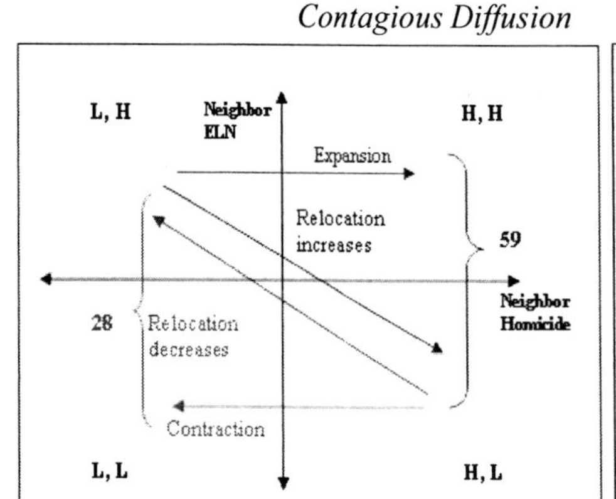

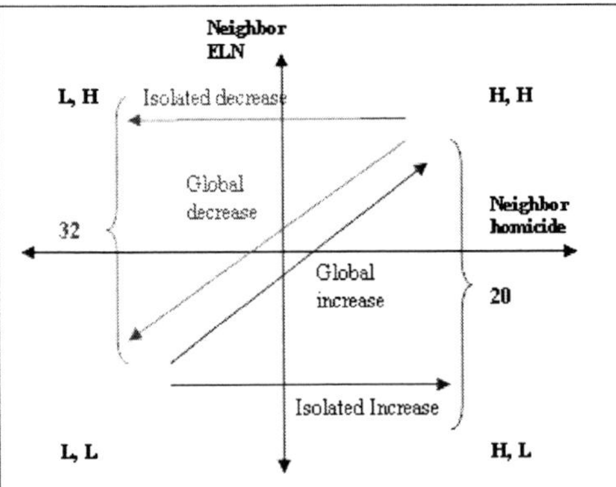

Graph 17. Neighbor Homicide Rate - Neighbor Common Criminals (Number of Groups that Experienced Change Between 1995-98/1998-00)

Contagious Diffusion *Hierarchical diffusion*

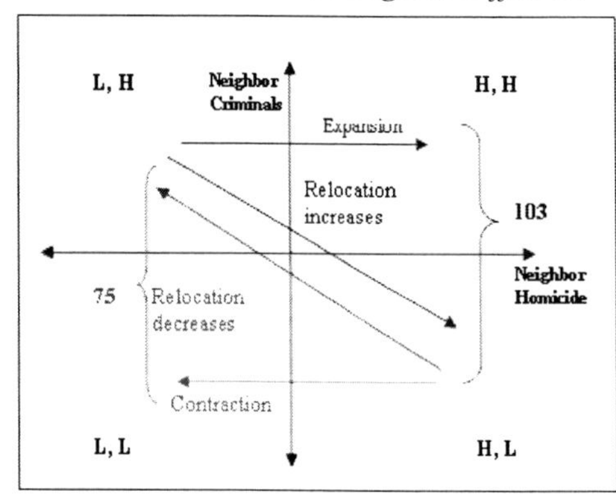

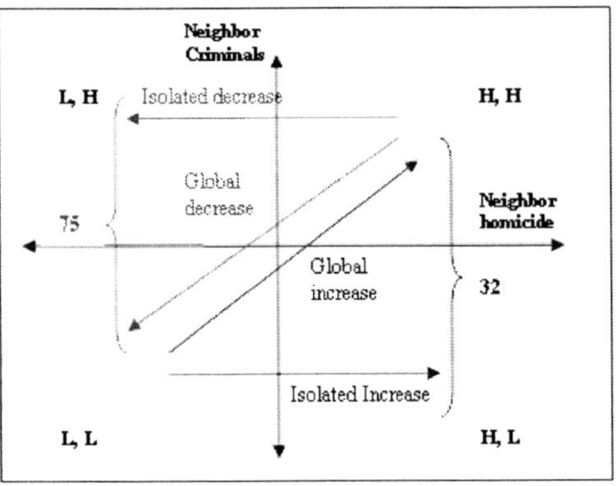

Finally, several exercises were carried out (Appendix 3) for combinations of. a) local homicides – local FARC; b) local homicides – neighbor FARC; c) neighbor homicides – local FARC; d) local homicides – local ELN, among others. These exercises show that most of the violence rate diffusion is caused by increasing contagious diffusion or relocation, which is always preceded by high indices of previous illegal armed group presence.

ECONOMETRIC EVIDENCE

Hypothesis

The presentation of the conflict history, the statistical evidence on the evolution of the different variables associated to the dynamics of conflict and criminal activity, and to the patterns of association and spatial diffusion of conflict and violent crime, allows stating some hypotheses on the relationship between conflict, violence and crime in Colombia. These hypotheses are:

Researchers have traditionally stated that Colombia is a violent country, as a result of culture or tradition. Although there is conflict and drug trafficking, only a small percentage of homicides (10% to 15%) are associated to these types of criminal activities (Commission of Studies on Violence, 1989). All other homicides are "common homicides" related to "intolerance" or to the "violent nature" of the Colombian population. The hypothesis of this paper is that *Colombia has experienced "cycles of violence" associated to conflicts between political parties during the 1950s, and to drug trafficking and conflict since the second half of the 1980s, with specific patterns of diffusion in time and space.*

Homicide is one of the high impact crimes associated to conflict. It is a intermediate product of the objectives of territorial control of illegal armed groups (Kalyvas, 2000). *In this sense, there is a clear correlation between the spatial presence of these groups and the violent crime rate, especially of civilians who are not combatants. The initial shock of violent crime generates persistence throughout time and a spatial diffusion that increases the homicide rate permanently, both in the local geographic unit and in the neighbors.*

The increase in kidnapping is clearly related to the growth of the financing needs of illegal armed groups. Although some of the kidnappings have "political" objectives, most of them are aimed at obtaining a ransom. In addition, kidnapping generates innovation and imitation patterns from other criminal organizations, which creates its persistence as a crime.

Drug trafficking is another crime related to the expansion of illegal armed groups. In particular, the growth of illicit crops is the result of the geographic expansion of these organizations, insofar as it generates sources of finance (Collier, 2001). The drug cartels, mainly in the 1980s, shattered and debilitated the judicial system, creating favorable conditions for other types of crimes.

The existence of illegal armed groups, which debilitates State presence through intimidation, annihilation or expulsion, can facilitate the rise of groups of common criminals and the increase of other types of crimes, in particular property crimes.

Social conditions such as inequality, poverty, and the lack of social services could be the origins of both violent crime and property crimes (Fanzylber et al, 1998), as well as of the rise of rebel groups. However, the *dynamics of conflict trigger a particular dynamics both of violent and common crime, losing most of its relationship with the original social conditions.*

Data

The dependent variables of the different econometric exercises are the municipal homicide rates between 1990 and 2000, and departmental kidnapping rates, rates of road piracy and of property crimes between 1985 and 2000. A probabilistic model is also estimated to determine the presence of kidnappings on a municipal level for the 1995/2000 period. The quantitative methodology used in this paper is spatial econometrics pool data.

The explanatory variables are departmental and municipal guerrilla attack rates, both for the local spatial unit and the neighbors, departmental per-capita drug trafficking income, and justice inefficiency measured as the number of homicide arrests divided by the number of homicides in each department. In addition, we include socioeconomic variables such as poverty, which is measured using the Unsatisfied Basic Needs index (UBN), inequality in the distribution of rural property, which is measured using the Gini index, and departmental and municipal education coverage.

Methodology

Given the geographical character of the dependent variables used here, there may be a certain degree of correlation between the dependent local variable and the dependent variable in neighboring departments or municipalities, and between the dependent local variable and the explanatory variables of local and neighboring municipalities or departments. Thus, the homicides rate in a geographical unit can be correlated with the homicide rate of neighboring geographical units, with the social condition of the neighbors, or with factors that generate violence in the neighbors. In this sense, econometric techniques that identify and account for these relationships must be implemented. This was shown in the previous section, where different indicators of local concentration of violence were presented. Therefore, the homicide rate or the kidnapping rate of each municipality or department not only depends on the characteristics of each municipality (or department), but also on the rates and the value of other variables in neighboring municipalities (or departments)[16].

Spatial autocorrelation is very similar to the temporal autocorrelation observed in time series. However, in time series this econometric problem is exclusively unidirectional, i.e. the past explains the present, and this can be corrected with a lag operator. In contrast, space dependency is multidirectional, i.e. all regions can affect one another. This does not allow the use of the time series lag operator and force the implementation of the contiguity spatial (or spatial lag) matrix[17] in order to obtain a right estimation. Additionally, the maximum likelihood methodology is used in order to correct the spatial autocorrelation problems. The use of this methodology and the inclusion of the contiguity matrix in econometric models allow capturing the spatial diffusion and spillover effects of the homicide rate, the kidnapping rate and other crimes. Thus, the spillover that is exerted from one municipality to another by the homicide rate, the kidnapping rate, and other crimes can be analyzed, as well as the influence of independent variables of neighboring spatial units on the local dependent variables.

---

[16] Spatial autocorrelation in the dependent variable is not considered by standard econometrics (OLS, cross section); this violates the econometric principle of the observations' independence. Such an incorrect specification generates correlated residuals and leads to an overvaluation of the variance of the estimator's vector. It also biases the variance of the residuals, invalidating the results of the statistical inferences based on the test of t-student, and leading to an R2 value that is higher than it should.

[17] A contiguity matrix for N geographic units is symmetrical, of dimension (NxN), with values of zeros in the diagonal (since there is no vicinity of each geographical unit with itself) and in the other elements of this matrix the vicinity criteria of the other spatial units Ni and Nj are included (for i≠j). These values differ according to the vicinity criterion that is used. If the matrix that is used is 1/Distance, elements i and j of the matrix, for i different from j, are filled with the inverse of the distance between municipalities i and j, so that geographical units that are farther away from one another have smaller values. If the matrix that is used is binary 1 km, only those elements of the matrix where the distance between the spatial units is smaller than 1 kilometer are filled with ones, and the rest of the matrix is filled with zeros. The diagonal is filled with zeros, and then all the matrices are standardized horizontally, so that the horizontal sum of the elements of the matrix equals 1 (Moreno y Vayas, 2001).

Estimation Results of Homicides and Kidnappings

Tables 2 and 3 display the results of the estimations for the crimes of homicide and kidnapping. In relation to homicide, the results confirm both the validity of Becker (1968) and Fanzylber et al's (1998) model of criminal behavior, and the hypotheses on the dynamic and spatial effects of conflict on criminal activity. Two models were estimated for the homicide rate: one for the 1990/2000 period and another one for the 1995/2000 period. As observed in table 1, the difference between both resides in the existence for the 1995/2000 period of variable for groups of common criminals and paramilitary. The results are the following:

Variables of temporal and spatial dynamics. The results show that the lagged homicide rate of the local municipality has a positive and significant effect on the homicide rate in the local municipality. This means that a shock on the homicide rate increases the homicide rate over time, although its effect is "stationary". On the other hand, the homicide rate of the neighbor has a positive effect upon the local homicide rate, which validates the hypothesis of contagious diffusion. Accounting for temporal and spatial effects, a one homicide shock generates approximately 4 homicides in the long run[18]. There is also a small but significant effect of the lagged homicide rate of the neighbor on the local municipality's homicide rate. Table 1 also shows a probit model to estimate the probability of occurrence or non-occurrence of a kidnapping in a local municipality. The coefficients obtained show that the criminal activity of kidnapping generates important effects of spatial and time persistence and spillover diffusion.

Table 2 presents a probit model for the periods 1946-1950 and 1958-1963 at a municipal level. [19] These periods correspond to the initial and final stage of the period called "La Violencia". It can be observed, that for the periods: early violence (1946-1950) and late violence (1958-1963), the lagged spatial variables are significant. Spatial effects are positive and significant in both periods which once more validate the diffusion hypothesis. In addition the political variables included in the models[20], show that the most violent municipalities were the ones with political polarization in the 1946 elections. However in the 1958-63 period, the political variables lost all their significance, which indicates an important change in the patterns of violence.

The departmental homicide and kidnapping rate estimations for the period 1986-2000, is also included in table 2. The results confirm again the diffusion hypothesis at a departmental level. The lagged homicide rate in the neighboring department is negative and significant for the 86-00 period (with a coefficient of -0.35). This result shows the possible existence of a

---

[18] The 0.6 coefficient in the lagged variable implies that a one additional homicide generates 2.5 homicides, in the long term. Similarly, a one homicide shock causes a spatial increase (in al municipalities) of 1.6 homicides. Taking space and time into account, one homicide generates 4 homicides in the long run. The spatial effect increases by more than 60% the purely temporal effect of a homicide shock.

[19] The spatial autoregressive probit models predict the probability of violent deaths for the periods 1946-1950 and 1958-1963. The models include beside the spatial variables, political, geographical and land conflicts variables. These models were taken of Chacón and Sanchez (2003).

[20] The political variables were constructed using the 1946 municipal elections. The municipalities were classified according to the percentage of votes in favor to a political party (municipalities with 80% or more votes for a party were classified under supremacy of that party, between 60 and 79% under control and with 40 and 60% for any of the parties under electoral competition) . All these political variables were include as dummy variables For the 1958-1963 period, the presence of local and neighbor guerrillas, were also included.

Table 2. Departmental Estimations of Homicides and Kidnappings

Dependent Variable	**Early Violence 1946-1950**	**Late Violence 1958-1963**	**Homicide Rate 1986-2000**	**Kidnapping Rate 1986-2000**	**Kidnapping Rate 1990-2000**
Variables	Coefficient	Coefficient	Coefficient	Coefficient	Coefficient
Constant	-1,51 ***	-1,61 ***	33,37 ***	-1,28	-4,58
Spatial and Temporal Dynamic					
Neighbor Violence	0,18 ***	0,18 ***			
Dep. Homicide Rate 1946	0,01 *				
Early Violence		0,42 ***			
Neighbor Homicide Rate			0,27 ***		
One year Lagged Homicide Rate			0,68 ***		
Neighbor one year lagged Homicide rate			-0,31 ***		
Neighbor Kidnapping Rate				0,20	0,11
One year Lagged Kidnapping Rate				0,61	0,57
Neighbor one year lagged kidnapping rate				0,02	0,01
Illegal Armed Groups					
Guerrilla presence		1,37 ***			
Neighbor Guerrilla presence		1,95 ***			
ELN presence			-1,92	1,53	1,84
Neighbor ELN presence			12,71 *	1,05	2,79
FARC presence			0,48	0,12	0,34
Neighbor FARC presence			11,80 ***	1,79	2,04
Justice and Drug Trafficking					
Justice efficiency			-40,06 ***	-1,83	-1,79
Drug trafficking incomes			6,98 ***	-0,08	-0,29
Economic and Social					
Departmental agricultural and livestock GDP			27,53 ***	5,70	7,50
Poverty rate			0,04	-0,01	0,00
Education coverage			-43,50 ***	-0,22	-0,28
GINI inequality index of area			0,000002 *	1,20	2,71
Neighbor GINI inequality index of area			0,000004 **		3,54
The period of "La Violencia"					
Land Conflicts	0,02	0,04			
Granted Hectares	0,34 *	1,03 ***			
Peripheral					
Political Variables					
Liberal Supremacy	0,59 ***	-0,07			
Liberal Control	0,85 ***	0,23			
Consevative Control	0,72 ***	0,19			
Electoral Competition	0,95 ***	0,21			
Estimation Method:	Probit Spatial Autoregressive	Probit Spatial Autoregressive	Spatial Autoregressive	Spatial Autoregressive	Spatial Autoregressive
Interaction	NO	NO	YES	NO	NO
R^2			0,7916	0,6179	0,6135
No of observations	755	755	480	480	320
log-likelihood			-3149,57	-2338,36	-1521,01

†. Calculations taken of Chacón and Sanchez (2003)
*** significant at 99%
** significant at 95%
* significant at 90%

Table 3. Departmental Estimations of Property Crimes and Road Piracy

Dependent Variable	Property Crimes Rate 1986-2000		Road Piracy 1986-2000	
Variables	Coefficient		Coefficient	
Constant	2.55	2.70	0.004	0.03
Temporal Dynamics				
One year lagged property crimes rate	0.88 ***	0.88 ***	0.942 ***	0.96 ***
Armed Actors				
ELN presence	0.04	0.04	0.033	0.02
FARC presence	-0.03 **	-0.04 **	0.006	0.02
Justice and Drug Trafficking				
Justice efficiency	-2.84 **	-3.58 ***	-0.030	-0.02
Drug trafficking incomes	0.25	0.36	0.004	-0.002
Economic and Social				
Poverty rate	-0.02	-0.03	0.000	-0.001
GINI inequality index of area	6.11	6.18	0.073	0.22
Spatial Dynamics				
Neighbor property crimes	0.03 *	0.30 ***	0.106 ***	0.31 ***
Neighbor one year lagged property crimes rate		-0.30 ***		-0.32 ***
Neighbor ELN presence		-0.06		0.03
Neighbor FARC presence		0.04		0.06
Neighbor justice efficiency		1.74		-0.11
Neighbor drug trafficking incomes		-1.82 *		0.02
Neighbor poverty rate		0.04		0.00
Neighbor GINI inequality index of area		0.00		0.08
Estimation Method:	Spatial Autoregressive	Spatial Autoregressive	Spatial Autoregressive	Spatial Autoregressive
R^2	0.8372	0.8507	0.7821	0.796
No of observations	448	448	448	448
log-likelihood	-2480.5899	-2465.24	-900.59	-889.81

*** significant at 99%
** significant at 95%
* significant at 90%

spatial-temporal relocation mechanism of violent crime, because increases of the neighboring department's homicide rate in the previous year predict decreases in the local department's homicide rate in the current year. Similarly, the departmental kidnapping rates show persistence (with a 0.6 coefficient) and of spatial diffusion (with a 0.2 coefficient). On the other hand, the relocation effects are not significant (table 2).

Variables of illegal armed groups. The results confirm the hypothesis that there is a positive and significant relationship between conflict and homicidal violence. The local presence of illegal armed actors has a positive and significant effect for all the groups. This means that these groups are not only a very important factor in the generation of violence, but also that the fulfillment of their strategic objectives of territorial control is accompanied by the use of violence. The presence of illegal armed groups in neighboring municipalities is only positive and significant in the case of the FARC. This implies that this group has "influence areas" that go beyond municipal borders. The interaction between paramilitary groups and the guerrilla is negative although small, which would suggest that mutual dissuasion exists at a municipal level. The presence of illegal armed actors, in particular the FARC, increases the probability of kidnapping. A similar result is obtained with the presence of groups of common criminals in the local and the neighboring municipality.

In the departmental estimations, neither local ELN nor FARC had significant coefficients. However, the neighboring variables of both the FARC and ELN have the expected positive sign and are statistically different from zero (table 2)[21]. On the other hand, the presence of illegal armed groups have a positive and significant effect on the departmental kidnapping rates, especially local ELN, neighboring ELN and neighboring FARC.

Variables of justice and drug trafficking. As was expected, the effect of justice efficiency, measured as the number of homicides captures divided by the number of homicides, has a significant negative effect in the explanation of the municipal homicide rate. A greater action of justice dissuades and incapacitates the criminal. On the other hand, departmental drug trafficking income is positive and significant in the explanation of violent crime. Due to the nature and size of illegal profits generated by this activity, a positive effect on the homicide rate is expected. The justice variables were not significant for the case of municipal kidnappings.

As obtained for municipalities, at a departmental level justice efficiency negatively affects the homicide rate, while drug trafficking income affects it positively and significantly (table 2). In the case of the departmental kidnapping rate, justice efficiency has the expected negative sign.

Variables of social conditions. Among the social variables, only poverty is significant and negative in the explanation of the homicide rate. The Gini coefficient has the expected effect, although it is not significant. In the case of the probability of kidnapping cases, the coefficient of local poverty is negative (as expected) and significant. Poverty in the neighbors is positive and significant, suggesting that if poverty in a neighboring municipality changes, expected income of crime decreases in that municipality, increasing the probability of kidnapping in the local municipality.

In the case of the departmental homicide rate for the 1986-2000 period, the coefficient of poverty, measured by UBN, was not significant. Both the local and the neighbor property Gini are significant and positive in the explanation of violence, although the magnitude of the coefficient is quite small. For the period of La Violencia, the existence of previous land ownership conflicts positively affected the violence probability, but the effect was not significant. In addition, the percentage of the distributed hectares as the total municipality surface was related to a higher violence probability (table 2). On the other hand, none of the departmental social variables has a significant effect on the kidnapping rate.

---

[21] The aggregation of variables from small regional units (municipalities) to large units (departments) decreases the variance of the aggregated variables, and therefore its statistical importance. In the regressions for

Property Crimes and Road Piracy

The results of the econometric exercises for departmental property crimes and road piracy[22] are shown in table 2. The effects of the different variables are the following:

Variables of temporary and space dynamics. The estimations show that the departmental property crime rate has high temporal persistence (0.89) and experiences a diffusion effect from neighboring departments (0.3). There are also relocation effects, because an increase in the rate in the neighboring departments predicts a decrease in the rate in the local department. Road piracy persistence is very high (0.94) with diffusion effects from neighboring departments (0.1).

Variables of illegal armed groups illegal. The variables of local illegal armed actors do not have statistically significant effects on property crimes or on road piracy. Only neighboring ELN presence affects road piracy.

Variables of justice and drug trafficking. The variable of justice efficiency has negative effects on property crimes at a departmental level. The effect of this variable on road piracy, although negative, is not significant. Drug trafficking income does not affect the behavior of property crimes or road piracy, because the coefficient that resulted from the estimation is not statistically different from zero.

Variables of social conditions. Social conditions affect property crimes as suggested by crime theory. While poverty has a negative impact on these crimes by decreasing expected loots, wealth concentration (measured as property concentration) increases them. On the other hand, neighbor poverty increases property crimes in the local department; this shows that a relocation effect exists. Finally, none of the social variables are significantly associated to property crimes.

Decompositions

In order to quantify the contribution of the different explanatory variables in the homicide and kidnapping rate dispersion, between the different geographic units, several decomposition exercises were made, using the coefficients obtained in the econometric exercises. This decomposition exercise uses the regressions made to explain the municipal homicide rates for the periods 1990-2000 and 1995-2000, and the departmental kidnapping rate for 1990-2000 period.

The methodology used to carry out the decomposition exercise starts off taking the complete data sample (dependent and independent variables) and order it from the values of the dependent variables (homicide and kidnapping rates), then the total sample is divided in five parts (quintiles) and the average value of all the variables in each one of these quintiles is obtained. We calculated the differences between quintiles base on the following identity:

$$TH_{t,i} - TH_{t,j} = \sum \beta_k \times MET \times (X_{t,i} - X_{t,j})$$

departmental homicides we controlled for the spatial interaction of illegal armed groups and drug trafficking income, among other variables.

[22] Unfortunately, data of municipal property crimes do not exist.

Where $TH_{t,i} - TH_{t,j}$ is the difference of the estimated average rate between the i and j quintiles, the expression $(X_{t,i} - X_{t,j})$ is the difference in the average value of the explanatory variables between the i and j quintiles, β_k is the coefficient of the k variable, whereas MET is the temporary spatial multiplier, which allows us to calculate the long-term persistence and contagious effects.

$$MET = \frac{1}{(1-\alpha)} + \frac{1}{(1-\rho)^2} + \frac{1}{(1-\delta)^2}$$

Where α is the temporary coefficient (the one that accompanies the lagged dependent variable), ρ is the spatial coefficient (the one that accompanies the neighbors dependent variable) and δ is the relocation coefficient (the one of the lagged neighbors dependent variable)[23].

The descriptive statistics by quintile of the municipal homicide rate for the periods 90-00, and 95-00 and the departmental kidnapping rate for 90-00, show that these variables present a high variance. Thus, the homicide rate of the less violent municipalities for period 90-00 was in average 3.1hpch and of 2.56hpch for the 95-00 period whereas the same variable in the 20% more violent municipalities was 167.97hpch and of 156.10hpch for first and the second period respectively. This pattern of high oscillation is similar in the lagged, neighbor and lagged neighbor homicide rates, corroborating then the: persistence, contagious or spillover effects and relocation hypotheses. The behavior of the armed actors activity is similar to the one of the dependent variables, high differences between quintiles. Thus, the conflict activity indicator for the FARC is of 0,92 for the most violent quintile (compared with 0,33 for the less violent quintile), 0,42 for the ELN group (compared with 0,15 for less violent quintile) in the period 90-00. For the 95-2000 period this indicator took a value of 1,23 for the FARC for the most violent quintile (0,43 for the less violent), 0,55 for the ELN (0,19 for the less violent), The delinquency activity indicator[24] was 0,29 in the higher quintile (0,06 for less violent) for the 95-00 period, being much more considerable the differences between quintiles for the FARC activities[25]. On the other hand, the justice and drug trafficking variables indicate big differences in both quintiles ends, the efficiency of justice is considerably higher in the lower homicides rates quintile and the drug trafficking income have a greater magnitude in the most violent quintile for the both periods. The social variables used to explain the homicides were NBI (Uncover basis necessities index), Educative Cover, GINI and neighbor GINI. The statistics show that the NBI index (poverty) in the less violent municipalities is greater than the same index in most violent. The rest of social variables do

23 The temporary spatial multiplier of the municipal homicide rate for the period 1990-1995 is 4,72, for period 1995-2000 is 3, whereas for the kidnapping rate for 1990-2000 is 3.

24 The delinquency variable is included only in the regression that explains the municipal homicide rate for the period 1995-2000, there isn't information for previous periods.

25 The neighbor illegal armed actors variables do not maintain in a strict way the patterns of greater activity in quintiles with high homicide rates and minor activity in those with low rates, the same as the interaction variables ELN and Delinquency, ELN and FARC, and FARC and Delinquency included only in the 1995-2000 period.

not show any type of behavior pattern, they show similar numbers in all the quintiles without any tendencies of increase or diminution.

On the other hand, the descriptive statistics of the departmental kidnappings for the 1990-2000 period show that the average kidnapping rate in Colombia is about 5.46 spch and oscillates between 0.46spch in the quintile with smaller kidnappings rates and 14.82spch between the greater rate quintile. The lagged, neighbor and lagged neighbor kidnapping rates, behave the same way as the dependent variable. The variables of illegal armed actors activity FARC, ELN, neighbor FARC and neighbor ELN is higher in the departments with greater kidnappings rates. The quintile with the greater kidnappings rates has in an equal way greater activity of the illegal armed actors. The justice efficiency shows to be of special importance, the quintile with greater kidnapping rates has indicators of justice efficiency considerably smaller and the opposite for the quintile with smaller rates. For this exercise not only social variables were included an economic variable was also included, the agricultural GIP as a percentage of the departmental GIP. This variable gathers the rural effect over the region. The social variables behave in a very similar way in all the quintiles without showing any type of special tendency and like in the case of the homicides the poverty is greater in the quintile with smaller kidnapping rate. The agricultural GIP, on the other hand, follows the same behavior of the dependent variable, greater agricultural GIP in quintiles with greater rates of kidnapping and the opposite in those with smaller rates.

Table 4. Municipal Homicide Rate Decomposition, 1995–2000

% of the long term difference between the most violent and the least violent quintile	Q5-1	Q4-1	Q3-1	Q2-1	Mean-1
Long Term diference Qi-Q1 i=2,3,4,5,mean	41,33%	27,98%	11,88%	1,96%	16,63%
Ilegal Armed Groups	***52,65%***	***43,62%***	***30,64%***	***-56,65%***	***43,89%***
FARC Activity	26,1%	12,7%	1,2%	-54,5%	16,1%
ELN Activity	7,6%	5,3%	0,1%	-12,1%	5,3%
Delinquency Activity	19,5%	19,6%	17,2%	38,3%	19,6%
Neighbors FARC Activity	5,8%	3,8%	1,2%	-73,7%	2,6%
Neighbors ELN Activity	0,7%	0,8%	0,4%	1,2%	0,7%
Neighbors Delinquency Activity	3,2%	4,8%	5,9%	11,7%	4,3%
ELN and Delinquency neighbors	-2,1%	-2,7%	0,0%	-1,4%	-2,0%
ELN and FARC neighbors	0,8%	0,1%	-0,1%	0,5%	0,4%
FARC and Delinquency neighbors	-8,8%	-0,9%	4,8%	33,3%	-3,2%
Juustice and Drug Trafficking	***35,6%***	***41,1%***	***37,0%***	***48,3%***	***37,9%***
Justice Efficiency	13,1%	16,3%	20,9%	41,2%	16,0%
Drug Trafficking incomes	22,4%	24,8%	16,1%	7,1%	22,0%
Social Variables	***11,8%***	***15,8%***	***32,4%***	***108,4%***	***18,2%***
Poverty rate	11,8%	15,1%	31,8%	106,5%	18,0%
Education Coverage	0,1%	0,2%	0,5%	0,8%	0,2%
Gini of property value	1,4%	2,0%	4,8%	14,5%	2,4%
Neighbors GINI of Property Value	-1,5%	-2,0%	-4,7%	-13,4%	-2,4%

Temporary spatial multiplier = 3,25

The decomposition exercises (tables 4 and 5) show that percentage of the difference between the homicide and kidnapping rates between the first quintile (lower quintile) and all the others quintiles and the average, is explained by each one of the independent variables (including the persistence and contagious effects). Thus, the differences in the homicide rates between quintiles of municipalities for the 1990-2000 period are explained by the justice and drug trafficking variables. These explain more than 50% of the difference between the quintile with minor and greater number of homicides, followed by the armed conflict variables which contribute 31% to the explanation and where the FARC activities are those that have a greater effect. Finally, the social variables like poverty, educative cover, neighbor GINI and GINI have a contribution of 17%, being the poverty the only one that contributes in a significant way to the explanation of the difference between both extremes quintiles.

Table 5. Departmental Kidnapping Decomposition, 1990-2000

% of the long term difference between the most violent and the least violent quintile	Q5-Q1	Q4-Q1	Q3-Q1	Q2-Q1	Mean-Q1
Long Term diference Qi-Q1 i=2,3,4,5,mean	8,42%	5,06%	4,34%	2,83%	4,16%
llegal Armed Groups	***54,82%***	***31,51%***	***15,87%***	***-3,82%***	***33,02%***
FARC Activity	2,3%	1,0%	-0,5%	-4,0%	0,5%
ELN Activity	29,7%	12,1%	9,0%	4,8%	17,7%
Neighbors FARC Activity	3,6%	4,2%	-7,3%	-20,7%	-1,9%
Neighbors ELN Activity	19,3%	14,2%	14,7%	16,0%	16,7%
Juustice and Drug Trafficking	***19,6%***	***28,2%***	***29,9%***	***31,0%***	***25,4%***
Justice Efficiency	13,6%	21,4%	24,2%	30,1%	20,0%
Drug Trafficking incomes	6,0%	6,8%	5,6%	0,9%	5,4%
Social	***25,6%***	***40,3%***	***54,3%***	***72,8%***	***41,6%***
Agro GDP	***16,8%***	***25,2%***	***28,5%***	***29,4%***	***23,0%***
Poverty rate	0,8%	1,2%	1,9%	5,8%	1,8%
Education Coverage	9,7%	15,4%	17,7%	28,4%	15,3%
Gini of property value	-2,0%	-3,2%	1,3%	1,9%	-1,1%
Neighbors GINI of Property Value	0,3%	1,6%	5,0%	7,3%	2,5%

Temporary spatial multiplier = 3

This same analysis for the 1995-2000 period was made. In this period the contribution of the illegal armed group's activities variables explains 53% of the difference between the quintile of higher homicide rates and the one with lower rates. The FARC group continues being the armed group with greater effects, followed by the delinquency (paramilitary) and the ELN. The justice and drug trafficking variables take a second place in contribution, explaining now a 36% of the difference. The effect of the social variables is explained almost in its totality by the poverty; as in the previous case, the social factors continue being those with a smaller explanatory percentage.

The last exercise made was the analysis of the departmental kidnapping rate for the 1995-2000 period. The armed conflict explains a considerable 55% of the long term difference between the quintiles with greater and smaller rates, being the ELN for the case of kidnappings, the most influential actor in the explanation. In second place we found the social and economic variables, where the departmental agricultural GIP stands out. This variable measures the rural effect (that is a proxy of the geographic difficulties of the region) and the educative cover. Finally, the justice and drug trafficking variables contribute 20% of the explanation of the differences.

CONCLUSIONS

Ever since the 19th Century, Colombia has experienced several civil wars and domestic conflicts that have caused both an increase of global rates of violent crime and the rise of other criminal activities. During the Thousand Day War (1899-1902) more than 70 thousand people perished, of whom only a small percentage was combatants. All other deaths were the result of the global increase in violence originated in the diffusion and contagion mechanisms described in this paper. During this same period, looting, robbery and arson crimes grew, and were perpetrated by the guerrilla and groups of soldiers who had lost all ideals.

The first cycle of violence occurred during "La Violencia" (1948-1962) and was mainly caused by political polarization and party confrontations. The second cycle of violence of the second half of the 20th Century began in the mid-1980s, mostly in urban than in rural areas, and related to the activity of cocaine traffic. At that time, although the guerrilla had begun an expansion consolidation process, its effects on violence only began be felt at the beginning of the 1990s. The existing data allowed carrying out an analysis of spatial patterns of conflict and violence, as well as its diffusion and contagion dynamics. The methodology of spatial analysis shows: a) the existence of a strong spatial correlation between the conflict and violence indicators, and b) that the changes in local or neighboring municipal violence indicators are preceded by previous activities of illegal armed groups.

The econometric results showed the existence of persistence and spatial diffusion in all types of crimes. The existence of such dynamics implies that, for example, for the case of homicides, a one homicide shock generates 4 homicides in the long run term after accounting for the effects of time and space. The efficiency of justice, drug trafficking and, to a great extent, the activity of illegal armed groups appear among the explanatory factors of violence. In addition, kidnapping is mostly explained by the presence of such groups.

Property crimes, in addition to the factors of persistence and diffusion, are explained by the efficiency of justice (negatively) and by social variables such as the distribution of land (positively) and poverty (negatively), as predicted by the economic theory of crime. An important result of this paper is that property crimes are not directly affected by the presence of illegal armed groups. There are several factors that discourage guerrilla and paramilitary groups from perpetrating property crimes. Among them, the existence of common criminal bands that specialize in property crimes and the difficulties of trading stolen objects when there is not a support criminal network. Finally, the only illegal group that had an effect on road piracy was ELN.

The relationship between conflict, violence and criminal activity is complex. However, the results of this research paper strongly show that the dynamics of conflict not only determines the deaths directly caused by conflict, but also the dynamics of *global* violence in the country. This happens because the diffusion mechanisms of criminal activity, which begin with an initial shock on the homicide rate, are transmitted through space and time, increasing the homicide rate both of the local and neighboring spatial unit. This is a fundamental finding since it questions the false separation between conflict homicides and "common" homicides, and bases the explanation of violence on a unique cause. This false separation (which has also been questioned by other authors; Llorente et al, 2001) has lead to explaining Colombia's high rates of violent crime as motivated by "the culture of violence" or the "intolerance" of Colombian citizens.

References

Alape, Arturo (1985). *La Paz, la Violencia: Testigos de excepción.* Bogotá, Editorial Planeta.

____, Arturo (1989). *Las Vidas de Pedro Antonio Marín, Manuel Marulanda Vélez, Tirofijo,* Bogotá, Editorial Planeta Colombiana.

Becker, Gary (1968) "Crime and Punishment: An Economic Approach", Journal of Political Economy 76, No. 2: pp. 169- 217

Bejarano, Jesús Antonio et.al. (1997). *Colombia: Inseguridad, Violencia y Desempeño Económico en las Áreas Rurales,* Bogotá, Universidad Externado de Colombia. Fondo Financiero de Proyectos de Desarrollo.

_______, Jesús Antonio (1995). *Una Agenda para la Paz,* Bogotá, TM Editores.

Bottía, Martha (2002). "La Presencia Municipal de las FARC: es Estrategia y Contagio, mas que Ausencia del Estado", Mimeo, Universidad de los Andes.

Cohen, Jacqueline and Tita, George (1999). "Diffusion in Homicide Exploring a General Method for Detecting Spatial Diffusion Processes", Journal of Quantitative Criminology, Vol. 15, No.4, pp. 451-494, 1999.

Collier, Paul and Hoeffler, Anne (2001). "Greed and Grievance in Civil War", Working Paper, World Bank, CSAE WPS/2002-01.

Comision de Estudios Sobre la Violencia (1987). *Colombia: Violencia y Democracia,* Bogota, Colciencias, Universidad Nacional de Colombia.

Cubides, Fernando, Olaya, Ana Cecilia and Ortiz, Miguel (1998), *La Violencia y el Municipio Colombiano 1980-1997,* Bogotá, Universidad Nacional de Colombia.

______, Fernando (1999) "Los Paramilitares y su Estrategias" in *Reconocer la Guerra para Construir la Paz,* Bogota, CEREC.

Chacón, Mario and Fabio Sanchez (2003). "Political Polarization and violence during "La Violencia", 1946-1963. In progress.

Deas, Malcom (1991). "Algunos Interrogantes sobre la Relación entre Guerras Civiles y Violencia", in Ricardo Peñaranda y Gonzalo Sánchez, (Compiladores), *Pasado y presente de la violencia en Colombia,* Bogotá, Fondo Editorial CEREC

Deas, Malcom and Gaitán, Fernando (1995). *Dos Ensayos Especulativos sobre la Violencia en Colombia,* Fondo Financiero de Proyectos de Desarrollo, Departamento Nacional de Planeación.

Delpar, Helen (1994). *Rojos contra Azules: El Partido Liberal en la Política Colombiana 1863-1899,* Bogotá, Procultura S.A.

Echandía, Camilo (1999). "Expansión Territorial de las Guerrillas Colombianas: Geografía, Economía y Violencia" in *Reconocer la Guerra para Construir la Paz,* Bogotá, CEREC.

_______, Camilo (2001). "La Violencia en Medio de Conflicto Armado en los Años Noventa", Opera 2001, publicación de la Facultad de Finanzas, Gobierno y Relaciones Internacionales de la Universidad Externado de Colombia.

Echeverry, Juan Carlos, Salazar, Natalia and Navas Verónica (2000). "El Conflicto Colombiano en el Contexto Internacional", in *Economía, Crimen y Conflicto,* Bogota, Universidad Nacional de Colombia.

Fajnzylber, Pablo, Lederman, Daniel and Loayza, Norman (1999).*¿Qué causa el crimen violento,* in Corrupción, Crimen y Justicia: Una Perspectiva Económica, Mauricio Cárdenas y Roberto Steiner, Bogotá, TM Editores, LACEA, pp.53 a 95

Fischer, Thomas (1991). "Desarrollo Hacia Afuera y Revoluciones en Colombia, 1850-1910", in Ricardo Peñaranda y Gonzalo Sánchez, (Compiladores), *Pasado y presente de la violencia en Colombia*, Bogotá, Fondo Editorial CEREC.

Fuerzas Armadas Revolucionarias de Colombia at www.farc-ep.org

Gaviria, Alejandro (2001). "Rendimientos Crecientes y la Evolución del Crimen Violento: el Caso Colombiano" in *Economía, Crimen y Conflicto*, Bogotá, Universidad Nacional de Colombia.

Gilodhés, Pierre (1985). "La Violencia en Colombia, Bandolerismo y Guerra Social" in Marta Cárdenas (Editora), *Once Ensayos sobre la Violencia,* Bogotá: Fondo Editorial CEREC.

Gómez Buendía, Hernando (1991). "*La Violencia Contemporánea en Colombia, un Punto de Vista Liberal"* in Ricardo Peñaranda y Gonzalo Sánchez, (Compiladores), *Pasado y presente de la violencia en Colombia*, Bogotá, Fondo Editorial Cerec.

Guerrero, Javier (1991). *Los Años del Olvido: Boyacá y los Orígenes de la Violencia.* Bogotá, Universidad Nacional de Colombia, Instituto de Estudios Políticos y Relaciones Internacionales. Tercer Mundo.

Guzmán, Germán, Fals, Orlando and Umaña, Eduardo (1962). *La Violencia en Colombia, Estudio de un Proceso Social*, Bogotá, Carlos Valencia Editores.

Hartlyn, Jonathan (1993). *La Política del Régimen de Coalición: La Experiencia del Frente Nacional en Colombia*, Bogotá, Tercer Mundo Editores.

Henderson, James (1984). *Cuando Colombia se Desangro: Un Estudio de la Violencia en Metrópoli y Provincia,* Bogotá, El Ancora Editores.

Jaramillo, Carlos. E (1991). "La Guerra de los Mil Días: Aspectos Estructurales de la Organización Guerrillera", en Ricardo Peñaranda y Gonzalo Sánchez, (Compiladores), *Pasado y Presente de la Violencia en Colombia*, Bogotá, Fondo Editorial CEREC.

Jaramillo, Carlos (2001). "Fin de Dos Guerras, Principio de dos Siglos", en Sánchez, Gonzalo and Aguilar, Mario (editores) *Memorias de un País en Guerra: Los Mil Días 1899-1902,* Bogotá, Editorial Planeta.

Kalmanovitz, Salomón. "La Evolución de la Estructura Agraria en Colombia", Boletín Mensual de Estadística, DANE, No. 276 pp 77-161

Kalyvas, Stathis (2000). "The Logic of Violence in Civil War". New York University, Estudio, Working Paper, 2000, 151.

LeGrand, Catherine (1986). *Frontier Expansion and Peasant Protest in Colombia: 1850 – 1936*, México, Alburquerque: University of New Mexico press.

Medina, Carlos (2001). *Elementos para una Historia de las Ideas Políticas del Ejercito de Liberación Nacional: La Historia de los Primeros Tiempos (1958-1978)*, Bogotá, Rodríguez Quito Editores.

Ministerio de Justicia (1961). *Cinco años de Criminalidad Aparente* 1955-1959. Vol 2, Bogotá.

Molano, Alfredo (1990). *Aguas Arriba: entre la Coca y el Oro*, Bogotá, El Ancora Editores.

Molina, Gerardo (1978). *Las Ideas liberales en Colombia, Tercer Mundo*, Bogotá.

Moreno, Rosina and Vaya, Esther (2001). *Técnicas Econométricas para el tratamiento de Datos Espaciales: La Econometria Espacial*, Barcelona, Universitat de Barcelona.

Pécaut, Daniel (1987). *Orden y Violencia. Colombia 1930-1954,* México, Editorial Siglo XXI.

_____, Daniel (1985). "Reflexiones Sobre el Fenómeno de la Violencia", en Marta Cárdenas (Editora), *Once Ensayos sobre la Violencia,* Bogotá: Fondo Editorial CEREC

Pizarro Leóngomez, Eduardo (1991). *Las FARC 1949-1966,* Bogotá, Universidad Nacional de Colombia, Tercer Mundo Editores.

_____, Eduardo (2002). "Colombia: ¿guerra civil, guerra contra la sociedad, guerra antiterrorista o guerra ambigua ? en Análisis Político No 46, IEPRI Universidad Nacional, Bogota.

Posada, Francisco (1968). *Colombia Violencia y Subdesarrollo*, Universidad Nacional, Bogotá.

Posada, Eduardo (2001). *¿Guerra civil?. El lenguaje del conflicto en Colombia.* Bogotá: Libros de Cambio. Alfaomega.

Offstein, Norman (2002) "An extortionary guerrilla movement" Documento CEDE 2002-09, Universidad de Los Andes, Facultad de Economía.

Ortiz, Carlos Miguel (1985). *Estado y Subversión en Colombia: La Violencia en el Quindío en los años 50,* Fondo Editorial CEREC.

Ramirez, William (2002). "¿Guerra civil en Colombia?, en Análisis Político No 46, IEPRI Universidad Nacional, Bogota.

Ramsey, Russell (1981). *Guerrilleros y Soldados*, Bogotá, Ediciones Tercer Mundo.

Rangel, Alfredo (1999). "Las FARC-EP: Una Mirada Actual" in *Reconocer la Guerra para Construir la Paz,* Bogota, CEREC.

Rubio, Mauricio (1999). *Crimen e Impunidad: Precisiones sobre la Violencia.* Bogotá. Editorial Tercer Mundo.

Rocha, Ricardo (2000), *La Economía Colombiana tras 25 años de Narcotráfico.* Bogotá: Siglo de Hombre Editores, UNDCP.

Salazar, Boris and Castillo, Maria del Pilar (2001). *La Hora de los Dinosaurios. Conflicto y deprecación en Colombia.* Fondo Editorial CEREC.

Sanchez, Fabio and Nuñez Jairo (2000). "Determinantes del Crimen Violento en un país altamente violento: el caso de Colombia" in *Economía, Crimen y Conflicto*, Bogota, Universidad Nacional de Colombia.

Sánchez, Gonzalo and Aguilera, Mario (1991). "Memorias de un País en Guerra. Los Mil Días 1899-1902", en Ricardo Peñaranda y Gonzalo Sánchez, (Compiladores), *Pasado y presente de la violencia en Colombia*, Bogotá, Fondo Editorial CEREC.

Sanchez, Gonzalo and Donny Meertens (1983). *Bandoleros, gamonales y campesinos: El caso de la Violencia en Colombia.* Ancora.

Steiner, Roberto (1997), *Los Dólares del Narcotráfico*, Cuadernos de Fedesarrollo No.2, Bogotá.

Thoumi, Francisco E. (2002). *El Imperio de la Droga- Narcotráfico, economía y Sociedad en los Andes*, Bogotá, Editorial Planeta.

Vicepresidencia de la Republica (2002). *Colombia, Conflicto Armado, Regiones, Derechos Humanos, DIH 1998-2002*, Bogotá.

In: Focus on Urban and Regional Economics
Editor: Lawrence Yee, pp. 39-52
ISBN 1-59454-740-8

Chapter 2

PROVINCIAL CONVERGENCE IN SPAIN: A SPATIAL ECONOMETRIC ANALYSIS[1]

José Villaverde [2]
University of Cantabria, Avda. de los Castros, s.n., 39005- Santander (Spain)

ABSTRACT

This paper examines the process of provincial convergence that has taken place in Spain between 1985 and 2002. By taking labour productivity as its variable of analysis, the paper estimates the so-called "classical" models of convergence, concluding that, contrary to what has been suggested by previous work, convergence has not stagnated. After stressing the limitations of this type of approach, the paper attempts to overcome them, by, on the one hand, estimating the density function and the degree of internal mobility in the provincial productivity distribution; and on the other, by considering the influence of possible spatial effects on the aforementioned distribution. The conclusion arrived at is three-fold: we confirm the existence of provincial convergence of productivity; we reveal the low level of intradistributional mobility; and we do indeed find spatial effects, although they do not seem to be too relevant for the convergence process.

Keywords: Convergence, Productivity, Provinces, Spatial effects, Distribution.

Regional economists and, in particular, macroeconomists have been recently interested in territorial convergence for more than a decade, since the topic was again taken up for economic analysis in the late 1980s and early 1990s and used as a test bank for discriminating between competing growth theories: neo-classical models versus endogenous growth models. There have been a large number of empirical studies on the phenomenon of spatial convergence, and although it is frequently considered that the rate of convergence (wherever it occurs) is approximately 2% annually, the results are not conclusive. In the Spanish case,

[1] I would like to thank A. Maza for his useful comments and suggestions.
[2] Email: villavej@unican.es, Phone: 00 34 942 201629

most research carried out to date has taken the autonomous region as its unit of analysis, with relatively few looking at convergence at the provincial level[3]. Moreover, practically none of these studies has attempted to accurately evaluate the influence of space on the convergence process, something which can also be said for research using other scopes of reference[4].

Despite this relative lack of attention for the spatial phenomenon, one of the stylised facts of regional analysis is that economic activity tends to concentrate in certain areas[5], with obvious examples in the European case being the so-called "hot banana", and in Spain, the "Mediterranean arch"[6]. The existence of these corridors or axes of growth underlines the fact that space undoubtedly matters[7]. Space plays a significant role in the process of economic growth and convergence, since, for instance, the probability to reach a higher state of economic development is greater for poor areas surrounded by richer areas than for poor areas surrounded by poor areas.

This being so, it is a fact, however, that the traditional approach to convergence do not in general take spatial characteristics of the distribution into account, since it treat their objects of study (geographical units such as states, regions, provinces, etc.) as if they were absolutely independent from each other. This implies, logically, that this type of analysis has some important limitations, a fact which becomes particularly clear in estimations of σ and β-convergence. As we considered that empirical models developed to analyse real convergence should include the possibility of spatial effects, this study attempts to some extent to get round this problem, as well as some others common to what Sala-i-Martín (1996) calls the "classical approach to convergence". With this in mind, our analysis is focused on the distribution of labour productivity[8] in the 50 Spanish provinces[9], for the sample period that goes from 1985 to 2002.

The paper is structured as follows. In Section 2, following the aforementioned classical approach, we carry out a convergence analysis, with the aim of determining the existence or otherwise of β and σ convergence. In the next section, and in view of the limitations of this type of approach, we attempt to overcome it by analysing the distribution of the provincial productivity in more detail. Initially, our interest is devoted to the overall shape

---

[3] Among the pioneering work on provincial convergence since the early 1990s – which generally revealed that the convergence process had slowed (or stagnated) in the second part of the 1980s– we might mention Dolado, González Páramo and Roldán (1994), García Greciano, Raymond and Villaverde (1995), Villaverde (1996) and Villaverde and Sánchez-Robles (1998). More recent work of interest includes, among others, Goerlich and Mas (2001).

[4] In these cases, the units of analysis tend to be either European regions (see, for example, López Bazo *et al.*, 1999; Villaverde (2003) and Villaverde and Maza, 2003, among others) or US states (Rey and Montouri, 1999).

[5] One of the aims of the "new economic geography" is trying to explain industrial location and, in particular, why firms often cluster together provoking substantial agglomeration or concentration effects.

[6] The "hot banana" comprises the area from the South East of England to Northern Italy, containing Southern Germany, South East of France, the Ruhr area, the Ile de France and the Benelux. The "Mediterranean arch" is made up of the Mediterranean provinces of Gerona, Barcelona, Tarragona, Castellón, Valencia, Alicante, Murcia and Almería.

[7] The "manufacturing belt" in the USA is another example of these agglomeration effects.

[8] Labour productivity was calculated, in real terms (constant 1986 pesetas), as the quotient of GDP and employment, using for both variables series from FUNCAS (Spanish Savings Banks Foundation). With regards the GDP – and given the changes introduced in the SEC-95 methodology – we had to link the 1985-1999 series (at factor prices) with the 1995-2002 series (at basic prices). For employment, we should mention a jump in 1995 as a consequence of changes in the EPA (Spanish labour force survey).

[9] From a political-territorial perspective Spain is organised, since 1978, in 17 regions (called "autonomous communities") which are made up of 50 provinces (See Fig. 1 and the Annex).

characteristics of the provincial productivity distribution and its evolution over time. Afterwards, we are interested in elucidating the internal mixing or rank mobility that occurs within this distribution over time. Subsequently, in Section 4, we examine the possible presence of spatial dependence in the provincial productivity distribution, for which we undertake both an exploratory data analysis and –employing a strategy based on the modelling of spatial dependence- a confirmatory one. Finally, the last section presents our main conclusions.

PROVINCIAL PRODUCTIVITY CONVERGENCE IN SPAIN: THE CLASSICAL APPROACH

Most of the empirical studies on territorial convergence take per capita GDP as variable of reference; less frequently, productivity is used. It is important to remember, however, that from a theoretical point of view, economic growth models – particularly those with neoclassical roots, on which the hypothesis of β-convergence is based[10]– refer exclusively to productivity. As Paci (1997), points out, only in the case of full employment, and under the assumption that the relation between population and employment remains constant over time and is equal for all the territorial units considered, is it irrelevant whether the analysis is carried out with per capita GDP or productivity. In practice, however, it is virtually impossible to fulfil these assumptions, which means that the results obtained in the convergence analyses naturally differ depending on whether the variable under study is per capita GDP or labour productivity. A slightly extreme example of this situation is seen for the sample period (1985-2002) for the case of Spain compared to the European Union (EU): as we can see in Figure 2, there is a process of convergence of per capita GDP at the same time as one of divergence in terms of productivity[11]. Faced with a situation such as this, caused by an obvious divergence in the ratio of employment to population between Spain and the EU, and taking into consideration what we have said about the choice of the dependent variable in neoclassical growth models, we have opted to take labour productivity as our variable of reference. This variable, at the national level, experienced an accumulated growth of almost 26%, which represents an annual average rate of 1.3%.

With regards to the empirical question, there are two measures of convergence habitually used in regional analysis: β and σ-convergence[12]. Applied to our case, the first (β-convergence) occurs when provinces with lower initial levels of productivity tend to grow, on average, faster than those with higher initial levels and eventually catch up with them; the

[10] In the neoclassical growth models, economic growth is driven by factor (capital and labour) accumulation and technical progress, which is assumed to be endogenous. In this type of models convergence occurs due to diminishing returns to capital; this means that policy actions to correct income or productivity differentials are viewed as unnecessary.

[11] The figure makes use of data from the publication "Summary of Indicators" from the Bank of Spain; the GDP is expressed in purchasing power parities.

[12] A detailed account of the most commonly used convergence indicators is provided by Villaverde (2004). Generally speaking, β-convergence has been more popular with macroeconomists while σ-convergence has been mainly the focus of regional economists.

second (σ-convergence), which is a more restrictive concept of convergence[13], is seen when the cross-sectional dispersion of the provincial productivity diminishes over time.

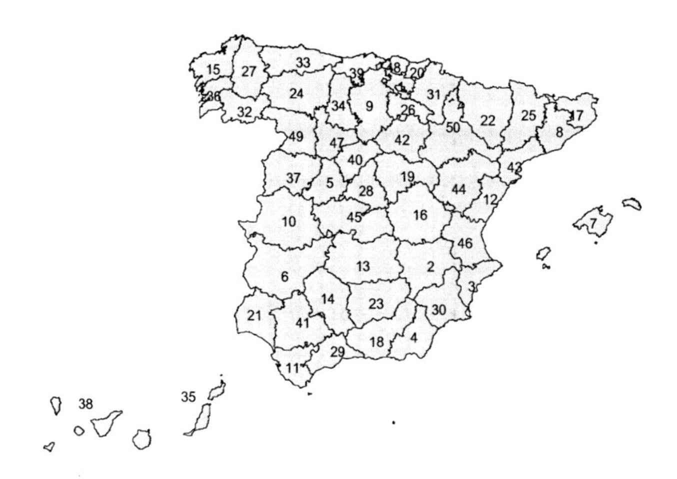

Figure 1. Spanish provincial organization

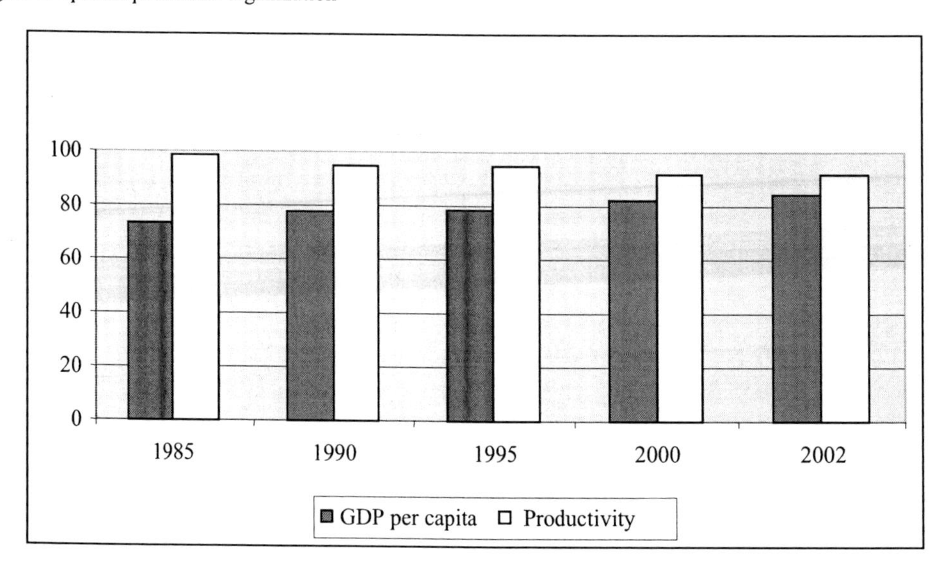

Figure 2. Real convergence Spain (EU= 100)

Our starting point consists of estimating an equation of absolute β-convergence, as follows:

---

[13] It is widely known that β-convergence is a necessary but not sufficient condition for σ-convergence. The presence of σ-convergence implies not only that $\beta<0$, but also that $-1<\beta<0$.

[15] The rate of convergence is calculated using the expression: $-\text{Log}(1+\beta T)/T$. In turn, the expression used to calculate the time required to close half the gap separating the productivity of the provinces from their corresponding steady state is: $\tau = -\text{Log}(2)/\text{Log}(1+\beta)$.

$$\frac{1}{T}\text{Log}\left(\frac{Y_{i,02}}{Y_{i,85}}\right) = \alpha + \beta\ \text{Log}\left(Y_{i,85}\right) + u_i \qquad (1)$$

where $Y_{i,t}$ is the labour productivity of province i in year t, T is the number of years of the sample and u the error term. In accordance with conventional analysis, if the coefficient β is negative and statistically significant, we can conclude that absolute β-convergence exists. The results obtained, shown in Table 1, allow us to say that between 1985 and 2002 there was a process of absolute β-convergence in labour productivity between the Spanish provinces. This process of convergence –explained by the regression in more than 66%– occurred at a rate of 1.9% per year, which implies that the time required for the provinces to close half of the productivity gap between their initial values and their steady state is 21.9 years[15]. Considering that the majority of provinces with low productivity are found in the south of the country, we re-estimated the previous equation introducing a dummy variable to control for their lower level of development[16]; although the dummy is in fact significant, its low value (the coefficient is equal to 0.0015) leads us in fact to ignore it when we consider the spatial influence later on.

Table 1. Ols Estimation Results for the Unconditional β-Convergence Equation

Dependent variable: $\frac{1}{T}\text{Log}\left(\frac{Y_{i,02}}{Y_{i,85}}\right)$

	Coefficient	t-Statistic
Constant	0,20521	10,242428
β	-0,0311554	-9,885057
Adjusted R-squared	0,6637	
LIK	240,526	
AIC	477.052	
SC	-473,228	

With the existence of β-convergence confirmed, Figure 3 shows the results for σ-convergence, calculated as the coefficient of variation of the logarithm of productivity. As can be seen, throughout the time period under study, the dispersion in the provincial distribution of productivity has diminished, and at an extremely fast rate: the drop in the coefficient of variation between 1985 and 2002 was no less than 41.6%, which implies an annual rate of convergence of 3.2%, clearly superior to that estimated by the β-convergence.

[16] This is the case of "conditional" $\beta -$ convergence, in which a set of variables is introduced in equation (1) conditioning the steady state of each province. In a somewhat arbitrary way, the provinces included in our"south" dummy variable are all the provinces of Andalusia and Extremadura, along with Murcia, Alicante, Ciudad Real, Toledo, Cuenca and Albacete.

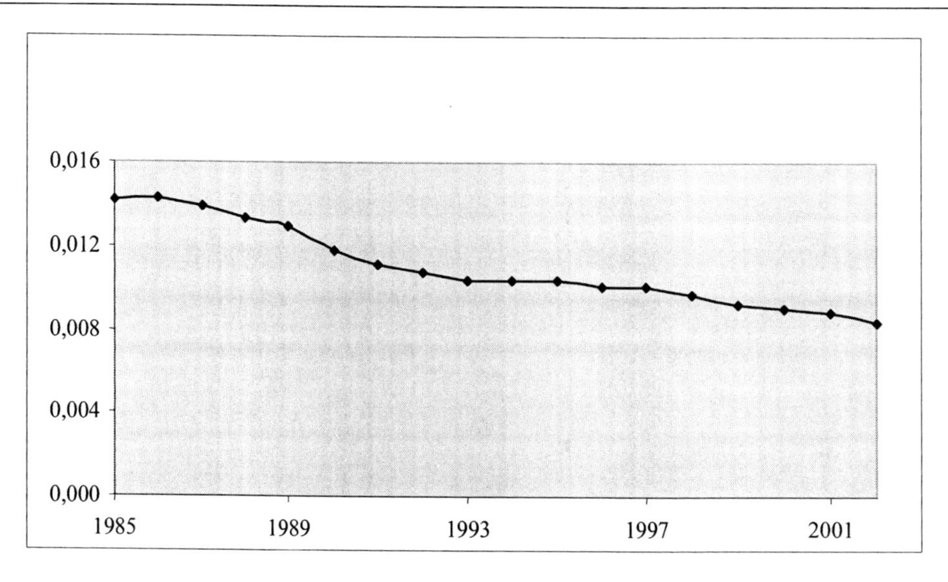

Figure 3. σ - convergence in (LOG) productivity

Having confirmed the presence of both types of convergence, an important question from the socio-economic perspective –but which, nevertheless, is rarely given much attention– is the way in which this convergence has occurred. In our case, the process has taken place as a consequence of an increasing concentration of production and employment in the provinces that initially had the highest levels of productivity; and correlatively, of a reduction in the participation, in both variables, of the provinces that were least efficient (least productive) in the base year. Logically, for convergence to have occurred the process of concentration has been more intense in employment than in production (see Table 2).

Table 2. Provincial Contribution to Spanish GDP and Employment (Selected Years)

	Ten Most Productive Provinces 1985-2002		Ten Less Productive Provinces 1985-2002	
GDP	47,1	47,4	8,1	7,9
Employment	39,5	42,7	12,3	9,7

Provincial Productivity in Spain: Distributional Dynamics

Although it does illustrate some important features of the provincial distribution of productivity in Spain, the analysis of the previous section does suffer from some significant limitations: in particular, as various authors have pointed out –see, especially, Quah, 1993, 1996a and 1996b– the "classical approach" does not capture the richness of the dynamic of the distribution, since it only encompasses some of its moments: its mean, in the case of β-convergence, and its variance, in the case of σ-convergence.

With a view to getting round some of these limitations, and to deepen our understanding of the provincial distribution of productivity in Spain, we proceeded to estimate the associated density functions for the first and last years of the sample period. By offering an approximation of the external form of the distribution, these density functions summarise the distribution more precisely than the previously calculated measures of position (β-convergence) or dispersion (σ-convergence). In particular, density functions can reveal, for each year, important insights as to the current situation of provincial productivity disparities while, when viewed in a dynamic process, can explain some aspects of the provincial growth process.

Following the standard procedure, the density functions were obtained by carrying out a non-parametric[17] analysis, using the kernel method -in particular we have estimated a Gaussian kernel with optimal bandwidth[18]. The results obtained (Figure 4) reveal several important changes occurring over the sample period in the external form of the distribution, changes which doubly confirm the process of convergence mentioned previously: first, because of the overall decline in the level of dispersion of provincial productivity distributions; and second, because in 2002 there is a greater concentration of its probabilistic mass around its mean than in 1985[19]. In addition, and with regards to the potential for polarisation or stratification phenomena, a comparison of the two density functions reveals that a peak (mode) for low productivity levels disappears, while another appears for relatively high levels. We might conclude, therefore, that an incipient provincial polarisation at low levels of productivity has been replaced by another, also incipient, at high levels; to some extent, these poles can be assimilated to convergence clubs.

In spite of the supplementary information about the external form of the provincial productivity distribution (and its variation over time) provided by the density functions in Figure 4, they say nothing about any changes that might have occurred within the distribution. Occasionally, however, and particularly in the perspective of economic policy options, these intradistributional movements can be as significant as the changes seen in the external form of the distribution, or indeed even more so.

A simple way of dealing with this question consists of estimating transition matrices, which –by mapping the provincial productivity distribution from one period into the distribution for the next period- represent the probability that a province belonging to a group formed by particular levels of productivity jumps to another with different levels. When this occurs there is said to be mobility in the distribution (the more changes that occur, the more mobility there is); while, in contrast, when this does not occur there is said to be persistence. This type of analysis –which has the undeniable advantage of assigning percentages to the level of mobility and persistence– has however the disadvantage that the results obtained from it may depend critically on the number of groups or intervals of productivity chosen when estimating the transition matrix. In this sense, it seems clear that, *ceteris paribus*, the greater the number of intervals, the greater the level of mobility, and consequently the lower the level of persistence.

[17] In this type of analysis no functional form is imposed, *a priori*, on the distribution; as is said informally, non-parametric estimations "let the data speak".

[18] A kernel can be understood as being a smoothed version of a histogram; the bandwidth of the kernel reflects the smoothness degree employed in the estimation of the density function.

[19] The 1985 distribution is skewed to the left while the 2002 distribution is almost symmetric. At the same time, the relative kurtosis in the distribution has changed over time. In 1985 the distribution is platykurtic while in 2002 is leptokurtic.

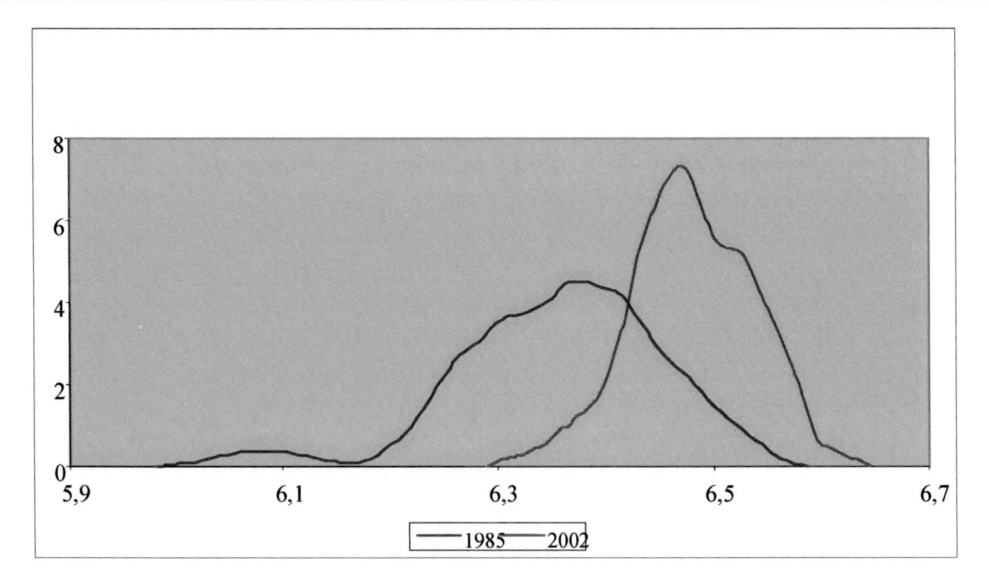

Figure 4. Density functions in (LOG) productivity

This problem is easily solved by estimating a stochastic kernel, which provides the probability of transiting between any two levels of value ranges of the provincial productivity distribution. A stochastic kernel is, therefore, conceptually equivalent to a transition matrix with the number of intervals tending to infinity. Figure 5 (Panel a) presents, for labour productivity (taking the national mean as base 100) and for the sample period 1985-2002, the stochastic kernel of the Spanish provinces corresponding to transitions of five years. In the 3-D graph of Panel a, the X-axis represents the productivity values in year t, the Y-axis the productivity values five years later, while the Z-axis represents the density (or conditioned probability) at each point in the X-Y plane. The lines running parallel to the t+5 axis show the probability of transiting from the point in the X-axis being considered to any other point in the Y-axis. Since the probability mass is concentrated on the positive diagonal, we can conclude that the distribution has a high level of persistence. This phenomenon is seen more clearly in the 2-D graph of Panel a, which shows the contour lines obtained by making cuts parallel to the X-Y plane: the lines obtained connect, therefore, points of equal height or density. Taking into account that these contour lines concentrate on the positive diagonal, we confirm our earlier conclusion that the level of mobility within the provincial productivity distribution is very low, or equally, that the level of persistence is very high. This result appears to be quite logical since it is likely that for transitions over five years changes in provincial rankings will not be very significant. In contrast, when we consider longer transitions –17 years in our case (Figure 5 Panel b) – the level of mobility within the distribution is, naturally, higher, despite the fact that the contour lines continue to show a high level of persistence. It is precisely this result that would seem to justify, at least in part, the application of a regional policy at the national level[20].

a) Five Years Transition Periods

[20] The suitability of such a policy is indeed reinforced in view of the increasing concentration of GDP and employment pointed out in Section 2. This type of policy is somewhat stressed by endogenous growth models, in which the presence of increasing returns to scale may lead to the possibility of persistent and even increasing real spatial disparities.

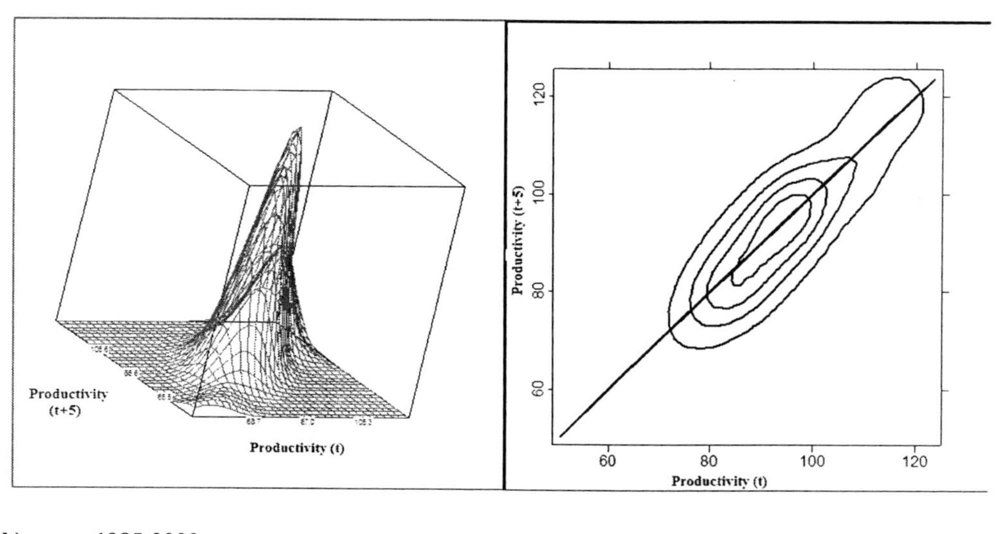

b) **1985-2002**

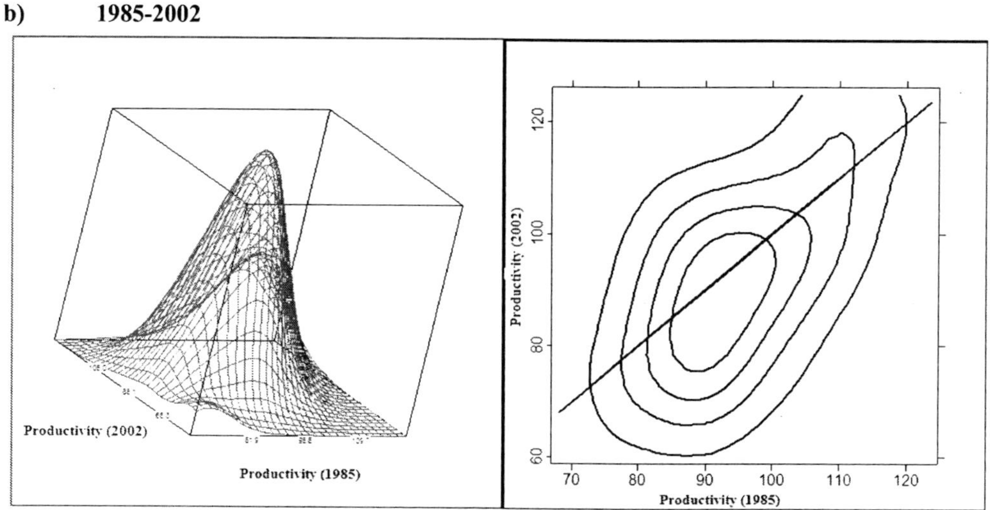

Figure 5. Distribution dynamics

Provincial Productivity Convergence in Spain: A Spatial Econometric Approach

The analysis carried out in the two previous sections did not take the geographical location of the Spanish provinces into account; it is, therefore, insensitive to their spatial distribution. Indeed, the results would not be modified in the slightest if for example, Asturias (in the north of the country) were located in Granada (south), or Huelva (southwest) in Tarragona (northeast). This is the case because the units of analysis –the provinces– are considered to be absolutely independent of each other, which ignores possible spatial interactions between them.

The spatial location can be –and in some cases undoubtedly is– of great importance for the processes of economic development and convergence; endogenous growth theory and the new economic geography provide interesting arguments in this respect (spillover effects, technological diffusion, economies of scale, market size, transport costs, etc.) to justify the potential relevance of space to development (or backwardness) and convergence (or divergence). Spatial econometrics provides, in this sense, various techniques of analysis that attempt to evaluate the impact of geography on the aforementioned processes[21].

Applying a spatial approach, in this section we carry out a new analyses of provincial convergence in productivity with two basic objectives: to offer, initially, a spatial perspective of the pattern of provincial growth in productivity; and to subsequently extend the model of β-convergence to include possible spatial effects that have been ignored previously.

In our case, this is a question of the existence or otherwise of autocorrelation or spatial dependence; this is understood to exist when there is some type of functional relation between what occurs in a province and what occurs in another or others. The so-called exploratory spatial data analysis (ESDA) allows us to show, at the univariate level, the presence or absence of spatial dependence by calculating a number of statistics[22]. The most familiar of all of them is Moran's I[23], which in addition has the advantage of allowing for an easily interpretable graphical representation in the form of a scatterplot or scattermap. In our case, we have opted to present the scattermaps for the first and last years of the sample (Figure 6), which allow us to clearly see the existence of a phenomenon of positive spatial autocorrelation between the Spanish provinces in terms of labour productivity: both maps show –the 2002 one even more clearly– that the provinces with a low (high) relative productivity tend to be close to each other –i.e., they are geographically concentrated.

Having shown the existence of global positive spatial dependence in the Spanish provincial distribution of productivity, it is more than likely that the equation of β-convergence previously estimated will also be affected by problems of spatial dependence, which will lead to some difficulties with the estimators (Anselin, 1988). To decide if this is the case, spatial econometrics has designed a whole series of tests, some of an *ad hoc* nature (such as Moran's I) and others based on the maximum likelihood estimation of a spatial model. Among these last are, for example: the Maximum Likelihood test, the Wald test, and above all those based on the Lagrange multiplier. With regards to these last ones, the LM-ERR test, along with the associated robust LM-EL, tests for the absence of spatial autocorrelation in the regression residuals; while the LM-LAG test, along with the associated robust LM-LE, tests for the absence of spatial autocorrelation in the variables, also called substantive spatial autocorrelation. The results obtained in our case (see Table 3) show that there is no substantive autocorrelation, but that there is residual autocorrelation[24]; this implies that a shock in a particular province spills over to all or part of the national territory.

---

[21] An analysis that illustrates spatial econometrics can be seen in Moreno and Vayá (2002), among others.

[22] All computations have been carried out by using the SpaceStat 1.91 software, by Luc Anselin.

[23] This indicator is used to test the null hypothesis that the variable analysed is distributed randomly in space.

[24] The robust test LM-LE is not rejected at the 95% level, so we conclude that there is no substantive autocorrelation. In contrast, the test LM-ERR and its robust LM-EL throw up p-values of less than 0.05, which indicates that the null hypothesis is rejected (absence of spatial autocorrelation) in the residuals. We conclude, therefore, that the equation of β-convergence estimated previously presents spatial dependence in the residuals. When, as in our case, there is residual autocorrelation, the estimations of the parameters are, like in a temporal context, inefficient although unbiased; as a result, statistical inference is not reliable.

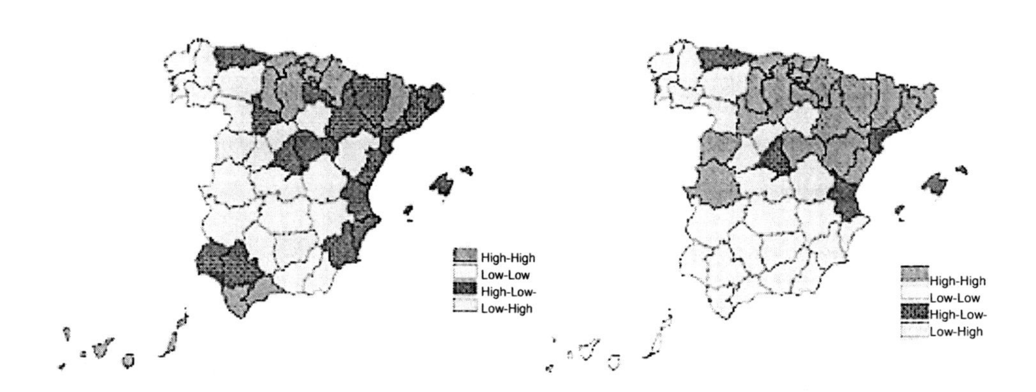

Figure 6. Moran scattermaps

Table 3. Diagnostic for Spatial Dependence

	Value	p-Value
Moran I	5,936381	0,000000
LM-ER	24,243674	0,000000
LM-EL	6,259792	0,012351
LM-LAG	19,441868	0,000000
LM-LE	0,266986	0,605361

The procedure for correcting the aforementioned autocorrelation in the residuals consists of including an autoregressive structure of spatial dependence in the error term of the model to estimate, so that the new regression equation is as follows:

$$\frac{1}{T}\text{Log}\left(\frac{Y_{i,02}}{Y_{i,85}}\right) = \alpha + \beta\,\text{Log}\left(Y_{i,85}\right) + \varepsilon \tag{2}$$

$$\text{where} \quad \varepsilon = \lambda W\varepsilon + u \quad \text{and} \quad u \approx N(0,\sigma^2 I)$$

In this new equation, λ is the autoregressive parameter expressing the intensity of spatial autocorrelation (interdependences) in the error term, while W represents the weights matrix, defined –like in the case of Moran's scattermap– in terms of the inverse of the standardised distance: its elements $w_{i,j}$ reflect the intensity of the interdependence between the provinces i and j. In this model the effects of the spatial dependence (diffusion) appear in two ways, since the rate of growth of the productivity of a province i is influenced, on the one hand, by the growth rates of the other contiguous provinces, and on the other, by its own initial level of productivity, weighted in both cases by W[25].

The results of the maximum likelihood estimation of this new equation of β-convergence are shown in Table 4. As can be seen, all the coefficients –including the one corresponding to the autoregressive parameter λ– are significant[26]. Moreover, this model presents better results compared to the previous one, whatever the goodness of fit measure is considered. This occurs, indeed, with regards to the maximum likelihood test (LIK) –which passes from 240.5 to 249.6– as well as in Akaike's Information Criterion (AIC) –which passes from –477.1 to –495.1– and Schwartz's Criterion (SC) –which jumps from –473.2 to –491.3.

Table 4. Maximum Likelihood Estimation Results for the Spatial Dependence Model

Dependent Variable: $\frac{1}{T}\text{Log}\left(\frac{Y_{i,02}}{Y_{i,85}}\right)$

	Coefficient	z-value
Constant	0,200307	10,242428
β	-0,0303736	-13,289972
λ	0,830104	8,088082
LIK	249,560	
AIC	-495,120	
SC	-491,296	

The process of convergence, once the presence of spatial autocorrelation in the residuals is taken into account, occurs at a slightly lower rate than in the classical model (1.8% compared to 1.9%)[27], which implies that the time required for provinces to close half the gap separating them from their steady state is now 22.5 years (compared to 21.9 years in the classical case). Thus, the relevant conclusion we obtain is that spatial effects –although present in the distribution- have not affected, to a great extent, the speed of provincial productivity convergence in Spain during the sample period.

CONCLUSIONS

In contrast to what the first works on provincial convergence led us to believe, the process of real convergence between Spanish provinces has continued throughout the period

---

[25] Manipulating Equation 2 (see Toral, 2002; or Anselin, 2003) allows us to obtain the following equation, in which the third and fourth terms on the right-hand side refer to the aforementioned spatial effects:

$$\frac{1}{T}\text{Log}\left(\frac{Y_{i,02}}{Y_{i,85}}\right) = \text{constant} + \beta\,\text{Log}\left(Y_{i,85}\right) + \rho W\frac{1}{T}\text{Log}\left(\frac{Y_{i,02}}{Y_{i,85}}\right) + \gamma W\frac{1}{T}\text{Log}\left(Y_{i,85}\right) + u$$

where $\rho = \lambda$; $\gamma = -\lambda\beta$

[26] The fact that the parameter λ is significant and positive confirms what the spatial dependence tests suggested about the ordinary least-squares estimation.

of analysis considered in this paper. This convergence, which has been of both types (β and σ) and which is confirmed examining the corresponding density functions, has occurred in parallel with a growing process of concentration of GDP and employment in the most efficient provinces, more intense, logically, in employment than in GDP. If this last result is worrying from a socio-economic perspective, thus justifying the application of a compensatory regional policy at the national level, the scarce mobility within the provincial distribution of productivity provides another argument in favour of this policy. Finally, the paper has revealed the existence of a certain spatial dependence between the Spanish provinces, a finding that led us to re-estimate the equation of β-convergence; the results obtained from this new model, which are better than those of the classical one, confirm the existence of β-convergence but at a slightly lower rate than that of the classical model.

ANNEX: SPANISH PROVINCES AND REGIONS

1. Alava (País Vasco)
2. Albacete (Castilla-La Mancha)
3. Alicante (C. Valenciana)
4. Almeria (Andalucía)
5. Avila (Castilla y León)
6. Badajoz (Extremadura)
7. Baleares
8. Barcelona (Cataluña)
9. Burgos (Castilla y León)
10. Cáceres (Extremadura)
11. Cádiz (Andalucía)
12. Castellón (C. Valenciana)
13. Ciudad Real (Castilla-La Mancha)
14. Córdoba (Andalucía)
15. Coruña (Galicia)
16. Cuenca (Castilla-La Mancha)
17. Girona (Cataluña)
18. Granada (Andalucía)
19. Guadalajara (Castilla-La Mancha)
20. Guipúzcoa (País Vasco)
21. Huelva (Andalucía)
22. Huesca (Aragón)
23. Jaén (Andalucía)
24. León (Castilla y León)
25. Lerida (Cataluña)
26. Rioja, La
27. Lugo (Galicia)
28. Madrid
29. Málaga (Andalucía)
30. Murcia
31. Navarra
32. Orense (Galicia)
33. Asturias
34. Palencia (Castilla y León)
35. Palmas, Las (Canarias)
36. Pontevedra (Galicia)
37. Salamanca (Castilla y León)
38. Tenerife (Canarias)
39. Cantabria
40. Segovia (Castilla y León)
41. Sevilla (Andalucía)
42. Soria (Castilla y León)
43. Tarragona (Cataluña)
44. Teruel (Aragón)
45. Toledo (Castilla-La Mancha)
46. Valencia (C. Valenciana)
47. Valladolid (Castilla y León)
48. Vizcaya (País Vasco)
49. Zamora (Castilla y León)
50. Zaragoza (Aragón)

The names in brackets refer to Autonomous Communities (Regions)

[27] This is a very general result in this type of analysis, as can be seen for example in Rey and Montouri (1999) and Moreno and Vayá (2002).

REFERENCES

Anselin, L. (1988) *Spatial Econometrics: Methods and Models*, Kluwer, Dordrecht.

Anselin, L. (2003) "Spatial Externalities, Spatial Multipliers, and Spatial Econometrics" *International Regional Science Review*, 26 (2), pp. 153-166.

Dolado, JJ., González Páramo, JM. and Roldán, JM. (1994) "Convergencia económica entre las provincias españolas: evidencia empírica (1955-1989)", Banco de España, *Documento de Trabajo*, No. 9406.

Garcia Greciano, B., Raymond, JL. and Villaverde, J. (1995) "La convergencia de las provincias españolas, *Papeles de Economía Española*, No. 64, pp. 38-53.

Goerlich, F. and Más, M. (200.) "*La evolución económica de las provincias españolas (1955-1998). Vol II, Desigualdad y Convergencia*", Fundación BBVA.

Lopez Bazo, E., Vayá, E., Mora, AJ. and Suriñach (1999) "Regional economic dynamics and convergente in the European Union", *Annals of Regional Science*, 33, pp. 334-370.

Quah, D. (1993) "Gallton's fallacy and tests of the convergence hypothesis" Scandinavian *Journal of Economics*, 95 (4) pp. 427-443.

Quah, D. (1996a) "Regional convergence clusters in Europe" *European Economic Review*, 40 (3-5), pp. 951-958.

Quah, D. (1996b) "Empirics for economic growth and convergence" *European Economic Review*, 40 (6), pp. 1353-1375.

Moreno, R. and Vayá, E (2002) "Econometría espacial: nuevas técnicas para el análisis regional. Una aplicación a las regiones europeas" *Investigaciones Regionales*, 1, pp. 83-106.

Paci, R. (1997) "More similar and less equal: Economic Growth in the Euroepan Regions" *Weltwirtschaftliches Archiv*, 133 (4), pp. 609-634.

Rey, S. and Montouri, B. (1999) "US Regional Income Convergente: A Spatial Econometric Análisis", *Regional Studies*, 33 (2), pp. 143-156.

Sala-i-Martin, X. (1996) "The classical approach to convergence analysis". *Economic Journal,* 106 (437), pp. 1019-1036.

Toral, A. (2002) "La mesure de la distance dans le processus de convergence regionale en Espagne", *Revue d'Économie Régionale et Urbaine*, No. 5, pp. 789-803.

Villaverde, J, (1996) Desigualdades provinciales en España, 1955-1991, *Revista de Estudios Regionales*, No. 45, pp. 89-108.

Villaverde, J. (2003) "Regional Convergence, Polarisation and Mobility in the European Union, 1980-1996". *Journal of European Integration*, No. 1, pp 73-87.

Villaverde, J. (2004) "Indicators of Real Economic Convergence. A Primer" *UNU-CRIS e-Working Papers* W-2004/2

Villaverde, J. and Sánchez-Robles, B. (1998) Disparidades provinciales y clubes de convergencia en España. *Revista de Estudios Regionales*, nº 52, pp.177-199.

Villaverde, J. and Maza, A. (2003) "Desigualdades regionales y dependencia espacial en la Unión Europea" *CLM-Economía*, 2, pp. 109-128.

In: Focus on Urban and Regional Economics
Editor: Lawrence Yee, pp. 53-64
ISBN 1-59454-740-8

Chapter 3

LABOUR MOBILITY FROM INDUSTRIAL COMPANIES

Juha Kettunen [1]
Turku Polytechnic, Sepänkatu 3, FIN-20700 Turku, Finland

ABSTRACT

This study analyses the effect of wages on the job tenure in the Finnish manufacturing industry using microeconomic data. The alternative channels out from a company to other industrial jobs or outside the industry are explicitly accounted for. Semi-parametric models of job tenure were estimated in a competing risk framework allowing for piece-wise linear hazards for the predefined intervals of job tenure. According to the results the relative wage of the worker is negatively related to the exit rate for the persons who leave industry. On average there are no remarkable wage gains at job changes within industry, but a closer analysis indicates that low-paid workers are able to gain higher wages whereas the high-wage workers incur wage decreases.

Keywords: Labour mobility, Job tenure, Wages, Industry

INTRODUCTION

Since the 1980's there has been a remarkable decrease in the number of workers in the Finnish manufacturing industry. This study analyses the transitions from employment using longitudinal data on industrial workers. Special emphasis is devoted to the effects of wages on the labour mobility and the rate of leaving industry.

Job-matching models of Jovanovic (1979, 1984), Miller (1984), Gottschalk and Maloney (1985) and a search model of Albrecht, Holmlund and Lang (1991) incorporate uncertainty of wages or unobservable job-specific characteristics and constitute a theoretical framework for job-to-job transitions. This study presents a search model of labour mobility, which is used to analyse the effects of various factors on the mobility of workers.

---

[1] tel: +358 10 553 5612, fax: +358 10 553 5791, e-mail: Juha.Kettunen@turkuamk.fi

The job tenure in the Finnish metal and forest industries is studied using microeconomic data on blue-collar workers. The longitudinal data were compiled from administrative files of the Confederation of Finnish Industry and Employers. The data cover a period of 11 years starting from the first quarter of 1980.

There is a huge body of literature on the duration of employment (see Kiefer, 1988, Björklund and Holmlund, 1989, Brown and Light, 1992, Gritz, 1993 and Becker and Lindsay, 1994). The empirical analysis of this study is carried out in the competing risk framework. It makes possible to take into account the feature that employment spells may be terminated by different outcomes. The data allow one to make a distinction between the workers who change their jobs within Finnish industry or leave it.

Special attention is paid to the duration-dependent changes in the hazard function. Semi-parametric models with piece-wise linear hazards are used to examine the non-monotonic job separation hazards. In these models job tenure is expressed in predefined intervals and separate constant baseline hazards are estimated for each of the intervals.

This study is organized as follows. In the next section the theoretical background of the determination of the wage is exposed briefly. The data of this study are presented in section 3. The econometric models and the results of estimations are presented in section 4. The concluding chapter summarizes and discusses the results of the study.

A Search Model of Labour Mobility

The simple search model of this study is based on a model presented by Stiglitz (1985), which is one of the efficiency wage models (see Krueger and Summers, 1988). An important characteristic of the model of labour mobility is that a person with long job tenure is more valuable to the company than a newcomer. The reason is that there are extra costs of labour at the beginning and end of an employment spell. It is more profitable for a company to pay high efficiency wages in order to reduce the costs of labour mobility.

From the point of workers it is assumed that the workers are continually searching for a higher paid job and that they quit when they find it. The quit function q is assumed to depend negatively on the present wage of the workers w. The workers leave the company at the rate of q(w), where $\partial q/\partial w < 0$. The quit rate function is assumed to be a decreasing convex function. Stiglitz (1985) gives arguments why the quit function should have the given shape.

From the point of the company the production is characterised by the fixed training costs T, which are creating an inflow per worker $f(T)$ and interest expenditures for training costs rT. The constant returns-to-scale property of the technology is assumed. The quit function acts like the depreciation factor on the human capital. It is assumed that the workers are replaced by an equal number of new workers and that there are fixed training costs T for workers when they are entering the company.

The managers of the company are maximizing the profits by avoiding unnecessary costs of labour mobility. A low wage will increase costs of labour mobility. On the contrary, a high wage will increase direct labour costs. The wage w is the only decision variable of the management. The profits can be written as follows:

$$P = f(T) - w - [q(w) + r)]T. \tag{1}$$

The zero-profit condition P = 0 is a natural technical simplification to analyse the implications of the model. This simplification can be relaxed if deemed necessary. As a consequence the market clearing wage $w = f(T) - [q(w) + r)]T$.

Clearly the wage is an increasing function of the production. If for some exogenous reason the productivity of the workers decreases the wage level will become lower. The decrease of the productivity may depend on the change of technology, motivation or health of the workers. The wage is a decreasing function of the quit rate function, interest rate and training costs.

In order to analyse the effect of the training costs, let the subscripts denote the derivatives. Then the implicit-function rule of differentiation gives:

$$w_T = -P_{wT} / P_{ww} > 0, \qquad (2)$$

since $P_{wT} = -q_w > 0$ and $-P_{ww} = q_{ww}T > 0$. Hence, the sign of w_T is determined by the sign of P_{wT}, which is positive. Consequently, the wage is an increasing function of the training costs.

The reasons for quitting a company can be classified into two categories. The workers quit the industrial work or become voluntarily unemployed with probability $v(w)$ or alternatively they find better paid jobs in Finnish industry. It is assumed that $\partial v / \partial w < 0$. For some workers an intervening spell of unemployment is observed immediately after they quit their job. For others consecutive employment is observed, since they quit their job in order to accept immediately a new one.

The probability of changing jobs depends on the number of searchers during the search period s and on the unknown wage offers, which are characterized by the distribution function F(w). The quit rate function can be written as follows:

$$q(w) = v(w) + s[1 - F(w)]. \qquad (3)$$

The probability that a worker finds a higher paid job is a product of the search activity s and the probability of finding an acceptable offer $[1 - F(w)]$.

The model predicts that low-wage workers would have a higher quit rates and shorter spells of employment. The low-wage workers would seek better paid jobs and the job-to-job transitions would tend to be followed by higher wages. On the contrary, if the profit-maximizing company pays too high wages, the model predicts that high-wage workers would incur wage decreases in the new industrial jobs.

DESCRIPTION OF THE DATA

The investigation is based on data from the administrative files of the Confederation of Finnish Industry and Employers (TT). The data have been reported and analysed in various studies (Kettunen, 1993, 1998, 2000). Access to the reliable administrative data is a substantial advantage of this study. It can be observed from the data whether the workers immediately find another job in Finnish industry. Alternatively the workers leave the industry.

The sampling of spells of employment was made from the outflow of workers from the companies. In order to guarantee the random and seasonally representative sample, the workers were sorted into a random order and every 15th worker was picked from the outflow during 1990. The follow-up covers a period of 11 years backwards until the first quarter of 1980. About 14 % of the workers had longer lengths of spells. These observations are censored, because the length of employment is not known in the data. The job tenure is measured in years.

The data are representative, because 80 % of the Finnish industrial workers are working in the private member companies of the confederation. The workers in the three largest industries of the metal and forest industries were included to the final sample. The forest industry includes the wood and paper industries. The selection of these industries represents 79 % of all the industrial workers and leaves 2899 observations in the sample. A reason for selecting these industries is that the number of wage groups defined in the collective wage agreements is different between the industries, which causes problems to draw reasonable statistical conclusions using all the industries.

A well-known and simple nonparametric life table method introduced by Cutler and Ederer (1958) was first used to evaluate the distribution of job tenure. This nonparametric actuarial method was used separately for the workers who find new industrial jobs and workers who do not find new jobs in industry.

There is a remarkable difference between the two categories of the data. The hazard function of the workers who find new industrial jobs is clearly lower than the hazard function of the persons who leave Finnish industry. This phenomenon is especially pronounced during the first two years of employment. Starting from the second year the hazard functions of the two groups are rather similar. The exit rate from industry peaks during the second quarter. An obvious reason is that there are short tenures during the summer time when students fill short holiday vacancies.

The labour mobility is rather strong, because 46 % of the workers leave their jobs during the first year. About 35 % of the workers who change their jobs within industry leave their jobs within the first year, and 62 % of the workers who do not find new jobs within industry leave their jobs during the first year. These figures indicate that the labour mobility is clearly higher among the persons who leave industry.

Topel (1991) provides strong evidence that wages rise with job seniority. Persons with longer job tenures typically earn higher wages. He found that 10 years of current job seniority raise the wage of the typical male worker in the United States by over 25 %. Senior workers would suffer this amount if their jobs were to end exogenously. There are also other results in the empirical studies of job tenure that high-wage workers are less likely to terminate their employment spells (Kiefer, 1988, Brown, 1992 and Belzil, 1993).

The plotting of average relative wages against the job tenures was used to examine the relationship between the relative wage and job tenure. The relationship seems to be slightly increasing, which means that the persons with long spells of employment have higher wages than the others. It can also be seen that the relative wage of the persons who find new industrial jobs is during the first three years clearly higher than the relative wage of the persons who leave industry.

A more detailed analysis was made by calculating the wage profiles for groups of persons who have experienced equal lengths of employment. In this way it is possible to examine the proper development of wages of the identical persons. The wage profiles indicate that the workers are 'low paid' at the beginning of job tenure and 'overpaid' at the end of it.

The wage profiles are increasing for the short spells of four years or less. They are constant for the spells of five years or more. The workers with longer spells of employment have on average higher wages than the other. Also the starting wages of the high-wage workers are higher than the average. An increasing wage profile is related to the low starting wage, short employment and faster mobility of labour.

The wage profiles indicate that the relative wages are clearly lower for the short-term employed persons who leave industry than for the persons who find new industrial jobs. This can be seen as evidence for the discouragement of the workers. If the persons realize that they cannot obtain better paid jobs within industry, they leave the industrial companies. The opportunity cost of choosing unemployment is lower for a person who has a low wage. Therefore these figures can be seen in that respect as evidence for a search theory.

The wage level of the subsequent job is interesting from the point of on-the-job search. Better earnings opportunities in other companies may attract the workers to initiate a job search. There may, however, be other reasons for the termination of an employment than a search. Therefore the means of the wages in the subsequent jobs cannot necessarily be used in order to give very strong support to the wage gains implied by the search theory.

Topel and Ward (1992) studied the job mobility and the careers of young men using longitudinal data from the United States. It turned out that during the first ten years in the labour market a typical worker will hold about two thirds of his jobs in his total career. The wage gains at job changes account for at least a third of early-career wage growth. Job changing is a critical component of workers' movement toward the stable employment relations of mature careers. Also Farber (1994) found that mobility is strongly positively related to the frequency of job change prior to the start of a job. According to a Swedish study a majority of job leavers report that they have received higher pay on the new job (Björklund and Holmlund, 1989). The excess wage growth for job leavers is 7-8 %. On the contrary, a minority of job losers reported that they have received higher pay.

The analysis of the termination wages and starting wages of new jobs show that the persons who find new industrial jobs get on average only 1 % higher wages in Finnish industry. These average figures of the data do not support the theory of search for a better paid jobs within industry.

The distribution of the wage changes was analysed for the persons who change their jobs within industry. The wage level of most workers does not change very much when the workers change their jobs. The distribution of the wage changes indicate that the workers have got in a new job clearly higher wages than in the previous job if their previous job tenure has been short.

If the job tenure has been less than one year, the wage remains within the band of 5 % in 42 % of the cases and changes less than 15 % in 75 % of the cases. If the job tenure has been 1-3 years the wage change is clearly less than in the short job tenures. The wage remains within the band of 5 % in 48 % of the cases and changes less than 15 % in 85 % of the cases. If the job tenure has been longer than 3 years the change of jobs rather seldom imposes a large change of the wage. The wage remains within a band of 5 % in 52 % of the cases and changes less than 15 % in 87 % of the cases and there is a similar amount of observations in the lower and upper tails of the distribution of the wage changes.

Table 1 describes the characteristics of the workers that have changed their jobs within industry. The information has been classified by the wage change in three groups according to whether the wages have decreased, remained unchanged or increased. The changes that remain within the band of 10 % have been classified as unchanged wages in the table. About 13 % of the workers have lower wages in the new job. There have not been any remarkable wage changes in 69 % of the cases. Only 18 % of the workers have succeeded to obtain better paid jobs.

Table 1. The Characteristics of Workers by the Wage Change

	Wage of the new job / wage of the previous job:		
	<0.9	0.9- 1.1	1.1<
Job tenure, years	3.52	4.33	2.68
Sex, 1=male	0.87	0.81	0.80
Share of men	0.83	0.82	0.79
Age, years	33.73	35.31	28.42
Average age of men in a company	37.82	37.52	36.86
Average age in a company	38.52	38.25	37.89
High cost area, 1=yes	0.42	0.35	0.29
County of Uusimaa, 1=yes	0.10	0.15	0.14
Share of incentive hours[1]	0.33	0.25	0.14
Share of incentive hours[2]	0.23	0.27	0.31
Share of overtime hours, %	3.79	3.57	3.95
Share of Sunday hours, %	4.10	4.55	5.66
Quarter, 1=yes: 1	0.19	0.19	0.23
2	0.13	0.11	0.14
3	0.24	0.14	0.42
4	0.44	0.55	0.31
Wage group of metal industry, 1=yes: 1	0.30	0.21	0.10
2	0.27	0.29	0.23
(low) 3	0.09	0.08	0.12
Wage group of forest industry, 1=yes: 1	0.09	0.06	0.16
2	0.07	0.09	0.13
3	0.08	0.11	0.15
4	0.06	0.09	0.07
(high) 5	0.05	0.08	0.04
Relative wage in industry	1.15	1.09	0.98
The number of observations	222	1170	315

1. The incentive wage based on quantity, %.
2. The incentive wage based on quality and quantity, %

What are the characteristics of workers whose income increases when they change their jobs within industry? These workers have been working a relatively short time in their jobs. Women and young workers are more successful to find better paid work in industry. They have been working in a low cost area, which includes rural areas, villages and small towns. They have been working more often in an incentive work based on quality and quantity and in Sunday work, but more seldom in an incentive work based on quantity. The wages increase often if the workers change their jobs during the third quarter of the year, but those who change jobs during the fourth quarter incur wage decreases. The wage group is the required level of skill of the collective wage agreements. The workers who have been working in the lowest wage groups have gained from the change of jobs, but workers who have a rather high wage in their previous jobs have wage decreases.

SEMI-PARAMETRIC MODELS OF JOB TENURE

In this section an approach of piece-wise linear hazards is followed to analyse the effects of various factors on the exit rate. One reason for the flexible hazard function is that job separation hazards may not be non-monotonic. Farber (1994) found using monthly data that the probability of job termination increases to a maximum at 3 months of employment and declines thereafter. In our case the exit rate from industry peaks during the second quarter as shown by the life-table method.

Prentice and Gloeckler (1978) have presented a semi-parametric model, which has been analysed and used by Meyer (1990). In the semi-parametric approach the duration is expressed in intervals and separate constant baseline hazards are estimated for each of the intervals. The effect of time on the exit rate is estimated for the intervals. A nonparametric characterization of the baseline hazard ensures consistent estimation of simultaneously estimated structural parameters.

The hazard is specified assuming proportional hazards as follows:

$$h(t) = h_o(t)\exp[x(t)\beta], \tag{4}$$

where $h_0(t)$ is the unknown baseline hazard, x is a vector of explanatory variables for an individual and β is a vector of unknown structural parameters. It is assumed that $x(t)$ is constant during the specified intervals. The constant of the model is omitted. Therefore the matrix x does not include the vector of one. The shape of the baseline hazard is non-parametrically estimated and no parametric form is assumed.

Consider independent pairs of independent random variables which are the job tenure T and censoring time Z. Either a job tenure t or a censoring time c is observed for an individual, t = min(T, Z), with an indicator for the complete spells c. If T < Z, then c = 1 and c = 0 otherwise.

In the competing risks approach it is assumed that there are K different types of terminations of jobs (k = 1,...,K). It is assumed that the types of terminations are mutually exclusive and exhaust the possible destinations. In our case there are two types of job terminations. The workers can change a job within industry or leave industrial work.

Let $F^k(\cdot)$ be the distribution function of a job tenure for type k of termination. Then the survivor function is $S^k(\cdot) = 1 - F^k(\cdot)$. The probability that a job tenure terminates during a predefined interval (t, t+1] can be written as follows:

$$h^k(t) = 1 - S^k(t+1)/S^k(t). \tag{5}$$

The rate that the job tenure is terminated by time t+1 due to a type k, given that the person was still working at time t, is defined by the following discrete-time proportional hazards model:

$$h^k(t) = 1 - \exp[-\exp(x\beta)\int_t^{t+1} h_o{}^k(\tau)d\tau] = 1 - \exp\{-\exp[x\beta + \gamma^k(t)]\} \qquad (6)$$

where

$$\gamma^k(t) = \log[\int_t^{t+1} h_o{}^k(\tau)d\tau] \qquad (7)$$

is a parameter to be estimated consistently with the structural parameters β. An advantage of the constancy of $x(t)$ during the intervals is that h^k can be expressed in a closed form. In this case there are eight intervals predefined by the researcher. The selected intervals are (0, 1], (1, 2], (2, 3], (3, 4], (4, 5], (5, 6], (6, 8], (8, 11] years.

The likelihood function can then be written as follows:

$$l(\beta,\gamma) = \prod_{n=1}^{N}\{h^k(t)^c \prod_{u=0}^{t-1}\prod_{j=1}^{K}\exp[-\exp(x\beta + \gamma^j(u))]\}, \qquad (8)$$

where N is the size of the sample. The subscript n has been left out to simplify the notation. The log-likelihood function can be written using the hazard functions as follows:

$$\log\, l(\beta,\gamma) = \sum_{n=1}^{N}\{c\log[h^k(t)] + \sum_{u=0}^{t-1}\sum_{j=1}^{K}\log[1 - h^j(u)]\}. \qquad (9)$$

The maximum likelihood estimates of the unknown parameters β and γ are obtained by maximizing the log-likelihood using standard techniques.

It can be seen from (9) that the log-likelihood component can be partitioned into separate terms that are functions of cause-specific hazards. Therefore the parameters of any cause-specific hazard can be estimated separately by treating durations terminated by other types as censored with the true censored employment spells (see Kalbfleich and Prentice, 1980).

Table 2 presents the results of the estimations of the semi-parametric models of job tenure. The estimations have been done in a competing risk framework separately to both of the destinations. The explanatory variables are the same in both of the groups. The data of the models differ only with respect to the indicators of the destinations.

According to the results the sex of the workers does not have statistically significant effect. Similar results were obtained in both of the destinations. The share of men in a company has a positive effect on the probability of leaving an industrial company.

The age of the workers has a negative effect on both of the destinations. Older persons have longer spells of employment. The effect of age was studied also using the age squared and indicators for the age groups. These estimations show, however, a linear increasing effect of age. Therefore the age was included as a continuous explanatory variable.

Table 2. Results of Estimations of the Semi-Parametric Models of Job Tenure

(A) The persons who find new jobs (B) The persons who do not find new jobs	(A)	(B)
Sex, 1=male	-0.115	0.126
	(0.091)	(0.098)
Share of men	2.019	1.515
	(0.292)	(0.298)
Age, 10 years	-0.730	-0.474
	(0.036)	(0.035)
Average age of workers, 10 years	-1.528	-1.593
	(0.293)	(0.269)
Average age of men, 10 years	1.022	0.974
	(0.299)	(0.273)
High cost area, 1=yes	-0.027	-0.218
	(0.070)	(0.083)
County of Uusimaa, 1=yes	0.068	0.323
	(0.084)	(0.093)
Share of incentive hours[1]	-0.130	-0.261
	(0.132)	(0.167)
Share of incentive hours[2]	-0.164	-0.041
	(0.105)	(0.121)
Share of overtime hours	7.973	6.505
	(1.029)	(1.249)
Share of Sunday hours	-0.396	-0.901
	(0.940)	(1.224)
Quarter 2, 1=yes	0.039	0.334
	(0.097)	(0.105)
Quarter 3, 1=yes	0.346	0.827
	(0.081)	(0.091)
Quarter 4, 1=yes	-0.005	-0.598
	(0.083)	(0.113)
Wage group of metal industry, 1=yes: 1	-0.398	-0.419
	(0.122)	(0.133)
2	-0.125	-0.218
	(0.106)	(0.112)
(reference group, low) 3		
Wage group of forest industry, 1=yes: 1	0.152	0.138
	(0.149)	(0.157)
2	-0.022	0.019
	(0.133)	(0.139)
3	-0.515	-0.261
	(0.140)	(0.146)
4	-0.929	-0.900
	(0.166)	(0.210)
(high) 5	-1.147	-1.083
	(0.190)	(0.230)
Relative wage in industry	0.635	-1.330
	(0.163)	(0.188)
Seven duration-dependent parameters γ		
Log likelihood	-2847.6	-1977.4

1. The incentive wage based on quantity, %.
2. The incentive wage based on quality and quantity, %

The average age of the workers in a plant takes a negative coefficient. It indicates that the mobility of the labour force is small in the companies where the average age is high. It is, however, surprising that the average age of men has a positive effect in both of the destinations.

The high cost area is negatively related to the exit rate for the persons who leave industry. The high cost area is situated mainly in the prosperous southern part of the country, where the spells of employment are longer. In the county of Uusimaa the labour mobility is high for the persons who leave industry. There are usually plenty of vacancies in Uusimaa. Most of them are not in the metal and forest industry.

The incentive hours based on quality and quantity are negatively related to the exit rate for the persons who find new industrial jobs. The incentive work is better paid, but it is more effective. Another study shows that the incentive work is given to the skilled persons (Kettunen, 1998). Therefore one reason for the negative signs of the coefficients of incentive work is that experience and a rather long job tenure is required until the person is accepted into incentive work schemes.

The share of overtime hours is positively related to the exit rate. A laborious job may exhaust the workers and therefore increase the exit rate. The share of Sunday hours does not have statistically significant effects.

The quarterly indicators are included in the model in order to take the non-stationarity of the economic environment into account. The job-to-job transitions are frequent during the third quarter. The exit rate from industry is high during the second and third quarter. One reason is that there are short job tenures during the summer when the ordinary staff has their summer holiday. For example, students often fill short summer-time or holiday vacancies. During the last quarter the mobility of labour is low.

The wage group has been defined in the labour market agreements using the respective job requirements. In the metal industry the lowest wage group is denoted by the number three and in the forest industry it is denoted by the number one. The reference group in the models is the wage group number three of the metal industry. It turns out that the wage groups with high requirements are negatively related to the exit rate in both of the destinations. A wage group of a worker can be considered as an organisational position. The wage groups do not determine the wage level alone, because there are many other important factors. In practice the wage groups indicate only the minimum wage of the workers. These findings support the argument that highly skilled labour cannot be replaced easily and therefore they are better paid. The promotion of a worker spurs workers to remain in their jobs. In order to reduce the unnecessary mobility of labour the specification of the criteria of promotion turns out to be important. The possibility to make a career seems to be a significant factor in reducing labour mobility.

The relative wage in industry represents the average relative wage of the worker during the whole spell of employment. The relative wage of the worker is calculated in relation to the average wage of industrial workers. The relative wage is negatively related to the exit rate for the persons who do not find new jobs within industry. This is a result was expected by the economic theory. A low wage increases incentives to seek another job or go back to school.

On the contrary, the relative wage is positively related to the exit rate for the persons who leave the company in order to get another industrial job. These persons have on average higher wages than the persons who leave industry. Those moving from one job to the next within industry have on average 1 % higher starting wage in the new jobs than their wage was during the last quarter of their previous job.

CONCLUSIONS

Usually wage profiles of workers are estimated from the studies of cross-section data. In our study the wage profiles were calculated for groups of persons over their spells of employment. The wage profiles are increasing for the short spells of four years or less and thereafter they are constant. The wage differentials are rather small between the short- and long-term workers. The workers who have long spells of employment have on average higher wages than the workers who have short spells. The starting wage of the workers is important. High starting wages will typically lead to long spells of employment. An increasing wage profile is related to the low starting wages, short employment and faster mobility of labour.

In the data there are two kinds of transitions among the persons who left the companies. The workers can immediately find another job within Finnish industry or they may leave it. About 59 % of the workers found another industrial job and 41 % of workers left industry. The relative wage level is clearly lower for the persons who leave industry. This gives support to the search models. For the low-wage workers the opportunity costs of unemployment and non-participation are lower. Therefore the low-wage workers are expected to leave industry.

The required level of skill, which is the wage group of the collective wage agreements, is negatively related to the exit rate. The coefficients of the indicators are similar for workers who change their jobs within industry and those who leave industry. The mobility of workers is higher in the jobs, which have low requirements. This remark supports the argument that highly skilled labour cannot be replaced easily and therefore they are better paid.

The relative wage of the worker with respect to the aggregate wage level in industry is negatively related to the exit rate for the persons who do not find new jobs within industry. The negative effect was expected by the economic theory. A low wage increases incentives for seeking better paid jobs or going back to school. On the contrary, high-wage workers are able to change jobs in industry. On average there are no remarkable wage gains at job changes. It is, however, interesting that the low-paid workers have gained from the change of jobs, but the high-wage workers incur wage decreases.

ACKNOWLEDGEMENTS

I wish to thank Professor Andrew Chesher for his helpful comments.

REFERENCES

Albrecht, J.W., Holmlund, B. and Lang, H. (1991), Comparative Statics in Dynamic Programming Models with Application to Job Search, *Journal of Economic Dynamics and Control* 15, 755-769.

Becker, E. and Lindsay, C.M. (1994), Sex Differences in Tenure Profiles: Effects of Shared Firm-specific Investment, *Journal of Labor Economics* 12, 98-118.

Belzil, C. (1993), An Empirical Model of Job-to-job Transition with Self-selectivity, *Canadian Journal of Economics* 26, 536-551.

Björklund, A. and Holmlund, B. (1989), Job Mobility and Subsequent Wages in Sweden, In van Dijk et al. (eds.), *Migration and Labor Market Adjustment*, Kluwer Academic Publishers, 201-216.

Brown, J.N. (1992), Interpreting Panel Data on Job Tenure, Journal of Labor Economics 10, 219-257.

Brown, J.N. and Light, A. (1992), Interpreting Panel Data on Job Tenure, *Journal of Labor* Economics 10, 219-257.

Cutler, S.J. and Ederer, F. (1958), Maximum Utilization of the Life Table Method in Analyzing Survival, *Journal of Chronic Diseases* 8, 699-712.

Farber, H.S. (1994), The Analysis of Interfirm Worker Mobility, *Journal of Labor Economics* 12, 554-593.

Gottschalk, P. and Maloney, T. (1985), Involuntary Terminations, Unemployment and Job Matching: A Test of Job Search Theory, *Journal of Labor Economics* 3, 109-123.

Gritz, M.R. (1993), The Impact of Training on the Frequency and Duration of Employment, *Journal of Econometrics* 57, 21-51.

Jovanovic, B. (1979), Job Matching and the Theory of Turnover, *Journal of Political Economy* 87, 972-990.

Jovanovic, B. (1984), Matching, Turnover and Unemployment, *Journal of Political Economy* 92, 108-122.

Kalbfleisch, J.D. and Prentice, R.L. (1980), *The Statistical Analysis of Failure Time Data*, John Wiley and Sons, New York.

Kettunen, J. (1993), Förändringar i lönestrukturen inom den finska industrin under 1980-talet, *The Journal of the Economic Society of Finland* 3, 153-158.

Kettunen, J. (1998), Method of Pay in Finnish Industry, *Applied Economics* 30, 863-873.

Kettunen, J. (2000), Effects of Wages on Job Tenure, *Journal of Income Distribution* 9, 155-169.

Kiefer, N.M. (1988), Employment Contracts, Job Search Theory, and Labour Turnover: Preliminary Empirical Results, *Journal of Applied Econometrics* 3, 169-186.

Krueger, A.B. and Summers, L.H. (1988), Efficiency Wages and the Inter-industry Wage Structure, *Econometrica* 56, 259-293.

Meyer, B.D. (1990), Unemployment Insurance and Unemployment Spells, *Econometrica* 58, 757-782.

Miller, R. (1984), Job Matching and Occupational Choice, *Journal of Political Economy* 92, 1086-1120.

Prentice, R. and Gloeckler, L. (1978), Regression Analysis of Grouped Survival Data with Application to Breast Cancer Data, *Biometrics* 34, 57-67.

Stiglitz, J.E. (1985), Equilibrium Wage Distributions, *The Economic Journal* 95, 595-618.

Topel, R.H. (1991), Specific Capital, Mobility, and Wages: Wages Rise with Job Seniority, *Journal of Political Economy* 99, 145-176.

Topel, R.H. and Ward, M.P. (1992), Job Mobility and the Careers of Young Men, *The Quarterly Journal of Economics CVII*, 439-479.

In: Focus on Urban and Regional Economics
Editor: Lawrence Yee, pp. 65-88
ISBN 1-59454-740-8

Chapter 4

CITIES OF SIBERIA, RUSSIA: URBAN PHYSICAL ENVIRONMENT AND ITS EVALUATION BY CITY-DWELLERS

Boris A. Portnov[1]
Department of Natural Resources & Environmental Management, Faculty of Social Sciences, University of Haifa, Mount Carmel, Haifa, Israel 31905

ABSTRACT

Specially-designed questionnaires, published in major newspapers of five Siberian cities - *Novosobirsk, Kasnoyarsk, Barnaul, Norilsk*, and *Lesosibirsk,* - were used to rank residential neighborhoods in these cities according to their attractiveness for residence and business activity. The newspaper polls were supplemented by expert surveys, designed to investigate differences between environmental priorities of ordinary city-dwellers and local decision-makers. The factors affecting the environmental assessments of city-residents and city-officials were then investigated using multivariate statistical techniques. As the study indicates, social evaluations of the urban physical environment (UPE) do not appear to reflect genuine qualities of this environment. Instead they reflect a range of local conditions, such as the average level of urban development achieved in a particular city; the variation of environmental conditions across individual neighborhoods, and the socio-demographic composition of the local population. It was also revealed that priorities and assessments of ordinary city residents and of city officials (e.g., urban planners, designers, and city-engineers) differ prominently. While the specialists tend to put an emphasis on the spatial qualities of the UPE (e.g., access to the city center, and access to recreational areas), ordinary city-dwellers pay more attention to functional issues, such as the availability of services and facilities in residential neighborhoods, structural conditions of the housing stock, etc. A system of evaluation indices (the *Index of Prestige*, the *Residents' Evaluation Index*, and the *Business Attractiveness Index*) is proposed for use during the period of transition from a planned to market-oriented economy, for both long-term physical planning and urban land appraisal.

[1] E-mail: portnov@nrem.haifa.ac.il. Fax: +972-4-8249971

Keywords: Siberian cities; Urban environment; Attractiveness

INTRODUCTION

The response of city dwellers to various urban improvements (e.g., road construction and urban renovations), and the degree of the residents' satisfaction with the urban physical environment are important issues for urban planers. Quite often, urban improvements are not well met by city-dwellers simply because they do not meet their expectations and needs. Therefore, when local financial resources are considerably restricted, as often the case in most transitional economies, any future improvements in the urban physical environment must be *planned and prioritized according to their actual importance for city-dwellers.*

Figure 1. Geographic location of the cities surveyed A – West Siberia; B – East Siberia; C – latitude and longitude; D – cities in the sample

The residents' evaluations of the urban physical environment (UPE) may also assist in estimating *property values* during the period of transition from a planned to market economy. During this period, residential market transactions tend to be sparse and not always reflect actual property values. Social evaluations may thus be used to substitute, at least temporarily, genuine market assessments, sought by individual investors, property appraisers, and local authorities for taxation purposes.

In order to understand how city-residents' evaluations of the UPE may be used in urban physical planning and appraisal practice, three important questions should be answered:

1. How accurately does the social attractiveness of the UPE represent genuine qualities (i.e. amenities and disamenities) of this environment?

2. What factors determine the relative attractiveness of urban areas in cities of different sizes and geographic locations?
3. Do the evaluations of the quality of the UPE given by city-dwellers differ from those given by the professionals (e.g., city-planners, engineers, and local officials)?

To answer these questions, the present study was carried out in five Siberian cities: Novosibirsk (1.5 million residents), Krasnoyarsk (1.0 million residents), Barnaul (600,000 residents), Norilsk (180,000 residents), and Lesosibirsk (50,000 residents). The cities were selected so as to represent Siberian cities of different population sizes and geographic locations. The following regions of Siberia were covered by the study: the South-East (Krasnoyarsk), the South-West (Barnaul and Novosibirsk), the Center (Lesosibirsk), and the North (Norilsk) - see Fig.1. The study was carried under the present author's supervision in 1990-1994 by the Laboratory of Regional & Urban Planning at the Krasnoyarsk Civil Engineering Institute of Russia.

BACKGROUND STUDIES

The links between the urban physical environment and social behavior have long been discussed in urban psychology and sociology (Lynch, 1960, Glass et al., 1977; Timmermans, 1991; Hillier and Harrison, 1984; Teklenburg et al, 1993). Assessments of the urban environment through the use of computer techniques were conducted inter alia by Smardon (1986), Tugnutt and Robertson (1987), and Rahman (1992).

Specific forms of community life in relation to urban spatial characteristics were examined by Keane (1991), whereas the negative aspects of the 'urban environment - social behavior' interaction, such as the relationship between residential density and residents' environmental satisfaction, were studied by Bonnes et al (1991) in Rome, and by Lin and Hanlong (1990) in the Shanghai urban area.

In recent studies, the interactions between the urban physical environment and daily behavior of city dwellers (e.g., commuting, and the choice of residence places) have been investigated at both the entire city level and the level of individual neighborhoods (Rapoport, 2000; Kou and Sullivan, 2001; Evans et al, 2001; Michael, 2001). However, the *relative attractiveness* of different city neighborhoods for settling and business activity, and factors affecting it (e.g., development patterns, services and facilities, transportation, and ecological conditions), which is the main focus of the present study, has been received hitherto relatively little attention. Moreover, the cities covered by the present study (e.g., the cities of East and West Siberia of Russia) have been largely overlooked by previous urban studies. Though there have been fragment studies dealing with urban places in Siberia (see, *inter alia,* Krushlinskiy, 1986; Portnov, 1990), most of these studies are published in Russian and are largely unavailable for the Western audience.

THE REGION

According to a commonly-accepted definition, *Siberia* is a region of Russia which lies to the east of the Ural Mountains and west of the Russian Far East.[2] The region is composed of two unequal parts: East Siberia and West Siberia (see Fig.1). The total territory of the region amounts to some 2.4 million sq. miles, or ca. 36.5% of the entire Russian territory. The region is sparsely populated: it hosts only 23.0 million people or ca. 16.4% of the national total (Portnov and Maslovskiy, 1996).

The entire region is frigid in winter. Air temperatures stay below -30° (C) for approximately 80 days annually in *Norilsk* and *Dudinka* (East Siberian cities situated above the polar circle) and for 25-30 days in Krasnoyarsk and Irkutsk (the cities located in the southern part of the region). In *Dixson* (the north part of East Siberia), winds blow at a speed of 9 miles per hour for an average of 240 days a year, while winds of more than 25 miles per hour blow there for an average of 60 days (Krushlinskiy, 1986).

Nearly two-thirds of Siberian population live in urban areas. (10,000+ residents). Most of Siberian 107 cities and towns (10,000+ residents) are located along the Trans-Siberian Railway (the *Transsib*), in the southern part of the region. The planning layout of Siberian settlements differs considerably from that of the cities and towns located in other regions of Russia. These differences may be outlined as follows:

- First, the specific natural landscapes of the region (the presence of large rivers, steep slopes, etc.) have led to the spatial dispersion of residential neighborhoods and other functional areas in Siberian cities. Climatic harshness has been another factor contributing to the uniqueness of Siberian cities. Combined with a lack of engineering utilities and transport infrastructures, the extreme climate of the region (e.g., long periods of low winter temperatures, snow-drifts, and strong winds) called for sitting residential neighborhoods and industrial area near all-weather arterial roads. This was accompanied by sparse development between them. As a result, most Siberian settlements spread along major roads over considerable distances, sometime over 15-30 miles, with population density of urban areas staying as low as 5-15 persons per acre.
- Second, during the Soviet era, the spatial development of all cities and towns, including those in Siberia, was determined by long-term master plans. These plans regulated land use stringently, with little or no rezoning allowed. As a result, if a site, designated for construction of a public facility or a new road, was not developed (owing, for instance, to a lack of financial resources), it might have remained unused for years or was put to agricultural use. The absence of private land ownership and market pricing during the Soviet era also contributed to highly inefficient land use in urban areas. In particular, in the absence of market stimulus, public land-holders have little or no incentives to achieve more efficient use of land which was virtually a free resource. As a result, there were undeveloped land all over urban areas and

[2] According to another definition, Siberia extends from the Ural Mountains to the Pacific, i.e., includes the Russian Far East (see Webster's Encyclopedic Dictionary, 1996). However, this definition appears to be less accurate, since the Far East region of Russia, bordering on the Pacific shore, differs considerably by its geography, climatic conditions and urban patterns from its continental counterparts.

population density remained low. This countrywide trend was even stronger in Siberia because of a traditional notion about its land abundance.

- Third, as Show (1987) justly points out, the *Soviets,* like the *tsars* before the Bolshevik revolution, were determined to exploit the remote natural resources of Siberia as quickly and cheaply as possible. To achieve this goal, they had a tendency to skimp on even basic infrastructure where not absolutely necessary. In a book on Siberian urban planning, Portnov (1990) argues that the above tendency led to the concentration of extensive areas of single-family housing around industrial enterprises, leading to the formation of poli-nuclear settlements located far from each other and from the central city. These mixed industrial-residential structures had limited social facilities and deficient infrastructures. These residential-industrial conglomerates came into existence because this type of development allowed the central and local governments to house labor force close to the place of work without diverting state resources from industrial needs. In addition, such a type of development provided possibilities for subsistence agriculture for industrial workers and their families.

THE CITIES

Novosibirsk is the largest city of the region, 1.5 million residents, and the official capital of Russian Siberia. The city was founded in the turn of the 20th century, during the construction of the Trans-Siberian railway. A comparatively low level of air pollution, beautiful natural surrounding, and highly developed, at least for the region, social and cultural infrastructures (e.g., universities, research institutes, theaters, and museums) make the city attractive and desirable for settling and living.

Krasnoyarsk is one of the oldest, 370 years, and largest industrial cities of the region. It houses about one million residents. Despite its extremely favorable natural surrounding (e.g., the presence of the *Yenissei* river, natural forests, and the ridges of the *Sayany* Mountains, whose red natural color gave the name to the city: *Krasnoyarsk* means the Red Ridge, in Russian), the city is aesthetically poorly developed, and heavily polluted. The city's neighborhoods differ considerably in the level of social facilities and commercial services, with large areas of physically deteriorated, low-density development spread all over the city.

Barnaul is an industrial city of medium size, 600 thousand people, located in the southern part of the region. It is characterized by relatively new housing and industrial development. The social facilities and commercial services in the city are not as developed as in Novosibirsk, Krasnoyarsk and other large cities of the region.

Norilsk is the central city of the Greater Norilsk Metropolitan Area (GNMA). The city was founded in the 1930's as a part of Josef Stalin's Main Directorate for Corrective Labor Camps (GULAG). Norilsk's economy is based on primary industries, mainly on mining and ore-processing. Due to the location of most industrial plants close to residential neighborhoods and obsolete technologies used in production, the city is heavily polluted. Due to its extreme climate and geological conditions (the presence of permafrost), construction costs (specifically of roads) are extremely high. As a result, the city has virtually no open areas, and is very compact: about 2.1 miles long and 1.5 miles wide. The density of development in Norilsk reaches 42 residential units per acre, as opposed to 3-6 residential units per acre in other cities of the region. Norilsk has a typical flat landscape of Arctic latitudes. It is believed that the GNMA is the coldest and windiest urban area in the world.

Lesosibirsk is a small city with only 50,000 residents. It is aesthetically poorly developed and comparatively low polluted. The city is formed by a conglomerate of small villages grouped around two large timber-industry enterprises. The city stretches along the *Yenissei* river for about 35 miles, from north to south. Lesosibirsk has no other population centers in vicinity and has very few social, recreational and cultural facilities in its neighborhoods.

RESEARCH METHOD

The research was carried out in three phases: a) sociological polls and expert surveys; b) data processing, and c) multivariate analysis. Each of these phases will be discussed below in some detail.

Sociological Polls and Expert Surveys

During the first phase of the analysis, questionnaires were designed and disseminated among the residents of the cities under study. The questionnaires included five main questions. The first question was accompanied by a map, showing a generalized city plan and the location of main city districts. Each district was given a name, in order to facilitate its recognition by survey participants. For example, the map for Krasnoyarsk showed the *Center, Pokrovka, Nikolaevka,* and other city districts (see Fig. 2). The districts were chosen according to the following three criteria:

1. Development homogeneity (that is, similar patterns of land use within each district);
2. Similar population size (each district had between 20,000 to 40,000 people in Novosibirsk, Krasnoyarsk, Barnaul, and Norilsk, and about 5,000-10,000 residents in the smaller Lesosibirsk);
3. Familiarity to ordinary city-dwellers.

Small circles in which the attractiveness of each district's was supposed to be ranked were provided alongside the maps (see Fig. 2). The respondents were asked to evaluate *each district* according to the following two criteria:

- General attractiveness for residence, and
- Attractiveness for business activity.

The respondents were also asked to evaluate their own districts separately or simply underline the names of their "home" districts on the map. For ranking city-districts, a ten-point scale was offered - *1 through 10* (with 10 representing the highest level of attractiveness).

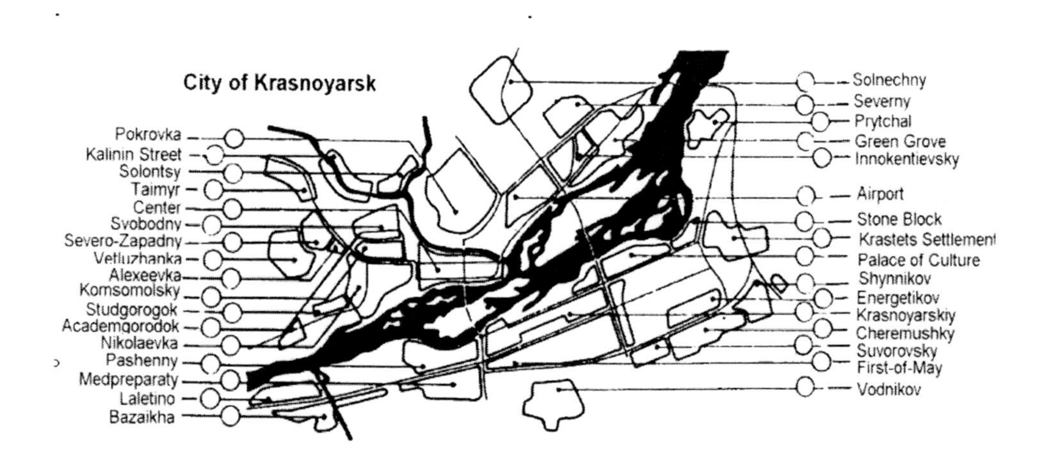

Figure 2. A generalized plan of the city of Krasnoyarsk analogous to that used in the newspaper survey

Other four questions (#2-#5) in the questionnaires were designed to determine the residents' opinions concerning the priorities of urban renewal, neighborhoods amenities and disamenities, etc. Basically, these questions served an auxiliary function and were added to the questionnaires in order to draw the respondents' attention to the main question (#1).

The respondents were also asked to indicate their gender, age, and education. This information was required to trace any bias that might have occurred in the representation of particular socio-demographic groups in the sample and then make necessary adjustments.

The questionnaires were published in major newspapers of the cities surveyed, with a total daily circulation of some 470,000 copies. The readers were asked to fill out the questionnaires and send them back, either to the editorial boards or to the local city councils. Approximately 8,500 filled out questionnaires (~1.8% of the total newspaper circulation) were received. Most questionnaires were received within two weeks after publication.

The survey technique employed in the present study deserves comment. The use of newspapers for disseminating research questionnaires was our original idea. Most likely, such an approach has not been used before in previous studies on the topic. Furthermore, to the best of our knowledge, city maps similar to those used in our study have not been used before as a tool for evaluating the relative attractiveness of individual city areas.

An obvious advantage of newspaper publications as a media for disseminating research questionnaires is a possibility to collect a considerable amount of relevant sociological information with minimal efforts and within a limited time-span. The approach in question may be weak, however, in making a valid representation of particular groups of the general city population in the sample. Since the newspaper survey is based on a self-selected population sub-set (i.e., respondents who, first, read newspapers, and, second, chose to fill out and return the questionnaires), a sampling bias may become an issue. However, as our analysis showed, the sample appeared to be fairly representative of the general population, with an error margin not exceeding 10-15 percent of specific population groups (grouped by age, gender, and education). Nevertheless, in order to correct a bias, which might have been caused by either overrepresentation or under-representation of particular population groups, a small number of questionnaires received from 'over-represented' groups were randomly excluded from the final set of questionnaires. In order to minimize sampling bias even further, we also used specially-designed computer software, which allowed us to apply a weighting scheme to the assessments given by different groups of respondents according to the actual percentage shares of these groups in the general population of a given city.[3]

In addition, in order to secure the comparability of the estimates obtained in individual cities, their socio-demographic compositions were mutually compared (see Appendix 1). Although we observed certain differences in the proportional shares of various population groups, disparities among the cities appeared to be minor, generally falling within an error margin established for the survey.

In addition to the newspaper surveys, identical questionnaires were distributed among the experts, i.e., city-planners, urban designers, and local decision-makers. As a result, between 40 and 60 additional 'expert' questionnaires were received in each city covered by the study.

Data Processing

During the second phase of the research, *four* separate indices were calculated for each district in each city covered by the study:

1. *The General Index of Prestige (the IP index).* This index measures the general attractiveness of a city district as a place of residence. The index was calculated as an average of values given by *all survey participants* to a particular city district. The index's values range from 1 to 10, with the upper threshold indicating the highest level of a district's attractiveness for residence.
2. *The Index of Residential Quality* (*the RE index*). The index was calculated in a similar manner to the IP index. However, in its calculation, only answers of respondents relating to their *own districts of residence* were taken into account. As assumed, while residents of other districts of the city may have only limited knowledge about a city-district in question, its local dwellers may have deeper insights concerning actual advantages and disadvantages of the district's physical environment.
3. *The Specialists' Evaluation Index* (*the SE index*). The index averaged the assessments of district attractiveness given by the 'specialists' (e.g., local planners, city engineers, and decision-makers) participating in the survey.
4. *The Business Attractiveness Index* (*the BA index*). The index averaged individual assessments of a district's attractiveness for business activity, given by all survey participants. As with all other indices used in the study, the index takes values between 1 and 10, with the latter value indicating the highest level of attractiveness.

[3] In order to illustrate the weighting procedure used in the study, let us consider the following example. Assume that the sample is formed by two groups of respondents, 'A' and 'B', whose proportional shares in the sample are equal. However, in the population, these groups are split as 40 to 60. Further assume that the attractiveness of a district as a place of residence is estimated by an average of 6.0 points by the group A and an average of 3.0 points by the group B. The adjusted attractiveness of the district at hand can thus be calculated as follows: 6.0x0.4 + 3.0x0.6 = 4.2 points.

Multivariate Analysis

During the final phase of the analysis, the objective physical characteristics of individual city districts and the evaluations of their social attractiveness were mutually compared. To this end, the Stepwise Multiple Regression Analysis (SMRA) was used. The following ten factors were included in the analysis as explanatory variables:

- F1: average access time from a district to the city center [minutes];
- F2: average access time from a district to main industrial areas of a city - workplace accessibility [minutes];
- F3: recreation accessibility - average access time to nearby natural amenities, i.e., parks, lakes, and riverfront [minutes];
- F4: the level of a district's functional development, measured as the number of major social facilities and businesses available in the district, such as schools, shopping facilities, healthcare, sports facilities, etc.;
- F5: the average annual level of air pollution, measured by a dimensionless index reflecting the year-wide surpass of major air pollutants over the accepted pollution standards;
- F6: the structural conditions of buildings [average percentage of physical depreciation];
- F7: engineering infrastructures [the number of engineering utilities available in a city district, such as water supply, sewage, electricity, gas, and central heating. The variable took value 1 if only one utility type was available; 2 for two types of utilities and so forth];
- F8: the aesthetic quality of a district's built environment [a categorical variable ranging from 1 to 10, with the latter number representing the highest level of attractiveness];
- F9: the aesthetic quality of a district's natural landscapes [1 through 10, with the latter value representing the highest level of landscape attractiveness].
- F10: building density [m^2 of gross building area per hectare of land].

The list of explanatory factors used in the study thus covers all the main features of the UPE that may affect, at least theoretically, the residents' assessments of individual city districts: location, utilities, services, structural condition of building, aesthetic appearance of development, and the quality of natural landscapes. These factors are commonly considered in urban studies as major determinants of urban land values and the overall quality of the UPE (see, *inter alia*, Hester, 1984; Rapoport, 1977; Wittick et al, 1977; Bonnes *et al.*, 1991).

In order to evaluate the districts' environmental qualities, the following analytical techniques were used: time measurements (F1, F2, F3); the analysis of available statistical data (F4, F5, F6, F7, and F10), and expert assessments (F8 and F9).[4]

---

[4] To minimize possible interdependencies, different groups of experts were used to grade overall attractiveness of districts (the SE index) and their aesthetic qualities.

RESEARCH RESULTS

Spatial Patterns of District Attractiveness

The analysis of the IP's values allowed us to classify residential districts in the cities surveyed into four typological groups of territories (TGTs).

- *TGT I* includes residential districts with the highest score of social attractiveness (above 6 points on a 10-point scale). This group covers both central city districts and new residential neighborhoods located in external suburban fringes, specifically those with most favorable landscape and ecological conditions - attractive natural landscapes, low levels of air pollution, etc.
- *TGT II* is formed by city districts with a medium-high level of social attractiveness. IP ranks of the districts in this group vary from 5 to 6 on a 10-point scale. This TGT mainly includes residential neighborhoods built in the 1940's through the early 1960's. These 'old city districts' are well established and provide numerous functional amenities (e.g., schools, shopping facilities, health, and sport facilities) to their residents.
- *TGT III* is formed by the districts with average levels of the IP (3 through 5 points on a 10-point scale). The districts in this group are represented by both low-density neighborhoods of single-family housing, located in external fringes of central city districts, and by suburban neighborhoods of four- and five-storey buildings constructed in the late 1950's through the early 1970's, and characterized by considerably low construction standards (e.g., small rooms, absence of storage spaces, and poor quality of construction). Most districts in this TGT are located in unfavorable ecological conditions: they are characterized by unattractive natural landscapes, close proximity to industrial areas, and relatively high levels of air pollution.
- *Lastly, TGT IV* incorporates city districts which received the lowest attractiveness rating (i.e., less than three points on a 10-point scale). In most cases, this TG includes residential districts located far away from the city center, and especially those whose ecological conditions are extremely unfavorable (e.g., high levels of air pollution, proximity to industrial areas, and plain natural landscapes). Small and poorly developed suburban villages, transformed into 'satellite' settlements of the central city due to its gradual territorial expansion, also belong to this TGT.

Geographically, the distribution of IP values in the cities surveyed follow three chief spatial patterns (see Fig. 3):

1. *A 'two-peak' pattern* is found in large polycentric cities with multiple urban disamenities located throughout the urban territory. The cities of Novosibirsk and Krasnoyarsk fall into this group. These cities have both major city centers and peripheral sub-centers formed by clusters of academic and research institutions surrounded by high-status residential areas (*Academgorodki*, in Russian).

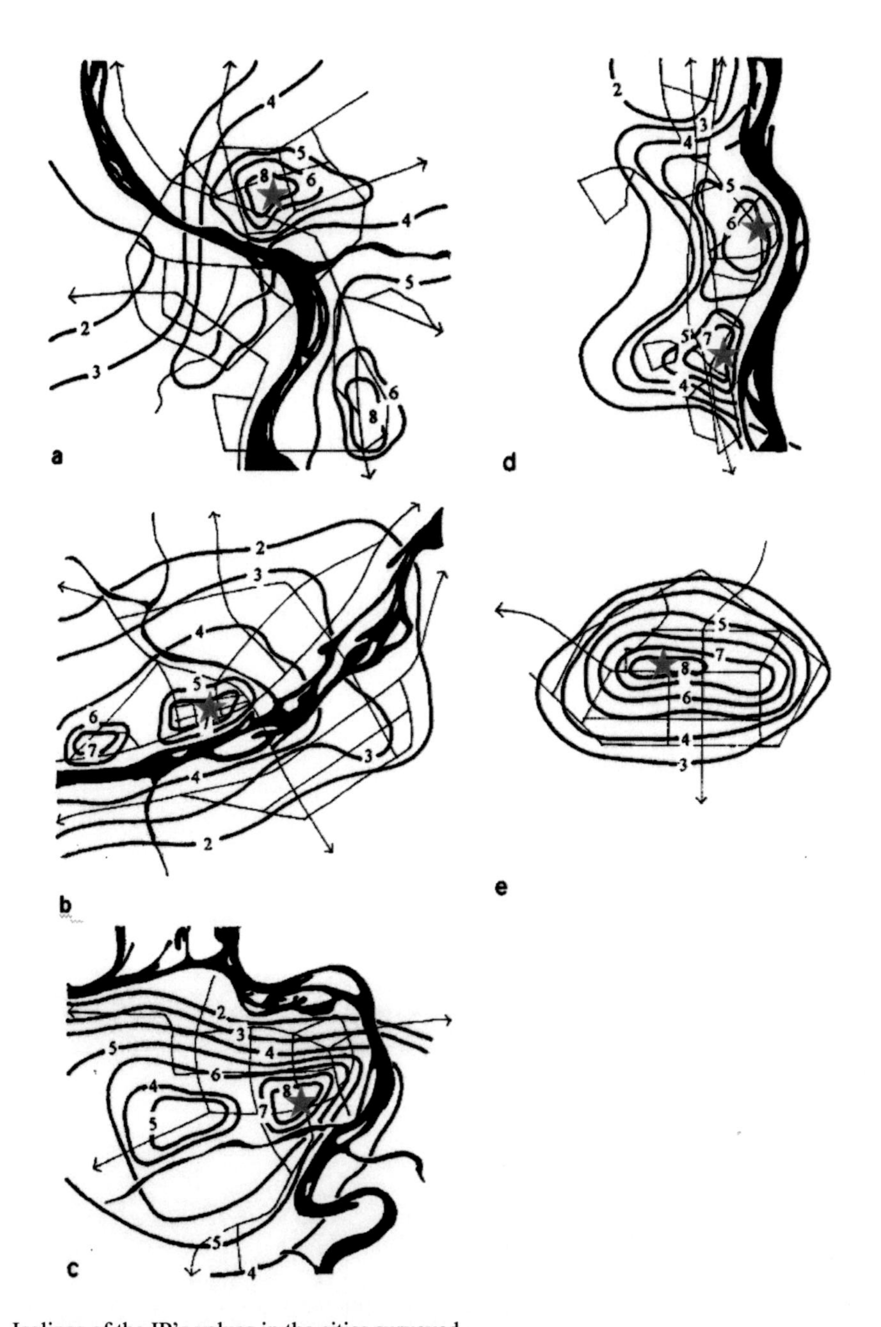

Figure 3. Isolines of the IP's values in the cities surveyed
a - Novosibirsk; b - Krasnoyarsk; c - Barnaul; d - Lesosibirsk; e - Norilsk
Stars indicate city centers; major rivers are colored in black; major thoroughfares are marked by thin solid lines and arrows

These high-status peripheral areas are marked by clearly pronounced peaks of IP values (see Fig. 3A-B). Somewhat surprisingly, the small Lesosibirsk also exhibits this spatial pattern. The explanation of this phenomenon is rather simple: The latter city is formed by two separate villages, which merged together decades ago, but have maintained separate public centers (Fig. 3D).

2. *A 'single-peak' pattern* is found in Norilsk, a compact mono-centric city with industrial disamenities located outside the city's boundaries.
3. *A 'peak-hollow' pattern* is found in Barnaul. This mono-centric city incorporates a large enclave of major urban disamenities (e.g., a industrial zones surrounded by large clusters of physically deteriorated, slam-type residential development) located just outside the city center. The location of this enclave is clearly marked by a negative peak of IP values in the bottom-left corner of the IP distribution map (see Fig. 3C).

Fig. 4 shows percentages of city districts included in each TGT. As we can easily notice, in the large cities covered by the study - Novosibirsk, and Krasnoyarsk (1,000,000+ residents), - the number of less attractive districts *(TGT III and TGT IV)* exceeds significantly the number of highly attractive residential districts *(TGT I and TGT II)*. For example, in Novosibirsk this ratio is 75.1% vs. 24.9%, while in Krasnoyarsk it reaches 78.4% vs. 21.6%. Notably, the smaller cities in the sample (Barnaul and Norilsk) appear to have the opposite ratios between attractive and unattractive districts (Barnaul: 56.0% vs. 44.0%; Norilsk: 62.5% vs. 37.5%).

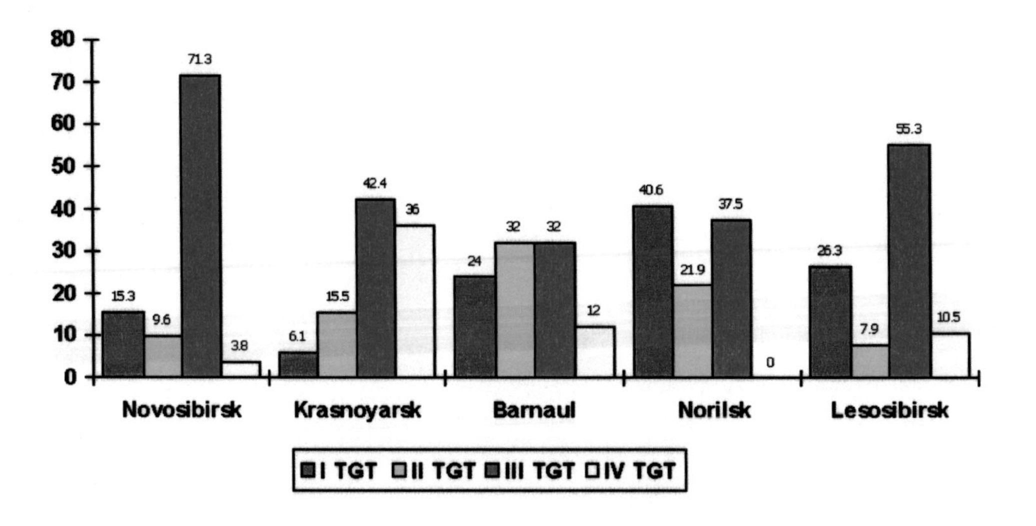

Figure 4. Percentage of districts included in different Typological Groups of Territories (TGTs) in the cities surveyed

This interesting phenomenon may easily be explained, if the relationship between city sizes and the heterogeneity of the UPE is taken into account. In a small city, the UPE is likely to be fairly homogeneous, with individual districts varying little in their development. The range of environmental qualities available to residents of a small city for evaluation and comparison may thus be fairly limited. As a result, the city's dwellers may appreciate even small differences among individual neighborhoods, viewing them as a simple dichotomy - 'good' vs. 'bad' neighborhoods. In the case of 'good' neighborhoods, the respondents may be very generous in their ranking. Concurrently, in a large, territorially sprawled city (e.g., Novosibirsk and Krasnoyarsk), development patterns may vary considerably, thus providing a wide choice of environmental varieties for both comparison and evaluation. Since no simple dichotomy of 'good' and 'bad' districts is no longer present here, the residents of big cities may tend to give high scores only to a limited number of city districts which they like best, while granting lower scores to all others.

Determinants of Attractiveness

Additional insights on the relationships between the IP and some physical characteristics of the cities surveyed can be gained from the data in Tables 1 & 2.

Table 1. General Characteristics of the Cities Surveyed

City	Population, 1,000 residents (as of 1995)	Land area, sq. miles	Index of climatic harshness*	Attractiveness of individual city districts on a ten-point scale (IP: residents' assessments)			
				Maximum	Minimum	Range	Mean
Novosibirsk	1,500	187	2.5	8.3	2.4	5.9	4.5
Krasnoyarsk	1,000	127	3.0	6.4	1.7	4.7	3.7
Barnaul	600	98	2.0	8.3	1.3	7.0	5.0
Norilsk	180	3	7.0	7.6	3.5	4.1	5.6
Lesosibirsk	50	19	5.0	7.2	2.8	4.4	4.8

* The indicator is suggested by Kruslinskiy (1986) and provides the integral assessment of various climatic features, including the average annual wind speed, relative humidity, and a number of days with discomfort winter temperatures. The index's values range from 1 to 10. High values indicate harsh climate, while low values indicate more moderate climatic conditions

Table 2. Selected Characteristics of the Cities Surveyed*

City	F1 (distance to the city center)		F4 (level of functional development)		F5 (level of air pollution)		F9 (aesthetic quality of natural landscapes)	
	Range	Mean	Range	Mean	Range	Mean	Range	Mean
Novosibirsk	55.0	33.7	88.0	61.3	2.8	1.1	9.0	5.1
Krasnoyarsk	50.0	35.1	166.0	44.3	9.2	2.6	6.5	4.4
Barnaul	55.0	25.8	80.0	38.6	7.0	2.8	6.0	4.1
Norilsk	15.0	11.0	196.0	103.5	1.5	6.7	0.2	3.5
Lesosibirsk	95.0	24.8	38.0	24.4	0.2	0.2	4.3	3.2

* see text for the factors' description

As Table 1 shows, the IP's ranges (i.e., the differences between IP's maximum and minimum values) do not appear to have any direct relationship with either city size (population) or its territory. As easily seen, the small Lesosibirsk (50,000 residents) does not exhibit smaller differences in the districts' attractiveness than Krasnoyarsk whose population is far larger. Although the city of Barnaul is much smaller than Novosibirsk (600,000 vs.

1,500,000 residents), the former city has a greater range of the IP's values than the latter (7.0 and 5.9 points, respectively).

However, the IP's range *does* seem to reflect the variation of local environmental qualities, specifically the differences in the districts' access to the city center (F1), the level of functional development (F4), and the level of air population (F5) - see Table 2. Thus, for instance, the relatively high range of the IP in the small Lesosibirsk can apparently be explained by the extremely high range of F1 (distance to the city center). It is also likely that the high range of F4 (the level of functional development) may be responsible for considerable differences between the IP's maximum and minimum values observed in the territorially compact Norilsk (see Tables 1-2).

The relationship between the IP's mean values and the values of some environmental factors is also worth noting. For example, the high average attractiveness of Norilsk's residential areas (IP(mean)= 5.6 vs. 3.7 in Krasnoyarsk; see Table 1) can be explained by an extremely low value of 'the location factor', F1 and by a relatively high level of the city's functional development F4 (see Table 2). Concurrently, the low average attractiveness of Krasnoyarsk's districts (IP(mean)= 3.7; see Table 1) can be due to unfavorable access conditions to the city's center (F1); a relatively low average level of functional development of individual city neighborhoods (F4), and a high level of air pollution (F5).

Summing up, we may conclude that the aforementioned differences in the social attractiveness of city districts are likely be caused by *the range of physical conditions in a particular city, and the level of the urban development achieved in it, rather than by the city's population size and land area.* Furthermore, it also appears that the *social attractiveness of various city districts can only partially be explained by objective qualities of the urban physical environment.* Indeed, the cities of the region, located in extreme climatic conditions (viz., Norilsk and Lesosibirsk) tend to exhibit higher average levels of the social attractiveness of their neighborhoods than Novosibirsk and Krasnoyarsk (see Table 1), whose climate is more moderate and social facilities more developed. As we shall see in the following section, the results of regression analysis further validate these preliminary conclusions.

Relative Importance of Influencing Factors

In order to identify and measure the relationships between IP values and the levels of environmental factors in the cities surveyed, the following linear regression model was used:

$$IP = B_o + B_1 \text{ x } F_1 + ... + B_{10} \text{ x } F_{10} + \varepsilon, \quad (1)$$

where B_o, B_1,...B_{10} are regression coefficients; F_1,...F_{10} are explanatory variables covered by the study (see Section 5.3), and ε is a random error term.[5]

[5] In order to insure the homoscedasticity of errors, a logarithmic transformation was applied to the explanatory variables. Hartley's F-Max test for violations of the homoscedasticity assumption confirmed that variances are indeed homoscedastic (Appendix 2). The test examines explanatory variables in order to avoid extreme departures of their variances, which may, theoretically, cause biased estimations of regression coefficients (Gravetter and Wallnau, 1992).

Table 3. Factors Affecting the Attractiveness of Residential Districts in the Siberian Cities Surveyed (Dependent Variable - the IP; Method - Stepwise Multiple Regression (SMR); Linear-Log Form)

Variable	Krasnoyarsk	Novosibirsk	Norilsk	Barnaul	Lesosibirsk
	B[a] (t[b])	B[a] (t[b])	B[a] (t[b])	B[a] (t[b])	B[a] (t[b])
F1 (distance to the city center)	-0.921	-	-4.687	-1.594	-1.413
	(-3.7**)	-	(-7.8**)	(-2.4**)	(-3.3**)
F2 (workplace accessibility)	-	-1.036	-	-	-
	-	(-2.4**)	-	-	-
F4 (level of functional development)	1.285	-	0.988	-	-
	(4.6**)	-	(2.2**)	-	-
F5 (level of air pollution)	-3.178	-	-	-5.600	-0.579
	(-8.1**)	-	-	(-6.8**	(-1.9*)
F6 (structural conditions of building)	-1.045	-		-	-1.231
	(-4.0**)	-	-	-	(-2.6**)
F7 (engineering infrastructures)	-	2.197	-	-	-
	-	(2.6**)	-	-	-
F8 (aesthetic qualities of the built environment)	-	1.576	-	-	1.680
	-	(2.1**)	-	-	(3.1**)
F9 (aesthetic qualities of natural landscapes)	-	1.321	-	2.535	1.056
	-	(1.7*)	-	(5.4**)	(2.8**)
(Constant)	6.916	5.279	8.954	0.673	2.094
	(5.6**)	(3.9**)	(8.3**)	(0.5)	(1.8*)
F-statistic	34.06	13.51	62.27	38.93	23.74
R^2	0.834	0.465	0.816	0.847	0.821

Note: Only statistically significant variables selected by the SMR procedure are reported.
[a] unstandardized regression coefficient;
[b] *t*-statistic (in parentheses).
** indicates a two-tailed 0.05 significance level;
* indicates a two-tailed 0.10 significance level

Table 3 shows the most statistically significant factors of district attractiveness selected on the basis of the *stepwise multiple regression* (SMR) procedure. Each of the factors reported in the table is significant at a 90% confidence level. As the table shows, the fits of the models, measured by their R^2 values, appears to be very high in four cities covered by the sample (R^2=0.834 for Krasnoyarsk, 0.847 for Barnaul; 0.816 for Norilsk, and 0.821 for Lesosibirsk). Although for Novosibirsk, the regression fit is somewhat lower, it is also relatively high (R^2=0.465). This indicates that the explanatory variables used in the analysis appear explain the variation of the dependent variable (the IP) quite well, thus implying that the models seem to cover all the most essential factors influencing the social attractiveness of residential districts in the cities surveyed.

Notably, the list of variables included in the models as statistically significant varies by city. Thus, '*access to the city center*' is statistically significant in Krasnoyarsk, Norilsk, Barnaul and Lesosibirsk, and statistically weak in Novosibirsk (see Table 3). Furthermore, the '*aesthetic qualities of built environment*' is statistically significant only in Novosibirsk and Lesosibirsk. As another example, in Norilsk, the *air pollution* variable is not statistically significant, whereas in Barnaul, this factor is highly statistically significant. The explanation of this interesting phenomenon may be fairly straightforward: individual environmental determinants emerge as statistically significant only in cities, in which the urban environment provides a sufficient inter-district variation (range) of their values. For instance, although Norilsk is heavily polluted, the levels of air pollution do not vary considerably across individual city districts (see Table 2). As a result, the air pollution variable does not appear in the list of factors influencing significantly the values of the IP (see Table 3). Concurrently, the variable in question is present in Lesosibirsk which is less polluted overall but in which the level of air pollution vary considerably across individual city districts (see Table 2).

The factors that determine the IP's levels in the cities under study warrant further discussion. They are: 1) access to the city center (this factor is statistically significant in four out of five regression models); 2) the level of functional development (two cities in the scope); 3) aesthetic qualities of the built environment (two cities); 4) aesthetic qualities of the natural landscapes (three cities), 5) structural conditions of buildings (two cities), and 6) the level of air pollution (three cities).

F_1 *(access time to the city center).* As expected, this factor has a negative relationship with the districts' attractiveness (the IP). That is, as the distance to the city center increases, the IP's level declines. The factor in question is of prime significance in the northern cities in the sample (i.e., Lesosibirsk and Norilsk) and statistically weaker elsewhere. The explanation is rather simple: in extreme climates, waiting time for public transportation becomes a crucial consideration for local residents (we should keep in mind that the level of private car ownership in Siberian cities is very low, at least by Western standards). In more mild climates (e.g., in Krasnoyarsk, Novosibirsk, and Barnaul), this factor loses, quite unsurprisingly, its prime significance.

F_4 *(the level of functional development)* is one of the most important variables influencing the level of a district's attractiveness in Siberian cities. This factor is included in two regression equations (Krasnoyarsk and Norilsk) as highly significant. Characteristically, this factor is of prime significance in Norilsk, while it is statistically weak in functionally underdeveloped settlements such as Lesosibirsk and Barnaul. This fact thus further validates the above conclusion that a factor's contribution to the IP's values is determined by the actual level of development achieved in a particular city.

F_5 *(the level of air pollution)* is statistically significant in three cites in the scope (i.e., Krasnoyarsk, Barnaul and Lesosibirsk). As expected, is has a negative sign in regression models tending to be highly statistically significant in cities whose built territory is sufficiently big to provide palpable difference in the levels of air pollution across individual city districts. This explains, for instance, why this factor *is not* statistically significant in the extremely polluted Norilsk which has similar levels of air pollution citywide (Table 2).

F_6 *(structural conditions of building)* is primarily important in the cities with historical buildings (e.g., Krasnoyarsk and Lesosibirsk). Concurrently, this factor is not statistically significant in the cities with newer development (e.g., Novosibirsk, Norilsk, and Barnaul).

F_8 *(aesthetic qualities of the built environment)* and F_9 *(aesthetic qualities of natural landscapes)* are statistically significant in Novosibirsk, Barnaul and Lesosibirsk. The statistical significance of these factors is especially notable since they are traditionally treated by urban planners and decision-makers as auxiliary factors, as opposed to other factors (e.g., access time, social facilities, and engineering infrastructures), whose significance is commonly emphasized.

'Experts' and 'Residents': Different Visions

Characteristically, ordinary city-dwellers and the experts evaluate individual city districts quite differently (see Table 4). In the city of Krasnoyarsk, for instance, the relationship between these evaluations is given to the following formula:

$$SE_i = 1.37 x IP_i - 1.31 \ (R^2=0.777), \qquad (2)$$

where SE_i is the attractiveness of district i estimated by the 'specialists,' and IP_i is the attractiveness of the same district estimated by ordinary city residents.

The values of the general attractiveness of a city district for residence (the IP) and its RE index (the Index of Residential Quality - see Section 5.2) are not identical either. The relationship between these two indices is captured by the following formula:

$$RE_i = 0.94 x IP_i + 0.95 \ (R^2=0.452) \qquad (3)$$

However, the mutual relationships between the indices in question (the IP, the SE and the RE) are not linear, as indicated by relatively low fits of the models (R^2=0.777 and 0.452, respectively). Furthermore, a more thorough statistical analysis shows that the factors influencing the values of the IP, SE and RE indicators are different. The regression models computed for the latter two measures of district attractiveness are as follows (the models report only the factors which are significant at a 95% confidence level):

$$SE = 17.5 - 1.29 x F_1 - 2.56 x F_3 - 3.15 x F_5 \ (R^2=0.831) \qquad (4)$$

$$RE = 3.76 - 4.46 x F_5 + 1.87 x F_8 \qquad (R^2= 0.545) \qquad (5)$$

Thus, compared to the IP (see Table 3), the SE index appears to have stronger relationships with F_1 and F_3 (i.e., access to the city centre and places of recreation). Concurrently, the SE index has no significant input from F_4 (the level of functional development) and F_6 (structural conditions of building), which are highly significant in the case of the IP (see Table 3: Krasnoyarsk). In other words, the 'specialists' appear to underestimate a number of qualities of the urban physical environment being important for the general city population, such as structural conditions of buildings (F6) and the level social services and facilities in the neighborhood (F4). On the other hand, the 'specialists' pay considerably more attention to location factors (F1 and F3; see (4)), which appear to be less essential for the general city population (see Table 3: Krasnoyarsk).

Table 4. Evaluation of Various Districts in Krasnoyarsk by City Residents (the IP and the RE Index) and by the Experts (the SE Index)

City district	IP	RE	SE	City district	IP	RE	SE
Center	1.00	1.00	1.00	Bazaikha	0.50	1.44	0.55
Academgorodok	0.97	1.51	0.86	Solnechny	0.48	1.47	0.32
Vetluzhanka	0.89	1.54	0.60	Severny	0.47	0.53	0.33
Nikolaevka	0.87	1.30	0.54	Vodnikov	0.47	0.53	0.20
Severno-Zapadny	0.85	1.32	0.66	Pokrovka	0.44	1.12	0.45
Airport	0.82	1.14	0.50	Palace of Culture	0.44	0.65	0.25
Svobodny Avenue	0.81	1.26	0.65	Green Grove	0.44	0.76	0.25
Studgorodok	0.73	1.04	0.79	Energetikov	0.42	0.40	0.17
Komsomolsky Gorodok	0.73	1.02	0.69	Laletino	0.42	0.36	0.53
Pashenny Island	0.73	0.88	0.31	Solontsy	0.40	0.80	0.36
Alexeevka	0.64	1.54	0.57	Cheremushky	0.39	0.73	0.19
Krasnoyarskiy Rabochy Avenue	0.62	1.03	0.45	Stone Block	0.35	0.61	0.22
Kalinin Street	0.59	0.64	0.30	Suvorovsky	0.34	0.40	0.18
Taimyr	0.58	1.04	0.39	Shynnikov	0.34	0.51	0.16
Innokentievsky	0.54	0.91	0.35	Prytchal	0.29	0.50	0.14
The First-of-May Settlement	0.51	0.78	0.26	Krastets Settlement	0.26	0.28	0.13
Medpreparaty	0.51	0.46	0.19				

Note: The values of the indices for the district 'Center' are set conditionally to 1; '-' indicates a lack of data.
IP = General Index of Prestige (the residents' evaluation of city districts)
RE = Index of Environment Quality (assessment of a district's attractiveness given by its permanent inhabitants).
SE= Specialists' Evaluation Index

The comparison between the RE and SE indices also indicates that the 'specialists' tend to underestimate the importance of the air pollution factor (F5), which influences significantly the residents' evaluations (see Table 3).

In order to understand the nature of the differences between the factors influencing the IP's values and the RE's levels (see Table 4), we should remind that the IP was evaluated by residents of the entire city, whereas the district's RE reflects only evaluations given by its own residents. It is thus unsurprising that the latter index emphasizes the importance of 'localized' environmental qualities, such as *the level of air pollution and the aesthetic qualities of the built environment* (see (5)), which appear to be overlooked by the 'outsiders' (see Table 3: Krasnoyarsk).

The models introduced in this section (see (4)-(5) and Table 3) make it possible to outline the '*perfect urban environment,*' as depicted by specialists and ordinary city dwellers. To this end, we shall rank statistically significant factors in a descending order according to their standardized regression coefficients (see Fig. 4). [factors are introduced in the order of their statistical significance, while signs in the parentheses indicate the direction of a particular factor's influence on a district's attractiveness, i.e. either positive or negative):

- *Specialists (the SE index):* remoteness from recreational areas (-); low levels of air pollution (+); closeness to the city center (+).
- *Ordinary city residents (the IP):* clean air (+); numerous community services and facilities in the neighborhood (+); new buildings in the neighborhood (+); remoteness from the city center (-).
- *Local residents of the district (the RE index):* low level of air pollution (+); attractive natural landscapes (+).

District Attractiveness for Business Activity

The regression model for the business the BA index, calculated for the city of Krasnoyarsk, is as follows [the model includes only factors which are significant at least at a 0.05 significance level]:

$$BA = 25.54 - 8.75xF_2 + 12.92xF_4 - 9.17xF_7 \quad (R^2 = 0.792) \qquad (6)$$

Comparing to the general index of a district's attractiveness for residence (the IP; see Table 3: Krasnoyarsk), the BA index appears to have stronger links with variables reflecting the functional and location qualities of city districts, viz., workplace accessibility, the level of functional development, and the availability of engineering utilities in the district. Concurrently, the influence of the aesthetic qualities of the urban environment (F8 and F9), and of the level of air pollution (F5) on the values of this index appears to be negligible.

Socio-Demographic Differences

Characteristically, different socio-demographic groups of city dwellers differ in their evaluations of district attractiveness (see Table 5). Since any detailed analysis of these relationships falls beyond the main thrust of the present study, only most general trends will be discussed. As Table 5 shows, the central city districts got the highest ratings from female respondents, and young people (14-16 years old). At the same time, peripheral districts were most popular among males, middle-age respondents, and, specifically, respondents with primary education. In contrast, the inner city fringes were most popular with female respondents, young adults (the 17-26 age group), the seniors (60+ years old), and high-school graduates. Apparently, central city districts and inner-city fringes tend to be more attractive for women because these districts are saturated with shopping and cultural facilities, whereas peripheral districts are often void of such facilities. The high attractiveness of suburban districts to people of middle age, and especially to those with primary education may be due to the fact that this category of city residents may be composed by people who recently moved from the countryside, and are still oriented on farming. They are not fully accustomed to city crowdedness and may thus prefer quieter peripheral neighborhoods.

Table 5. The Influence of Socio-Demographic Factors on the IP's Values (Krasnoyarsk)

Socio-demographic group	City zone		
	Center	Central Area's Fringe	Suburban Neighborhoods
Gender:			
• male*	1.00	1.00	1.00
• female	1.04	1.11	0.98
Age, years:			
• 14-16	1.08	1.18	0.93
• 17-26	1.04	1.23	0.91
• 27-36*	1.00	1.00	1.00
• 37-60	0.92	0.94	1.07
• above 60	1.10	1.50	1.08
Education:			
• elementary school	1.10	0.71	1.27
• high school*	1.00	1.00	1.00
• college, university	1.06	0.90	1.08

* set conditionally to 1.0

Conclusions and Applications in Planning

A cornerstone assumption of urban sociology, rooting in the ground-braking studies of the Chicago school (Park et al., 1925), is that social evaluations of the UPE reflect accurately genuine qualities of this environment. The results of the present study make it possible to reconsider, at least in part, this popular notion. The comparative analysis of Siberian cities of different sizes and locations demonstrates that social evaluations, obtained during sociological polls and surveys, reflect a combination of different environmental qualities, such as the average level of urban development achieved in a certain city, the range of environmental qualities across individual city districts, and the socio-demographic makeup of city residents, rather than the objective qualities of the UPE *per se*. This conclusion explains why less developed urban settlements can exhibit higher average levels of district attractiveness than more developed and attractive for living urban localities.

The differences between environmental values and priorities of ordinary city residents and 'specialists' (e.g., city-planners and local decision-makers), highlighted by the present analysis, are also important. While the 'specialists' tend to assign paramount importance to the spatial qualities of the urban environment (e.g., access to the city center, and recreation accessibility), ordinary city dwellers tend to pay more attention to ecological and functional issues (e.g., the level of air pollution in city neighborhoods, structural conditions of building, and the availability of social services and facilities). This may explain why planning improvements often meet priorities and professional ambitions of 'planners-in-charge' and decision-makers, rather than genuine needs of ordinary city dwellers.

The research introduced a system of evaluation indices (the General Index of Prestige or the IP, the Residents' Evaluation Index, and the Business Attractiveness Index), which may be useful in two separate areas -- property valuation and long-term physical planning.

During the initial phase of formation of the residential land market, when both housing and land transactions are sparse and data on comparable sales are unavailable, the survey method developed and applied in the present study (i.e., publication of specially designed questionnaires in major city newspapers) can be used to grade city districts according to their attractiveness, and then use these assessments as a substitute for a location component of property values. In particular, such assessment may be applied to the Average Standard Fee (ASF), routinely set for different cities by the central government in Russia and other transitional countries, and thereby used for property pricing during privatization and for local property taxation. Technically, the attractiveness indices proposed and estimated in this study may take forms of either downward or upward coefficients set for individual city districts and applied to standard (city-wide) fees, as discussed in Portnov and Maslovskiy (1996).

The use of the results of the present study in long-term physical planning may be based on the hierarchy of the factors influencing the IP and other indices of district attractiveness. For instance, based on the hierarchy of factors influencing the district attractiveness in the city of Krasnoyarsk, shown in Fig. 5, the following planning strategies may be employed in order to achieve positive changes in the existing social status of individual city neighborhoods [the strategies are ranked in the order of their importance for city dwellers]: 1) reducing the level of air pollution across individual neighborhoods (F5); 2) saturating residential neighborhoods with community services and facilities (F4); 3) renovating obsolesced buildings (F6), and 4) upgrading the existing thoroughfare system. The latter strategy may include the construction of new access roads and improving public transportation, which will lead, in turn, to the reduction of the access time from remote city districts to the downtown area (F1).

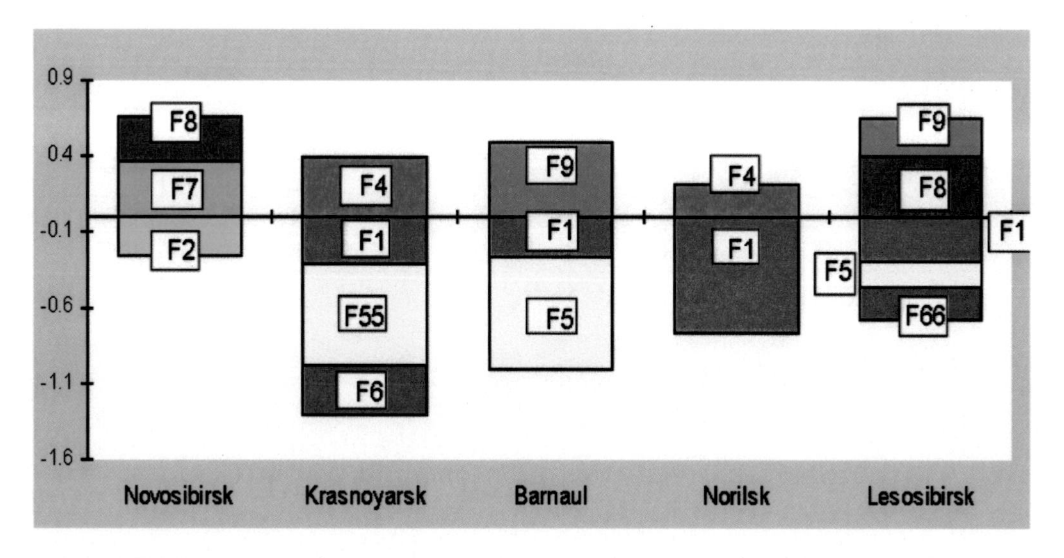

Figure 5. Relative importance of the factors influencing the relative attractiveness of residential districts in the Siberian Cities covered by the studyNote: The ranking is based on the values of the standardized regression coefficients; see text for the factors' definition

Finally, we should emphasize that this study's findings on the effects of spatial factors on the social attractiveness of the UPE are definitely specific to Siberian cities. However, the mode of the analysis (specifically, the use of newspaper publications for carrying out evaluation surveys and the system of evaluation indices proposed in the study) may be useful for similar studies carried out elsewhere. If it does, then this research may help planners and decision-makers formulate informed urban policies, especially for cities in economic transition.

APPENDIX 1

Population Composition of the Cities Surveyed (Percentages)

Parameter	Novosibirsk	Krasnoyarsk	Barnaul	Norilsk	Lesosibirsk
Gender:					
males	49.7	49.8	49.8	50.1	49.4
females	50.3	50.2	50.2	49.9	51.6
Age group:					
14-16	3.9	3.8	3.9	4.2	3.7
17-26	22.0	21.9	22.3	24.0	23.3
27-36	16.7	16.9	16.2	20.8	18.2
37-60	24.8	25.0	24.7	24.8	24.9
above 60	10.4	10.6	10.8	3.8	7.6
Education:					
elementary school	38.3	39.3	39.0	30.6	40.1
high school	24.1	24.8	26.7	36.9	28.3
college, university	37.6	35.9	34.3	32.5	31.6

APPENDIX 2

Hartley's F-Max Homogeneity-of-Variance (Homoscedasticity) Test

Factor	Variance after logarithmic transformation*				
	Novosibirsk	Krasnoyarsk	Barnaul	Norilsk	Lesosibirsk
F1	-	0.21	0.09	0.04	0.08
F2	0.12	-	-	-	-
F4	-	0.16	-	0.07	-
F5	-	0.08	0.05	-	0.16
F6	-	0.16	-	-	0.06
F7	0.05	-	-	-	-
F8	0.07	-	-	-	0.11
F9	-	-	0.12	-	0.11
F-Max	2.4	2.6	2.4	1.8	2.7
F-Critical (α=.01)	3.0	3.3	3.8	2.6	3.5

* The table reports the results of the test only for statistically significant variables (see Table 3).

REFERENCES

Bonnes M., Bonaiuto M., and Ercolani A.P. 1991. Crowding and residential satisfaction in the urban environment, *Environment and Behavior,* **23(5):** 531-552.

Evans G.W., Saltzman H. and Cooperman J.L. 2001. Housing quality and children's socio-emotional health. *Environment and Behavior,* **33(3):** 389-399.

Glass D., Singer J., and Pennlaker J. 1977. *Perspectives on Environment and Behavior.* New York: Plenum.

Gravetter F.J. and Wallnau L.B. 1992. *Statistics for the Behavioral Sciences.* St.Paul: West Publishing Company.

Hester R.T., Jr., 1984. *Planning Neighborhood Space with People*, 2nd Edition. New York: Van Nostrand Reinhold Company.

Hillier B. and Harison J. 1984. The Social Logic of Space. Cambridge: Cambridge University Press.

Keane C. 1991. Socio-environmental determinants of community formation, *Environment and Behavior*, **23(1):** 27-46.

Kou F.E. and Sullivan W.C. 2001 Aggression and violence in the inner city, effects of environment via mental fatigue. *Environment and Behavior*, **33(4):** 543-571.

Krushlinskiy V.I. 1986. *The Cities of Siberia.* Krasnoyarsk: The Krasnoyarsk University Press (in Russian).

Lin N. and Hanlong L. 1990. A structural model of social indicators and quality of life: a survey of life in the urban Shanghai, *Social Science in China*, **2:**180-211.

Lynch K.1960. *Image of the City.* Cambridge: Technology Press.

Michael S.E., Hull R.B. and Zahm D.L. 2001. Environmental factors influencing auto burglary a case study, *Environment and Behavior*, **33(3):** 368-388.

Park, R. E. Burgess E. W. and McKenzie R. D., eds. 1925 (1967 reprint). *The City,* pp. 47-62. Chicago and London: University of Chicago Press.

Portnov B.A. 1990. *Rational Use of Land in the Areas of Urban Renewal.* Krasnoyarsk: Stroyizdat Press (in Russian).

Portnov B.A., Maslovskiy V.P. 1996. Residential Land Attractiveness in an Emerging Property Market, *Netherlands Journal of Housing and Built Environment*, **11(2):** 107-130.

Rahman O.M.A. 1992. Visual quality and response assessment: an experimental technique, *Environment and Planning B: Planning and Design,* **19:** 689-708.

Rapoport A. 1977. *Human Aspects of Urban Form: Towards a Man-Environment Approach to Urban Form and Design,* London: Pergamon Press.

Rapoport A. 2000. Theory, culture and housing, *Housing Theory and Society,* **17(4):** 145-165.

Show D. 1987 'Siberia: Geographic Background' in A. Wood (Ed.) *Siberia: Prospects for Regional Development,* pp. 9-34. London: Croom Helm.

Smardon R.C. 1986. 'Review of agency methodology for visual project analysis,' in R.C. Smardon (Ed.) *Foundation for Visual Project Analysis.* New York: John Wiley.

Teklenburg J.A.F., Timmermans H.J.P. and van Wagenberg A.F. 1993. Space syntax: standardized integration measures and some simulations, *Environment and Planning B: Planning and Design,* **20:** 347-357.

Timmermans H.J.P. 1991. Decision-making process, choice, behavior, and environmental design: Conceptual issues and problems of application, in T. Garling and G. Evans (Eds) *Environment Condition and Action: An integrated Approach,* NY: Oxford University Press.

Tugnutt A. and Robertson M. 1987. *Making Townscape.* London: Mitchell Press.

Wittick A. (Ed.-in-chief) 1977. *Encyclopedia of Urban Planning, NY:* McGraw-Hill.

In: Focus on Urban and Regional Economics
Editor: Lawrence Yee, pp. 89-105
ISBN 1-59454-740-8

Chapter 5

STABILITY STUDY OF MIGRATION DYNAMICS[1]

Dao-Zhi Zeng [2]
Graduate School of Management, Kagawa University

ABSTRACT

Stability has been an essential topic in economic theory, particularly in the analysis of general equilibrium. A recent mainstream research area of urban and regional economics, called "New Economic Geography" (NEG), sets up a general equilibrium framework to explain how regional economic activities agglomerates or disperses. A dynamic approach plays an important role in describing the migration behavior of this study, and we need to know whether an equilibrium is stable. Since the literature of traditional stability research in the general equilibrium theory does not provide us enough results, this chapter aims to fill this gap and summarize some recent stability results that might help us to enrich the study of NEG, for example, from two regions to multiple regions and from a specific dynamic system to a class of dynamic systems. Furthermore, the evolutionary stability of game theory and the potential function approach are investigated. Surprisingly, we show that they are closely related to the asymptotical stability.

INTRODUCTION

In the absence of enough data, economists are required to infer analytically the qualitative direction of movement of a complex system. For this reason, stability has been an essential topic in economic theory since 1939, when Hicks published "Values and Capital." Originally, Hicks proposed imperfect stability and perfect stability (which are called Hicksian stability later) without explicit dynamics. Samuelson (1941, 1942) pointed out that Hicksian stability is essentially static in character, and true stability should be derived from explicit dynamical

[1] The author gratefully acknowledges the supports from the Japanese Ministry of Education, Sports, Science and Technology (Grant-in-Aid for Science Researchs 14730017 and 13851002). The comments from T. Tabuchi and X.-P. Zheng are very helpful.
[2] Phone & Fax: +81 87 832 1905, e-mail: zeng@ec.kagawa-u.ac.jp.

considerations. In other words, Samuelson suggested use the asymptotical stability of an explicit dynamical system to analyze the stability of a general equilibrium. As shown by Samuleson (1944), Hicksian stability is neither necessary nor sufficient for the asymptotical stability. Since then, the true stability research on general equilibrium developed very fast and there have been considerable interesting results, most of which are summarized in Hahn (1982).

The dynamic analysis of general equilibrium has a wonderful application in the field of urban and regional economics. In fact, theoretical urban economics has been almost entirely a study of equilibrium configurations: Where do the residents live and how do firms locate? Since most parameters (such as population, traffic means, environment, and etc.) are changing, the dynamic analysis is extremely important. Two decades ago, Miyao had done a vigorous study in analyzing the dynamic aspect of business and residential activities in the urban economy, and many interesting results are summarized in Miyao (1981). Needless to say, while the stability research in urban economics has been inspired and motivated by that of general equilibrium theory, it has contributed a lot and should contribute more to the stability study of general equilibrium in turn, and we need a summary of the recent development to activate the feedback.

Since Krugman (1991), the "New Economic Geography" (NEG) research has become a mainstream area in regional and urban economy. The main purpose of NEG is to explain the formation of a large variety of economic agglomeration (or concentration) in geographical space. Specifically, NEG discloses whether regional economy agglomerates or disperses when transport costs decrease. In its setup, the economic activity is described by industrial location, which is determined by the distribution of mobile workers. Assuming that a mobile worker migrates to a region with a higher utility level, some dynamic systems are applied to model the migration behavior. We need to judge whether the equilibria of such dynamics are stable or not. Furthermore, theoretically we also need to know whether such stable equilibria exist. Unfortunately, the results in traditional stability literature from general equilibrium theory (e.g., Hahn, 1982) do not take account of the features of regional migration and they are not directly applicable to this study. On the other hand, the results of Miyao (1981) are mostly devoted to the case of one region.[3] Therefore, their results are not enough for the study of NEG. For this reason, most of the NEG research has to be restricted to the case of two regions. However, such a setting makes the dynamic analysis very simple since moving away from one region automatically implies going to the other region. As revealed in Tabuchi et al (2005), the case of multiple regions is much more complicated and richer than that of two regions. The purpose of this chapter is to fill the gap and summarize the recent stability results, which are developed by authors from various fields, however, might be applicable to NEG.

A natural method to examine the asymptotical stability is checking the signs of all the eigenvalues of the Jacobian matrix. In this way, Tabuchi (1986) and Zeng (2002) provided stability conditions for a specific dynamic system of migration. Their results are now generalized to a class of dynamics in Tabuchi and Zeng (2004) by use of the Geršgorin Theorem.

---

[3] Chapter 6 of Miyao (1981) and Miyao (1978) provide the only model considering the case of multiple regions, however, the model is probabilistic instead of deterministic.

Meanwhile, the dynamics research obtained many results within the last two decades from the field of evolutional game theory. The concept of evolutionary stability came from ecology, but has been found strongly related to dynamics (particularly, the replicator dynamics) and their asymptotical stability. Hofbauer and Sigmund (1998, 2003) offer a systematic study of replicator dynamics and many other game dynamics. At the same time, many authors find that various stabilities are quite related to the maximizers of potential functions. Those results are put together here and we show how they can be applied to obtain stability results, in a way easier than checking the eigenvalues.

This chapter is organized as follows. Section 2 establishes a dynamic system describing migration behavior across multiple regions, and illustrates the stability result of Tabuchi (1986) and Zeng (2002). Section 3 generalizes the specific dynamic system to a class of dynamics and shows that the stability result of Section 2 is true for many dynamics. Section 4 summarizes how the evolutionary stability is related to asymptotical stability, which can be used to generalize the stability result of Section 2. On the other hand, the concept of potential function has been applied to analyze asymptotical stability since 1970s. Section 5 shows that the potential function can be used not only to generalize the result of Section 2, but also to obtain the existence of a stable equilibrium.

STABILITY OF A SPECIFIC DYNAMIC SYSTEM

As in Samuelson (1947, P. 262), an equilibrium is defined to be *stable* if sufficiently small displacements from equilibrium are followed by returns to equilibrium. The problem of stability of equilibrium cannot be discussed except with reference to dynamical considerations. We, therefore, first establish a suitable dynamic system. Then, the stability is equivalent to the asymptotical stability of that dynamic system.

Let us consider a country consisting of n separate regions. The total population of the country is chosen at unity for simplicity. Let $\mathbf{x} = (x_1, \cdots, x_n)$ be a population distribution, where x_i is the population in region i. Denote the whole set of x by:

$$S_n = \left\{ \mathbf{x} = (x_1, \ldots, x_r)^T \mid x_i \geq 0, \sum_{i=1}^{n} x_i = 1 \right\}$$

Although a resident's utility depends on many factors, this section assumes that the utility depends only on where the resident lives and how many people live in the same region. We denote the utility function by $u_i(x_i)$. All the residents are homogeneous, in the sense that the utility function does not depend on the names of residents. Assume that residents are free to choose regions and there is no migration cost. Then at equilibrium $\mathbf{x}^*$, it should hold that:

$$\begin{cases} u_i(x_i^*) = u^* & \text{if } i \text{ is a region such that } x_i^*>0, \\ u_i(0) \le u^* & \text{if } i \text{ is a region such that } x_i^*=0. \end{cases}$$

Suppose that $u_i(x_i)$ is a continuously differentiable function and hence continuous. Then there always exists an equilibrium according to Ginsburgh et al (1985). Equilibrium $\mathbf{x}^*$ is called *interior* if each $x_i^* > 0$ for $i = 1,...,n$, and *corner* if some $x_i^* = 0$. In the following, we focus on interior equilibia. Zeng (2002) shows that the stability of a corner equilibrium can be analyzed similarly.

To activate the dynamic approach, we sometimes denote the population distribution at time t by $\mathbf{x}(t) = (x_1(t),...,x_n(t))$. For an interior equilibrium $\mathbf{x}^*$, we limit our concern to a neighbor of $\mathbf{x}^*$ such that $x_i(t) > 0$. Let Δt be a small time period such that $x_i(t+\Delta) > 0$ for all of region i and denote $x_{ji}(t,t+\Delta t)$ as the population moving from region $j \neq i$ to region i during the time period from t to $t+\Delta t$. A positive value of $x_{ji}(t,t+\Delta t)$ means that some residents move from j to i, and a negative value means that some residents move from i to j, therefore, $x_{ji}(t,t+\Delta t) = -x_{ij}(t,t+\Delta t)$. Since residents move from a low-utility region to a high-utility region, we suppose that the migration population is proportional to the utility discrepancy. Then for sufficiently small Δt, it holds that:

$$x_{ji}(t,t+\Delta t) = \kappa_{ji}\Delta t[u_i(x_i(t)) - u_j(x_j(t))], \quad \text{for } i,j = 1,...,n, i \neq j, \tag{1}$$

where κ_{ji} is the so-called *speed of adjustment* (Metzler, 1945), which measures the speed with which residents migrate between regions i and j corresponding to a given utility discrepancy between regions i and j. Since $x_{ji}(t,t+\Delta t) = -x_{ij}(t,t+\Delta t)$, it holds that $\kappa_{ji} = \kappa_{ij}$. Because all the features of a region are included in its utility function and all residents are homogeneous, residents' decisions to migrate depend on the utility discrepancy alone. Therefore, independently of the names of regions, residents in region i respond to the utility discrepancy of any other region with the same speed of adjustment. That is $\kappa_{ij_1} = \kappa_{ij_2}$ for all $j_1, j_2 \neq i$. Therefore, $\kappa_{ij} = \kappa$ for all i and $j \neq i$. We can simply normalize residents' utility function so that $\kappa = 1/n$. Thus, in the following arguments, we always let $\kappa_{ij} = 1/n$.

For convenience, define $x_{ii}(t,t+\Delta t) = 0$ for any i, t and Δt. Then (1) holds for all i and j. Hence,

$$x_i(t+\Delta t) = x_i(t) + \sum_{j=1}^{n} x_{ji}(t, t+\Delta t) = x_i(t) + \frac{\Delta t}{n}\sum_{j=1}^{n}[u_i(x_i(t)) - u_j(x_j(t))],$$

and we obtain the following dynamic system:

$$\dot{x} = \lim_{\Delta t \to 0} \frac{x_i(t+\Delta t) - x_i(t)}{\Delta t} = u_i(x_i(t)) - \frac{1}{n}\sum_{j=1}^{n} u_j(x_j(t)). \tag{2}$$

This dynamic system is first utilized in Tabuchi (1986). Since we have supposed that $u_i(\cdot)$ is continuously differentiable, we know that there is a unique and continuous solution of (2) with any initial value around $\mathbf{x}^*$ (Hirsh and Smale 1974, P. 164).

Denote $u_{ii} = u_i'(x_i^*)$. To examine the asymptotical stability of interior equilibrium $\mathbf{x}^*$ of (2), we expand the RHS of (2) in a neighborhood of $\mathbf{x}^*$ (Samuelson, 1942). Since $\mathbf{x}^*$ is an equilibrium, the first term of the Taylor expansion is the linear term given by:

$$\begin{pmatrix} \dot{x}_1 \\ \dot{x}_2 \\ \vdots \\ \dot{x}_n \end{pmatrix} = \mathbf{A} \begin{pmatrix} x_1 - x_1^* \\ x_2 - x_2^* \\ \vdots \\ x_n - x_n^* \end{pmatrix},$$

where

$$\mathbf{A} = \begin{pmatrix} \frac{n-1}{n} & -\frac{1}{n} & \cdots & -\frac{1}{n} \\ -\frac{1}{n} & \frac{n-1}{n} & \cdots & -\frac{1}{n} \\ \vdots & \vdots & \ddots & \vdots \\ -\frac{1}{n} & -\frac{1}{n} & \cdots & \frac{n-1}{n} \end{pmatrix} \begin{pmatrix} u_{11} & 0 & \cdots & 0 \\ 0 & u_{22} & \cdots & 0 \\ \vdots & \vdots & \ddots & \vdots \\ 0 & 0 & \cdots & u_{nn} \end{pmatrix}$$

is the Jacobian matrix. Without loss of generality, we assume that:

$$u_{11} \geq u_{22} \geq \cdots \geq u_{nn}. \tag{3}$$

After investigating all the eigenvalues of matrix $\mathbf{A}$, Tabuchi (1986) shows that the following condition is necessary for the equilibrium $\mathbf{x}^*$ to be asymptotical stable:

$$(n-1)u_{11} + u_{22} \leq 0. \tag{4}$$

On the other hand, Zeng (2002) show that either of the following conditions:

$$(n-1)u_{11} + u_{22} < 0, \tag{5}$$

$$\text{If } u_{11} = 0 \text{ then } u_{22} < 0 \tag{6}$$

is sufficient to ensure the stability. Inspired by Tabuchi and Zeng (2004), the above conclusions can be generalized a little and summarized in a more concise way as follows:

Proposition 1. *Interior equilibrium* $\mathbf{x}^*$ *is asymptotically stable with respect to dynamic system (2) if either (7) or (8) holds.*

$$u_{11} \leq 0 \text{ and } u_{22} < 0, \tag{7}$$

$$u_{11} > 0 > u_{22} \text{ and } \sum_{i=1}^{n} \frac{1}{u_{11}} > 0 \tag{8}$$

The equilibrium is asymptotically unstable with respect to dynamic system (2) if either (9) or (10) holds.

$$u_{11} > 0 \text{ and } u_{22} \geq 0, \tag{9}$$

$$u_{11} > 0 > u_{22} \text{ and } \sum_{i=1}^{n} \frac{1}{u_{11}} < 0 \tag{10}$$

One will soon realize that the necessary conditions are very close to the sufficient conditions. Nevertheless, there are some situations remain unclear. For example, we are not sure about the case that $u_{11} = u_{22} = 0$, in which the Jacobian matrix has at least two zero eigenvalues. Fortunately, such cases are not typical in the view of *regular economy* (Debreu 1970). In other words, those cases are not generic and they are not expected to be observed (Mas-Colell, 1985, Chapter 8).

The above conditions have a very intuitive explanation. At equilibrium $\mathbf{x}^*$, call region i *underpopulated* if $u_{ii} > 0$ and *overpopulated* if $u_{ii} < 0$. If there are at least two underpopulated regions, then the equilibrium is unstable, because a resident in one underpopulated region feels happy to migrate to another underpopulated region. On the other hand, the equilibrium is stable if all regions are overpopulated because a resident's utility decreases if he/she migrates. The remaining case is that only one region is underpopulated. According to (3), the underpopulated one is region 1. To increase the utility level by one unit, region 1 should have $1/u_{11}$ residents moving in and region $i = 2, \cdots, n$ should have $-1/u_{ii}$ residents moving out. If (8) holds, then:

$$\frac{1}{u_{11}} > -\sum_{i=2}^{n} \frac{1}{u_{ii}},$$

i.e., the moving-out residents from regions $i = 2, \cdots, n$ are not enough to increase the utility in region 1 by one unit even if all of them move into region 1 together. Therefore, the equilibrium is stable. In contrast, if (10) holds, then the moving-out residents are enough and there is an incentive for some residents in regions $2, \cdots, n$ to migrate into region 1.

Proposition 1 is useful in at least two ways. First, there are some situations in which the interactions within regions are much stronger than those among regions, so that u_i can be treated as only related to x_i. Second, even if the interactions among regions are not negligible, it may happen that the dynamic system (2) can be simplified and the stability result applies. See Tabuchi et al (2005) for an example.

Stability of a Class of Dynamics

Proposition 1 is extended by Tabuchi and Zeng (2004). In their general setting, utility function of region i depends not only on its own population, but also on the population of other regions. The utility function of region i is, therefore, denoted by $u_i(\mathbf{x})$. Furthermore, they use general dynamics derived as follows.

The migrating population of (1) can be more generally described by:

$$x_{ji}(t, t+\Delta t) = f_{ij}(\mathbf{x})\Delta t[u_i(\mathbf{x}(t)) - u_j(\mathbf{x}(t))], \tag{11}$$

where $f_{ij}(\mathbf{x}) > 0$ is interpreted as the adjustment speed of migration or distance between regions. The symmetry holds evidently: $\dot{x}_{ij} = -\dot{x}_{ji}$ and $f_{ij}(\mathbf{x}) = f_{ji}(\mathbf{x})$. Summing up (11) over j yields

$$\dot{x}_i = \sum_{j=1}^{n} f_{ij}(\mathbf{x})[u_i(\mathbf{x}) - u_j(\mathbf{x})], \tag{12}$$

which can be rewritten in the following matrix form:

$$\dot{\mathbf{x}} = \mathbf{F}(\mathbf{x}) \cdot \mathbf{U}(\mathbf{x}) \tag{13}$$

where

$$\mathbf{F}(\mathbf{x}) \equiv \begin{pmatrix} f_1(\mathbf{x}) & -f_{12}(\mathbf{x}) & \cdots & -f_{1n}(\mathbf{x}) \\ -f_{12}(\mathbf{x}) & f_2(\mathbf{x}) & \cdots & -f_{2n}(\mathbf{x}) \\ \vdots & \vdots & \ddots & \vdots \\ -f_{1n}(\mathbf{x}) & -f_{2n}(\mathbf{x}) & \cdots & f_n(\mathbf{x}) \end{pmatrix}, \quad \mathbf{U}(x) \equiv \begin{pmatrix} u_1(\mathbf{x}) \\ u_2(\mathbf{x}) \\ \vdots \\ u_n(\mathbf{x}) \end{pmatrix}$$

and

$$f_i(\mathbf{x}) \equiv \sum_{j \neq i}^{n} f_{ij}(\mathbf{x}) \text{ for } i = 1, \ldots, n.$$

The dynamic system (12) or (13) is quite general. For example, (12) returns to (2) if $f_{ij}(\mathbf{x}) = 1/n$ for $i \neq j$. If we let $f_{ij}(\mathbf{x}) = x_i x_j$, then the following replicator dynamic system is obtained:

$$\dot{x}_i = x_i [u_i(\mathbf{x}) - \sum_{j=1}^{n} x_j u_j(\mathbf{x})], \tag{14}$$

which is widely used in evolutionary game theory (see next Section) and NEG (see Fujita et al, 1999).

To examine the asymptotical stability of an interior equilibrium $\mathbf{x}^*$, we expand the RHS of (13) around $\mathbf{x}^*$, and obtain the following linear approximation:

$$\dot{\mathbf{x}} = \mathbf{F}(\mathbf{x}^*) \cdot \partial\mathbf{U} \cdot (\mathbf{x} - \mathbf{x}^*) \tag{15}$$

where

$$u_{ik} = \left. \frac{\partial u_i(\mathbf{x})}{\partial x_k} \right|_{\mathbf{x}=\mathbf{x}^*}, \quad \partial\mathbf{U} = \begin{pmatrix} u_{11} & u_{12} & \cdots & u_{1n} \\ u_{21} & u_{22} & \cdots & u_{2n} \\ \vdots & \vdots & \ddots & \vdots \\ u_{n1} & u_{n2} & \cdots & u_{nn} \end{pmatrix}.$$

The Jacobian matrix of (13) or (15) is $\mathbf{F}(\mathbf{x}^*)\partial\mathbf{U}$. Let us denote it by $\mathbf{A} = [a_{ij}]_{n \times n}$ again, where

$$a_{ij} = \begin{cases} \displaystyle\sum_{k=1, k \neq i}^{n} (u_{ii} - u_{ki}) f_{ik}(\mathbf{x}^*) & \text{for } i = j \\ \displaystyle\sum_{k=1, k \neq i}^{n} (u_{ij} - u_{kj}) f_{ik}(\mathbf{x}^*) & \text{for } i \neq j \end{cases}.$$

Furthermore, denote the cofactor of u_{ij} in $\partial\mathbf{U}$ by $U_{ij} \equiv (-1)^{i+j}\left|\partial\tilde{\mathbf{U}}_{ij}\right|$, where $\partial\tilde{\mathbf{U}}_{ij}$ is a submatrix formed from $\partial\mathbf{U}$ by deleting the i-th row and the j-th column. After examining the eigenvalues of matrix $\mathbf{A}$ by use of the Geršgorin Theorem, Tabuchi and Zeng (2004) obtain the following stability condition.

Proposition 2. *Spatial equilibrium $\mathbf{x}^*$ of (15) is stable if either(i) or (ii) holds.*

(i) Inequality $\min_{i=1,\ldots,n,\, i\neq j}\{a_{ij}\} > 0$ holds for all j.

(ii) Inequality $\max_{i=1,\ldots,n,\, i\neq j}\{a_{ij}\} < 0$ holds for one j while the reverse inequality $\min_{i=1,\ldots,n,\, i\neq j}\{a_{ij}\} \geq 0$ holds for all other j. In addition, $(-1)^n\sum_{i=1}^{n}\sum_{j=1}^{n}U_{ij} < 0$ holds.

On the other hand, x^* is unstable if either (iii) or (iv) holds.

(iii) Inequality $\max_{i=1,\ldots,n, i\neq j}\{a_{ij}\} < 0$ holds for at least two j, and furthermore $\sum_{i=1}^{n}\sum_{j=1}^{n}U_{ij} \neq 0$.

(iv) Inequality $\max_{i=1,\ldots,n,\, i\neq j}\{a_{ij}\} < 0$ holds for one j, while the reverse inequality $\min_{i=1,\ldots,n,\, i\neq j}\{a_{ij}\} \geq 0$ holds for other j. In addition, $(-1)^n\sum_{i=1}^{n}\sum_{j=1}^{n}U_{ij} > 0$ holds.

What do we know from the above general result? Consider the special case that $u_i(x) = u_i(x_i)$ again. In this case,

$$a_{ij} = \begin{cases} u_{ii}f_i & \text{if } i=j, \\ -u_{jj}f_{ij} & \text{if } i\neq j, \end{cases}$$

$$U_{ij} = \begin{cases} \prod_{k\neq i} u_{kk} & \text{if } i=j, \\ 0 & \text{if } i\neq j. \end{cases}$$

Then conditions (i)~ (iv) are simplified to conditions (7)~ (10), respectively[4]. Therefore, we obtain:

Proposition 3. *Interior equilibrium x^* is asymptotically stable with respect to any dynamic system of (13) if either (7) or (8) holds. The equilibrium is asymptotically unstable with respect to any dynamic system of (13) if either (9) or (10) holds.*

The above proposition generalizes Proposition 1 in thc sense that the conclusion does not depend on the specific form of (2). In other words, all the dynamics of (13) share the same stability conditions when $u_i(x) = u_i(x_i)$. That is, we can use either (2) or (14) or any other

[4] Strictly speaking, we here omit the case of $u_{11} = 0$ in (7) and the case of $u_{22} = 0$ in (9). Both cases are not typical in all admissible environments in the sense of regular economy (Debreu, 1970).

form of (13) to obtain the same stability conditions. Generally speaking, $f_{ij}(\mathbf{x})$ are though to be important because they contain the geographyic factors among regions such as their distances. However, to our surprise, the stability turns out to be independent of $f_{ij}(\mathbf{x})$ when $u_i(\mathbf{x}) = u_i(x_i)$. We shall clarify this point more in subsequent two sections.

EVOLUTIONARY STABILITY AND POSITIVE DEFINITE DYNAMICS

ESS of Game Theory

The concept of evolutionary stable state (ESS) was proposed by Maynard Smith and Price (1973) and Maynard Smith (1974). The basic idea of ESS is originated from biology and then game theory, which considers what kind of states or strategies are robust to evolutionary selection pressures. More precisely, suppose that individuals are repeatedly drawn at random from a large population to play a symmetric two-person game, and suppose that initially all individuals are genetically or otherwise "programmed" to play a certain pure or mixed strategy in this game. Now inject a small population share of individuals who are likewise programmed to play some other pure or mixed strategy. The incumbent strategy is said to be evolutionarily stable if, for each such mutant strategy, there exists a positive invasion barrier such that if the population share of individuals playing the mutant strategy falls below this barrier, then the incumbent strategy earns a higher payoff than the mutant strategy.

For any matrix $\mathbf{B} = (b_{ij})_{n\times n}$, we form a symmetric two-player game, in which player 1's payoff matrix is $\mathbf{B}$ while player 2's payoff matrix is $\mathbf{B}^T$. Given player 1's strategy $\mathbf{x}$ and player 2's strategy $\mathbf{y}$, the payoff of player 1 is $x^T\mathbf{B}\mathbf{y}$ and the payoff of player 2 is $\mathbf{x}^T\mathbf{B}^T\mathbf{y}$. Then strategy $\mathbf{x}^* = (x_1^*,\ldots,x_n^*)^T$ is an ESS if:

$$\mathbf{x}^T\mathbf{B}\mathbf{x}^* \le \mathbf{x}^{*T}\mathbf{B}\mathbf{x}^*, \quad \forall \text{ strategy } \mathbf{x}, \tag{16}$$

$$\mathbf{x}^T\mathbf{B}\mathbf{x}^* = \mathbf{x}^{*T}\mathbf{B}\mathbf{x}^* \Rightarrow \mathbf{x}^T\mathbf{B}\mathbf{x} < \mathbf{x}^{*T}\mathbf{B}\mathbf{x}, \quad \forall \text{ strategy } \mathbf{x} \ne \mathbf{x}^*. \tag{17}$$

Note that (16) says that $\mathbf{x}^*$ is a Nash equilibrium strategy of the matrix game. For convenience, we focus on the case that $\mathbf{x}^*$ is an interior point in the strategy space. In other words, $x_i^* > 0$ for all $i = 1,\ldots,n$. Such an ESS is called *regular* in evolutionary game theory.

Hines (1980b) summarizes (16) and (17) as:

$$(\mathbf{x}^* - \mathbf{x})^T(\mathbf{B} + \mathbf{B}^T)(\mathbf{x}^* - \mathbf{x}) < 0, \quad \forall \text{ strategy } \mathbf{x} \ne \mathbf{x}^*. \tag{18}$$

Let:

$$\mathbf{R}_0^n = \left\{ (z_1, \ldots, z_n)^T \middle| \sum_{i=1}^{n} z_i = 0 \right\},$$

which is the subspace of $\mathbf{R}^n$ perpendicular to vector $1^T = (1, \ldots, 1)$. Then $\mathbf{x}^* - \mathbf{x} \in \mathbf{R}_0^n$ for any $\mathbf{x} \in S_n$ and condition (18) is intuitively explained as follows:

$$\text{Matrix } \mathbf{B} + \mathbf{B}^T \text{ is negative definite in } \mathbf{R}_0^n. \tag{19}$$

Another way to explain (18) is that $\mathbf{y}^T(\mathbf{B} + \mathbf{B}^T)\mathbf{y}$ attains its maximum at 0 when $\mathbf{y} = \mathbf{x}^* - \mathbf{x}$ is restricted in $\mathbf{R}_0^n$. To clarify this condition, we form the following borded determinants:

$$\mathbf{B}^\dagger[i_1 i_2 \cdots i_m] \equiv \begin{vmatrix} 0 & 1' \\ 1 & \dfrac{\mathbf{B}(\{i_1 i_2 \cdots i_m\}) + \mathbf{B}(\{i_1 i_2 \cdots i_m\})^T}{2} \end{vmatrix}, \qquad m \geq 2, \tag{20}$$

where

$$\mathbf{B}(\{i_1 i_2 \cdots i_m\}) = \begin{pmatrix} b_{i_1 i_1} & b_{i_1 i_2} & \cdots & b_{i_1 i_m} \\ b_{i_2 i_1} & b_{i_2 i_2} & \cdots & b_{i_2 i_m} \\ \vdots & \vdots & \ddots & \vdots \\ b_{i_m i_1} & b_{i_m i_2} & \cdots & b_{i_m i_m} \end{pmatrix}$$

is the submatrix of $\mathbf{B}$ with rows $i_1, \cdots, i_m$ and columns $i_1, \cdots, i_m$. Then, Theorem 1.E.17 of Takayama (1985, p.130) tells us that (18) is equivalent to:

$$(-1)^m \mathbf{B}^\dagger[i_1 i_2 \cdots i_m] > 0, \quad \forall m = 1, \ldots, n. \tag{21}$$

Similar to Hicksian stability, no dynamics is required in the definition of ESS. It subjects to the same criticisms of Samuelson if we cannot connect ESS to some specific dynamics. Fortunately, this work was well done by Taylor and Jonker (1978), who proposed the replicator dynamics (14), where:

$$u_i(\mathbf{x}) = (b_{i1}, \ldots, b_{in})(x_1, \ldots, x_n)^T, \quad i = 1, \ldots, n.$$

Differently from Hicksian stability, Taylor and Jonker found that the evolutionary stability is strongly related to the asymptotical stability:

Proposition 4. *If $\mathbf{x}^*$ is ESS, then it is asymptotically stable for (14), but the converse is not true.*

Therefore, ESS is stronger than the asymptotical stability of (14). Hofbauer and Sigmund (1998) provided many results on the relation between ESS and dynamic systems.

Positive Definite Dynamics and Adaptive Dynamics

In the appendix of Hines(1980a), the author provides the following mathematical result.

Proposition 5. *Given matrix $\mathbf{B}$, the following two statements are equivalent:*

(1) matrix $\mathbf{B}+\mathbf{B}^T$ is negative definite,

(2) for all positive definite symmetric matrices $\mathbf{Q}$, the eigenvalues of $\mathbf{QB}$ have negative real parts.

In the above proposition, the positive definiteness and negative definiteness are with respect to space $\mathbf{R}^n$. To connect with (19), Hopkins (1999a) reformulated the conclusion with respect to space $\mathbf{R}_0^n$.

Proposition 6. *If $\mathbf{B}+\mathbf{B}^T$ is negative definite in $\mathbf{R}_0^n$, then all the eigenvalues of $\mathbf{QB}$ have negative real parts where $\mathbf{Q}$ is positive definite in $\mathbf{R}_0^n$.*

Hopkins (1999b, P. 143) further defines positive definite dynamics as follows:

Definition 1. A positive definite dynamic system is a dynamic system of the form

$$\dot{\mathbf{x}} = \mathbf{Q}(\mathbf{x})\mathbf{B}\mathbf{x}, \tag{22}$$

where $\mathbf{B}$ is a constant matrix and $\mathbf{Q}(\mathbf{x})$ is a matrix function on the interior of S_n that possesses the following four conditions:

1. Positive definiteness with respect to $\mathbf{R}_0^n$, i.e., $\mathbf{z}^T\mathbf{Q}(\mathbf{x})\mathbf{z} > 0$ for all nonzero $\mathbf{z} \in \mathbf{R}_0^n$.
2. Symmetry.
3. $\mathbf{Q}(\mathbf{x})$ maps $\mathbf{R}^n \to \mathbf{R}_0^n$.
4. Continuously differentiability with respect to $\mathbf{x}$.

Positive definiteness ensures that the angle between vector $\mathbf{Bx}$ (the payoff vector of player 1) and the vector of the dynamic $\mathbf{Q}(\mathbf{x})\mathbf{Bx}$ must be less than 90°. The set of positive definite dynamics is quite large. For example, it takes the form of (15) if $\mathbf{B} = \partial\mathbf{U}$ and $\mathbf{Q}(\mathbf{x}) = F(\mathbf{x}^*)$. Note that $f_{ij}(\mathbf{x}) > 0$ is assumed in (15) but the elements of $\mathbf{Q}(\mathbf{x})$ are not required to be positive in Definition 1.

Then, combining the above conclusion with condition (19), Hopkins (1999a, P. 98) obtains the following conclusion.

Proposition 7. *A regular ESS is asymptotically stable for any positive definite dynamic system.*

Since the replicator dynamic system is a special case of (15), the above conclusion generalizes Proposition 4.

Hofbauer and Sigmund (1990, 1998, 2003) established a model for the mutant's learning strategy in an evolutionary game with homogeneous population, and obtained *adaptive dynamics* which is more general than (22). An adaptive dynamic system requires a symmetric matrix $\tilde{\mathbf{Q}}$ which is positive definite in $\mathbf{R}^n$. Such a matrix specifies another matrix,

$$\mathbf{Q} = \tilde{\mathbf{Q}}^{-1} - (\mathbf{1}^T\tilde{\mathbf{Q}}^{-1}\mathbf{1})^{-1}\tilde{\mathbf{Q}}^{-1}\mathbf{1}\mathbf{1}^T\tilde{\mathbf{Q}}^{-1},$$

which is positive definite with respect to $\mathbf{R}_0^n$ and maps $\mathbf{R}^n \to \mathbf{R}_0^n$. (One can easily prove the positive definiteness of $\mathbf{Q}$ by showing that any eigenvector in $\mathbf{R}_0^n$ of $\tilde{\mathbf{Q}}^{-1}$ is also an eigenvector of $\mathbf{Q}$.) After specifying the payoff function of the game to be linear, the adaptive dynamic system takes the same form of (22). Furthermore, the authors find that Proposition 7 is true for any adaptive dynamic system.

Equivalence of ESS and Asymptotical Stability

Let us return to special case considered in Section 2: $u_i(\mathbf{x}) = u_i(x_i)$. In other words, the utility level in a region depends only on that regional population. Then,

$$\partial\mathbf{U} = \begin{pmatrix} u_{11} & 0 & \cdots & 0 \\ 0 & u_{22} & \cdots & 0 \\ \vdots & \vdots & \ddots & \vdots \\ 0 & 0 & \cdots & u_{nn} \end{pmatrix}, \tag{23}$$

which is symmetric. Take $\mathbf{B} = \partial\mathbf{U}$, and assume that $u_{ii} \neq 0$ for all i for simplicity, then the LHS of (21) is

$$(-1)^m \begin{vmatrix} 0 & 1 & 1 & \cdots & 1 \\ 1 & u_{i_1i_1} & 0 & \cdots & 0 \\ 1 & 0 & u_{i_2i_2} & \cdots & 0 \\ \vdots & \vdots & \ddots & \vdots & \vdots \\ 1 & 0 & 0 & \cdots & u_{i_mi_m} \end{vmatrix} = -\sum_{j=1}^{m}\frac{1}{u_{i_j}}\prod_{j=1}^{m}(-u_{i_ji_j}).$$

Together with (3), the above shows that $\mathbf{x}^*$ is ESS if either (7) or (8) holds. Since (2) is a positive definite dynamic system, Proposition 7 implies to the following conclusion which generalizes the first part of Proposition 1:

Proposition 8. *Interior equilibrium* $\mathbf{x}^*$ *is asymptotically stable with respect to any dynamic system of (13) if either (7) or (8) holds.*

The above conclusion helps us to understand Proposition 8, that the conclusion of Proposition 1 does not depend on the specific form of dynamic system (2). Indeed, the conclusion crucially depends on two facts: the positive definiteness of matrix $\mathbf{F}$ and the symmetry of matrix (23).

The diagonal property of (23) is sufficient but not necessary for the symmetry. Therefore, Tabuchi and Zeng (2004) further generalized Proposition 8 to some extent:

Proposition 9. *If* $\partial\mathbf{U}$ *satisfies*

$$u_{ij} + u_{jk} + u_{ki} = u_{ik} + u_{kj} + u_{ji} \quad \textit{for all } i, j, k \in \{1, \ldots, n\}, \tag{24}$$

then the equilibrium $\mathbf{x}^*$ *is asymptotically stable with respect to any dynamic system of (13) if*

$$(-1)^i \begin{vmatrix} 0 & \mathbf{1}^T \\ \mathbf{1} & \dfrac{\partial\mathbf{U}_i + (\partial\mathbf{U}_i)^T}{2} \end{vmatrix} > 0, \ \forall i \geq 1,$$

where $\partial\mathbf{U}_i$ *is the principal submatrix of* $\partial\mathbf{U}$ *consisting of rows* $1, \ldots, i$ *and columns* $1, \ldots, i$.

Potential Function and the Existence of a Stable Equilibrium

The stability conditions obtained previously are complicated enough to think over the existence of a stable equilibrium. However, recent research shows that such an existence can be obtained from a potential function sometimes.

Many authors find that the stability of equilibrium is strongly related to potential function. Given potential function $P(\mathbf{x})$, early researchers like Dierker (1974, who named $P(\mathbf{x})$ as *height function* on P. 20 and P. 39), Hirsch and Smale (1974, who named the following as *gradient system* on P. 199), Wilson (1981), Zheng (1990), and Hofbauer and Sigmund (1998, P. 83) consider the stability with respect to the following dynamic system:

$$\frac{d\mathbf{x}}{dt} = \text{grad } P \equiv \left(\frac{\partial P}{\partial x_i} \right)_{n\times 1}.$$

Recently, Sandholm (2001) further extended the above dynamic system to a class of dynamics in the form of

$$\frac{d\mathbf{x}}{dt} = \mathbf{V}(\mathbf{x}), \tag{25}$$

where vector field $\mathbf{V}(\mathbf{x})$ is positively correlated with $\text{grad}P(\mathbf{x})$ in the following sense:

$$\mathbf{V}(\mathbf{x}) \cdot \text{grad}\, P(\mathbf{x}) > 0. \tag{26}$$

The differential equation (25) is called *myopic adjustment dynamic system*[5], in which (26) requires that population always moves toward a place with a higher potential value.

The myopic adjustment dynamic system is similar to but different from (22). They are similar because both of them require that the vector $\dot{\mathbf{x}}$ of the dynamic system must not be too different from $\text{grad}\, P(\mathbf{x})$ or $\mathbf{Bx}$. There are two differences. On the one hand, there are some dynamics of (22) without suitable potential functions when B is not symmetric. On the other hand, the positive definiteness of $\mathbf{Q}(\mathbf{x})$ is sufficient but not necessary to ensure (26). Interestingly enough, Hofbauer and Sigmund (1998, P. 83) show that dynamics (22) can be derived from the gradient system directly after re-defining the inner product when $\mathbf{B}$ is symmetric.

Extending the corollary on P. 200 of Hirsch and Smale (1974), Sandholm (2001) shows:

Proposition 10. *Any isolated local maximizer set of is a minimal asymptotically stable set of (25).*

According to Proposition 10, the asymptotical stabilities of all dynamics of (25) are equivalent to each other.

Given the positive definiteness of matrix $\mathbf{F}(\mathbf{x})$, the RHS of (15) is evidently positively correlated with $\partial\mathbf{U} \cdot (\mathbf{x} - \mathbf{x}^*)$. Therefore, Sandholm's result applies directly when $\partial\mathbf{U}$ is symmetric[6], in that case the potential function can be defined as:

$$P(\mathbf{x}) = \frac{(\mathbf{x} - \mathbf{x}^*)^T \cdot \partial\mathbf{U} \cdot (\mathbf{x} - \mathbf{x}^*)}{2}. \tag{27}$$

Remember that the ESS condition of (18) is equivalent to the fact that $\mathbf{x}^*$ is a maximum of:

$$(\mathbf{x}^* - \mathbf{x})^T [\partial\mathbf{U} + (\partial\mathbf{U})^T](\mathbf{x}^* - \mathbf{x}) = 2(\mathbf{x}^* - \mathbf{x})^T \partial\mathbf{U}(\mathbf{x}^* - \mathbf{x}) = 4P(\mathbf{x}),$$

we know that the maximum $\mathbf{x}^*$ of (27) is equivalent to the ESS property of $\mathbf{x}^*$ in the game with payoff matrix $\partial\mathbf{U}$. In this way, we obtain Proposition 8 again. Furthermore, as claimed in Proposition 3, the asymptotical stability of any dynamic system of (13) is equivalent to each other, which generalize Theorem 7.8.1 of Hofbauer and Sigmund (1998).

Now we turn to problem of examining the existence of a stable equilibrium. Since the stability conditions obtained in previous sections are complicated, it is hopeless to derive the existence directly from those conditions. However, due to Proposition 10, we only need to

---

[5] Strictly speaking, this name, first used in Swinkels (1993), only require a weak inequality in (26).

[6] This can be generalized slightly to the case of (24). See Tabuchi and Zeng (2004), Hofbauer and Sigmund (2003, P.491).

check the existence of a local maximizer of the potential function, if such a potential function exists. Based on this idea, Tabuchi and Zeng (2004) obtained the following conclusion.

Proposition 11. *If* $u_i(\mathbf{x}) = u_i(x_i)$, *then there generically exist at least one asymmetrically stable equilibrium for any PD dynamic system.*

Proposition 11 claims that the existence holds generically. A property is generic if it holds in an open and dense set of the whole topological space of parameters (Chapter 8 of Mas-Colell, 1985). To understand it, the existence may fail for some special parameters. For example, when $u_i(\mathbf{x}) = 1$ for all i and all $\mathbf{x}$, then each distribution form an equilibrium, but no equilibrium is (asymptotically) stable. However, the set of such exceptional parameters is small enough to be negligible. This is consistent with the fact that we have omitted the case that at least two eigenvalues of the Jacobian matrix are zero in the previous sections (see the comment after Proposition 1 and footnote 1).

The counterexample of Scarf (1960) shows that we need some conditions to ensure the existence of a stable equilibrium. On the other hand, the condition of $u_i(\mathbf{x}) = u_i(x_i)$ is clearly quite restrictive. It is a challenging task to obtain a more general result in the future.

REFERENCES

Debreu, G., 1970. Economies with a finite set of equilibria. *Econometrica* 38, 387-392.

Dierker, E., 1974. *Topological Methods in Walrasian Economics*. Berlin: Springer-Verlag.

Fujita, M., P. Krugman and A.J. Venables. 1999. *The Spatial Economy: Cities, Regions and International Trade*. Cambridge Mass.: MIT Press.

Ginsburgh, V., Y.Y. Papageorgiou and J.-F. Thisse. 1985. On Existence and Stability of Spatial Equilibria and Steady-States. *Regional Science and Urban Economics* 15, 149-158.

Hahn, F., 1982. Stability. *Handbook of Mathematical Economics* Vol. II, edited by Arrow and Intriligator, North-Holland Publishing Company, 745-793.

Hicks, J.R., 1939. *Value and Capital*, Oxford University

Hines, W.G.S., 1980a. Three characterizations of population strategy stability. *Journal of Applied Probability* 17, 333-340.

Hines, W.G.S., 1980b. Strategy stability in complex populations. *Journal of Applied Probability* 17, 600-610.

Hirsch, M.W. and S. Smale, 1974. Differential Equations, Dynamical Systems, and Linear Algebra. Academic Press.

Hofbauer J. and K. Sigmund, 1990. Adaptive dynamics and evolutionary stability. *Applied mathematics Letters* 3, 75-79.

Hofbauer J. and K. Sigmund, 1998. *Evolutionary Games and Population Dynamics*. Cambridge University Press.

Hofbauer J. and K. Sigmund, 2003. Evolutionary games and population dynamics. *Bulletin of the American Mathematical Society* 40, 479-519.

Hopkins, E., 1999a. Learning, matching and aggregation. *Games and Economic Behavior* 26, 79-110.

Hopkins, E., 1999b. A note on best response. *Games and Economic Behavior* 29, 138-150.

Krugman, P. 1991. Increasing Returns and Economic Geography. *Journal of Political Economy* 99, 483-499.

Mas-Colell, A. 1985. *The Theory of General Economic Equilibrium*. Cambridge: Cambridge University Press.

Maynard Smith, J., 1974. The theory of games and the evolution of animal conflicts. *Journal of Theoretical Biology* 47, 209-221.

Maynard Smith, J. and G.R. Price, 1973. The logic of animal conflict. *Nature* 246, 15-18.

Metzler, L.A., 1945. Stability of multiple markets: the Hicks conditions. *Econometrica* 13, 277-292.

Miyao, T., 1978. A probabilistic model of location choice with neighborhood effects. *Journal of Economic Theory* 19, 347-358.

Miyao, T., 1981. Dynamic Analysis of the Urban Economy, Academic Press.

Samuelson, P.A., 1941. The stability of equilibrium: comparative statics and dynamics. *Econometrica* 9, 97-120.

Samuelson, P.A., 1942. The stability of equilibrium: linear and nonlinear systems. *Econometrica* 10, 1-25.

Samuelson, P.A., 1944. The relation between Hicksian stability and true dynamic stability. *Econometrica* 12, 256-257.

Samuelson, P.A., 1947. *Foundations of Economic Analysis*, Harvard University Press.

Sandholm, W.H., 2001. Potential games with continuous player sets. *Journal of Economic Theory* 57, 363-391.

Scarf, H., 1960. Some examples of global instability of the competitive equilibrium. *International Economic Review* 1, 157-172.

Swinkels, J.M., 1993. Adjustment dynamics and rational play in games. *Games and Economic Behavior* 5, 455-484.

Tabuchi, T. 1986. Existence and Stability of City-Size Distribution in the Gravity and Logit Models. *Environment and Planning A* 18, 1375-1389.

Tabuchi, T., J.-F. Thisse and D.-Z. Zeng, 2005. On the number and size of cities. *Journal of Economic Geography*, forthcoming.

Tabuchi, T. and D.-Z. Zeng, 2004. Stability of spatial equilibrium, *Journal of Regional Science* 44, 641-660.

Takayama, A., 1985. *Mathematical Economics*. Cambridge University Press.

Taylor, P.D. and L.B. Jonker, 1978. Evolutionarily stable strategies and game dynamics. *Mathematical Biosciences* 40, 145-156.

Wilson, A.G., 1981. Catastrophe Theory and Bifurcation: Applications to Urban and Regional Systems. University of California Press, Berkeley and Los Angeles.

Zeng, D.-Z., 2002. Equilibrium Stability for a Migration Model, *Regional Science and Urban Economics* 32, 123-138.

Zheng, X.-P., 1990. The services sector and urban spatial structure: equilibrium versus catastrophe, *Environment and Planning A* 22, 1169-1182.

In: Focus on Urban and Regional Economics
Editor: Lawrence Yee, pp. 107-132
ISBN 1-59454-740-8

Chapter 6

EXTENDING ECONOMIC BOUNDARIES: A NOTE ON SINGAPORE'S GAMBIT IN INDONESIA AND INDIA

Caroline Yeoh* and Wong Siang Yeung#
*School of Business, Singapore Management University
#School of Accountancy, Singapore Management University

ABSTRACT

Singapore's regionalization stratagem led to the establishment of industrial parks in China, India and several South-East Asian countries. The strategic intent behind these overseas projects was two-fold: exporting Singapore's competencies such as management know-how, technological capabilities and corrupt-free administration to regions where such positive factors were lacking and secondly, exploiting comparative advantages that each region had to offer. This chapter revisits Singapore's flagship projects in Indonesia and India. Evidence from on-site surveys and interviews are presented. This chapter contends that progress in these privileged investment zones remains stymied by particular dependencies and challenges in the host environments.

Keywords: Regionalization,Singapore, Industrial parks, Indonesia, India

INTRODUCTION

Over the last four decades, Singapore, a city-state, has risen to be Southeast Asia's premier world-city, as well as an important base for multinational manufacturing. Singapore's reputation for corrupt-free administration and infrastructural efficiency, coupled with overall integrity of its legal and financial systems, have played a central role in attracting foreign direct investments to fuel the city-state's economic development (Chia, 1986; Pang, 1987; Perry, 1995; Yeung, 2001). However, rising business costs – in the late 1970s and early 1980s - rendered it an imperative for Singapore's economic planners to expand the island's

investment horizons[1] and potential economic growth through an overseas direct investment program[2]. Singapore-based companies were goaded to form joint ventures with companies in North America and Europe, to accelerate access to new technology and foreign markets (Caplen and Ng, 1990; Balakrishnan, 1991; Ng & Wong, 1991). However, most of these investments proved unsuccessful, resulting in enormous losses by the early 1990s (Kanai, 1993; Regnier, 1993; Lee, 1994).

Table 1. Singapore's Total Direct Investment Abroad by Destination Millions of S$, Stock as at Year-End

Destination	1996	1997	1998	1999	2000
China	11.5	13.8	16.1	15.4	16.3
Malaysia	17.3	11.8	11.4	9.2	10.1
Hong Kong	10.8	10.7	10.1	11.2	8.4
United States	4.7	3.8	4.1	4.5	6.5
Indonesia	7.0	8.6	5.9	5.9	5.8
Mauritius	0.7	3.3	4.3	3.7	4.5
British Virgin Islands	2.6	3.8	5.3	5.2	4.2
Liberia	4.2	5.2	3.5	2.6	4.0
Total (%)	58.8	61.0	60.6	57.8	59.6
Total (S$m)	55,536	75,807	75,622	92,720	91,949

Source: Singapore Department of Statistics.

A new phase in the internationalization strategy re-focused on expansion within Asia. The strategic repositioning was deliberated at the 1993 Regionalization Forum (Singapore Economic Development Board (SEDB), 1993a), and encapsulated in the policy document, Singapore Unlimited (1995a; 1995b).This stratagem was endorsed by the Committee to Promote Enterprise Overseas (Singapore Ministry of Finance, 1993). The change from internationalization (or, in local parlance, outer globalization) to regionalization (inner globalization) was rationalized by the liberalization of foreign investment controls occurring at the time in countries like Indonesia, China and Vietnam, and the high growth rates these economies were achieving (SEDB, 1993b; 1993c; Mahizhnan, 1994; Pang 1995; Kwok, 1995; Tan, 1995; Okposin, 1999; Pereira, 2001; Blomqvist, 2002; Sitathan, 2002). The marked increase in outward direct investments into the region is reflected in Table 1.

---

[1] Stoever (1985), Dunning (1988) and Porter (1990), among others, illustrate that a country's relative level and composition of outward and inward investments are systematically related to its stage of development. Dunning's (1988) investment development path model suggests that countries advance through five stages of development which relate to different levels of net outward investment. The thesis suggests that countries in the more advanced stages of development will have to increase their outward FDI in order to achieve greater economic growth. An extension of this thesis is revisited in Dunning and Narula (1996).

[2] The main ideas were set out in the policy document, Gearing Up for an Enhanced Role in the Global Economy (SEDB, 1988). The 1990 Global Strategies Conference added new dimensions to these deliberations (SEDB, 1990).

Singapore's trans-border industrialization initiatives comprised state-led[3] infrastructure projects, and a range of incentives and regulatory innovations (Goh et al, 2001; Yeung, 2001), designed to create Singapore-styled industrial townships in regional sites where such positive factors may be lacking (Perry & Yeoh, 2000). A three-pronged 'Singapore Inc' approach was adopted (Zutshi and Gibbons, 1998): senior politicians and civil servants negotiated[4] the institutional framework for the project, which typically involved garnering special investment conditions in the host location; (Singapore) government agencies and government-linked companies took the lead in infrastructure development; and Singapore's Economic Development Board (SEDB) takes on the role of 'business architect' and 'knowledge arbitrageur' (SEDB, 1995a:42), by encouraging foreign multinationals to locate their regional headquarters in Singapore, whilst redistributing their lower-end operations to the Singapore-styled industrial parks.

This strategic maneuver was premised on the perception that the redistribution of economic activities to regional industrial sites would enhance the collective competitiveness (or *shakkei*[5]) of Singapore-based companies, as well as Singapore's own competitiveness as a high-value investment location with strategic linkages to the region (Figure 1). The strategic intent was for Singapore-based companies to tap into the markets, and resources, of regional economies. It was also intended to strengthen Singapore's MNC-linkages through co-investment in the region (SEDB 1993a; 1993b; 1995a; 1995b).

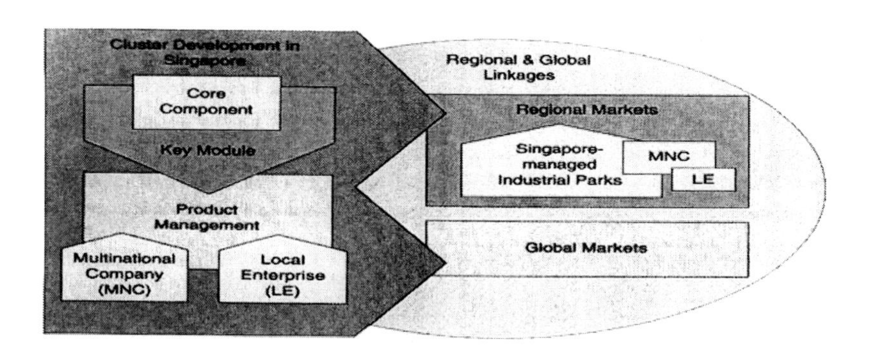

Source: Adapted from *Singapore Unlimited* (Singapore Economic Development Board, 1995).

Figure 1. Singapore's Transborder Industrialization

[3] The principles of government involvement are rationalized in the 1993 Report of the Committee to Promote Enterprise Overseas (chapter 4). For a scholarly discussion on the political economy of Singapore's development strategy, see Rodan (1989), Regnier (1991), Ng, et al. (1992); Huff (1995); Low (1998) and Blomqvist (2001). There is also an extensive political-economy literature on Singapore's regionalization program, succinctly summarized in Bellows (1995) and Yeung (1998).

[4] The stress on exploiting personal ties accords with business practice preferred by the linked communities of 'overseas Chinese' (Redding, 1990, Yeung, 1997; Brown, 1998; Lehmann, 1998), the 'bamboo network' which Singapore made use of in its industrial parks in Indonesia and China. Personal ties between Chairman, SEDB, and Ratan Tata (of the Tata Group) reportedly facilitated the move into India (Asian Review, 1996).

[5] Shakkei' is a Japanese landscaping strategy, where the scenery from one's garden is enhanced by incorporating the scenery from afar, such that the combined scenery is superior to each on its own. Extrapolated, the collective competitiveness approach envisaged that the development of regional economies, and sites, leads to positive complementary growth for Singapore.

This chapter will focus, specifically, on the first overseas industrial township project, in Batam Island (Indonesia), and the most recent project, in Bangalore, India's IT capital. To provide context to the discussion, the theoretical considerations underpinning these flagship projects are sketched in the next section, followed by an account of the origins and progress of the case study parks. The flagship projects are then evaluated in terms of the progress in attracting investment, the contributions to the strategic objectives associated with the park, as well as to Singapore's broader regionalization initiative. The analysis is reinforced by empirical data from our on-site surveys of the Parks' tenants, and in-depth case studies of selected tenants in both locations. The final section considers the implications of these experiences for Singapore's regionalization program, and evaluates the city-state's determined efforts to harness synergistic complementarities in its strategic intent to restructure the Singapore economy.

THEORETICAL CONSIDERATIONS

Prior to the 1960s, attempts to explain the activities of firms situated beyond their national boundaries represented an amalgamation of (i) the theory of (portfolio) capital movements (ii) empirical and largely country-specific studies on location factors influencing foreign direct investment (iii) modification to the neo-classical theories of trade, (iv) perceived gains of vertical or horizontal integration. Dunning's eclectic paradigm (1970, 1980, 1988, 2001) sought to offer a general framework for determining the extent and activities of MNE engaged in cross-border value-adding activities. The eclectic paradigm was used to explain the ability and willingness of firms to serve markets, and to look into the reasons for their choice of exploiting this advantage through foreign production rather than domestic production, exports or portfolio resource flows through the interaction of ownership-specific advantages, internalization-incentive advantages, and location-specific advantages (OLI). This theory has been extended, in more recent literature, to deliberations on the role of infrastructure in the attraction of new investments (Peck, 1996); the presence of immobile clusters of complementary value-added activities (Markusen, 1996), the transactional benefits of spatial proximity (Porter, 1996) and the business-government nexus in alliance capitalism (Dunning 1995, 1997; 2000; Evans, 1995; Dunning and Narula, 1996, 2000).

Not all advantages provided by the triumvirate of OLI will be evenly distributed across enterprises, industries and countries. These advantages are not static and may affect a firm's strategic response to any particular OLI configuration. Firms excogitate the O advantages through exploitation of firm-specific resources, simultaneously deriving I advantages through the diminution of transaction costs. As firms' core competencies become increasingly knowledge-intensive, MNEs seek locations (economic and institutional facilities) that are best utilizing their core competencies. In determining the propitious extent in which a firm strategically locates, we will examine, *inter alia*, Singapore's trans-border industrialization efforts, with particular focus on the regionalization of Singapore-based firms, and if the locations of these townships are indeed that strategically advantageous. A *survey questionnaire*, adapted from Yeoh, et al (2000), is applied to the tenants in the case-study parks.

Theories, from the perspective of the firm, have further argued that not only should the production process be viewed as a value chain (Kogut, 1985; Porter, 1986, 1994, 1996), but also, firms should identify comparative or location-specific advantages unique to each country/territory, which will serve to complement the competitive advantage they enjoy as a result of being placed higher up in the value chain. Additionally, in the face of globalization, the location-specific advantages need to be altered to suit the increasing spatial integration of complex and rapidly changing economic activities and to also consider the role of national and regional authorities in their influence over the extent and structure of localized centers of excellence. Thus, a holistic approach must be adopted that takes into consideration firm-oriented competitive advantages as well as comparative advantages offered by regions. Synergistic efforts will occur when a strategic fit between the competitive and comparative advantages exist. To address this aspect of our research, we will present *case studies* of eight firms located in the case-study parks to draw out empirical insights on the dynamics of the case-study parks as centers for value-added activities, inter alia, the strategic fit between the value-added chain of the firms and the competitive advantages of the sites.

SINGAPORE'S OVERSEAS INDUSTRIAL PARKS

Batamindo Industrial Park (BIP), Indonesia

The late 1960s witnessed Indonesia's ambition to develop the Riau islands when Batam was identified as a potential logistics and operational base to support offshore oil and gas fields. The first master plan for Batam was prepared by Nissho-Iwai, a Japanese consultancy firm, and Bechtel of the United States. The study was commissioned by the Indonesian state-owned oil company, Pertamina, to develop the island into a base for oil and gas exploration activities. The original master plan was reviewed by the American consultants CRUX in 1977. This study recommended guidelines for a more broad-based development of the island A significant step in the island's development was the assignment of Batam's development responsibility to the Batam Industrial Development Authority (BIDA) in 1978. BIDA's chairman, B.J. Habibie, favored attempts to engineer accelerated technological breakthroughs based on state-directed investment. This was reflected in the 1979 master plan, which focused on the development of transhipment facilities, the establishment of industrial estates, the development of marshalling areas for imports and exports, the construction of tourist facilities and the provision of infrastructural support. This master plan recognized that the Riau islands with its location-specific advantages such as abundant land cheap labor were well-positioned[6] to address Singapore's land and labor constraints and, more importantly, to take advantage of Singapore's established business and financial services network and the city-state's efficient facilities for communication, transportation and other services (Liew, 1990; Yeoh, 1990;

[6] The cataclysmic collapse of oil prices in the early 1980s impressed upon Indonesia's economic planners the need for a more broad-based development strategy. The Riau islands were an obvious choice to encourage investments not least because Singapore has shown interest in leasing these nearby islands to transcend the city-state's need for inexpensive land and labor. By the late 1980s, the perception from Jakarta was that Singapore was "bursting at the seams", and that the time was right to position Batam and the other Riau islands to take advantage of the spill-over from Singapore.

Regnier, 1991; Perry, 1991; Parsonage, 1992; Ho, 1994). A Memorandum of Understanding on bilateral cooperation in the development of Riau Province was signed on August 29, 1990.

BIP was launched in 1992. The Park started as a joint-venture between Singapore's GLCs[7] and the Salim Group of Indonesia. Salim was Indonesia's largest business conglomerate, and had close links to senior politicians and privileged access to the major investment projects in the Riau Islands (Sato, 1993; Hill, 1996). Singaporean GLCs were given control over the development and management of the Parks, while Salim's role was to facilitate operations and to provide a guarantee of priority over regulatory controls and administrative approvals. Singapore's reputation for transparent and efficient management of projects lent further credibility to the projects and maximized marketing leverage over Singapore-based multinationals (Yeoh, et al; 1992; Naidu, 1994; Peachey et al, 1998; Grundy-Warr, 1999).

Table 2A. Batamindo Industrial Park - Operational Statistics (June 2003)

General Information	
Investment by Developer	US$470 million
Committed Tenants	82
Area Taken Up	320 hectares
Investment by Tenants	> US$1 billion
Annual Export Value (for 2002)	> US$2 billion
No. of Employees	65,000

Source: SembCorp Industries.

Table 2B. Batamindo Industrial Park – Tenant Profile by Country of Origin (June 2003)

Country	Percent
USA	9
Japan	48
Europe	11
Singapore	30

Source: Batamindo Industrial Park, Tenants' List, June 2003

BIP was envisaged as a self-contained environment with its communication and business linkages through Singapore rather than through Indonesia. BIP, for instance, has its own power supply, water treatment plant, sewerage system, telecommunications facilities and social amenities. These, together with the location advantages that Indonesia offers, has resulted in an investment enclave offering facilities close to conditions in Singapore, in marked contrast to the conditions immediate outside the Parks.

---

[7] The Singapore consortium was led by Singapore Technologies Industrial Corporation (now SembCorp Industries) and Jurong Town Corporation, Singapore's main industrial estate infrastructure developer.

BIP's first tenants were mainly subsidiaries of American, European, and Japanese multinationals already operating in Singapore. Cumulative investments and export value in BIP topped US$1billion and US$2 billion in 2002 respectively, and the number of confirmed tenants increased from 17 in 1991 to 82 in 2003. Of these, 39 were Japanese companies with Singapore-owned companies the next largest concentration at 25. American and European investors have a limited presence. There is a concentration of electronics operations, mainly various component assembly processes, and supporting activities to the electronics sector such as plastic moulding and packaging. Out of total employment of 65,000, over 85% are female, most aged from 18-22. Table 2A shows the operational statistics in BIP, while Table 2B shows the tenant profile by origin and Table 2C, the tenant profile by sector.

Table 2C. Batamindo Industrial Park – Tenant Profile by Sector (June 2003)

Sector	Percent	Sector	Percent
Electronics	44	Packaging	6
Precision Parts	15	Medical	4
Plastic moulding	11	Pharmaceuticals	1
Electrical	11	Others	9

Source: Batamindo Industrial Park, Tenants' List, June 2003

International Tech Park Limited (ITPL), Bangalore, India

The idea to create a Singapore style park was first mooted by Singapore's Prime Minister Goh Chok Tong and India's Premier, P.V. Narasimha Rao, in 1992. Construction commenced in September 1994, and the park was officially inaugurated in 2000. ITPL is located 18km away from Bangalore in India's Silicon Valley[8]. The partners in the ITPL project are a Singapore consortium of companies[9] led by Ascendas International, the Tata Group and the Karnataka state government in a 40-40-20 arrangement. The Karnataka state government has since reduced its stake to 6 percent, while the Singapore consortium, and the Tata Group have increased their respective stakes to 47 percent each.

Marketed aggressively as an environment that "cuts through the red tape and bottlenecks that are a part of India's infrastructure and operating environment"[10], ITPL was slated to provide total business space solutions to multinationals and other conglomerates, within a state-of-the-art technology park. More distinctively, ITPL guarantees uninterrupted power supply and telecommunication facilities, immediate-occupancy business incubator space, and the formulaic 'one-stop' service. Its futuristic design comes complete with value added services like business/office support centers, medical center, food court, restaurants,

---

[8] Indian universities reportedly graduate about 20,000 to 30,000 software engineers every year, and Bangalore has been a 'hunting ground' for Singapore companies and Singapore-based multinationals seeking low-cost IT specialists.

[9] The Singapore consortium, Information Technology Park Investments Pte Ltd, includes RSP Architects, Planners and Engineers, L&M Properties, Sembawang Industrial, Technology Parks (a Jurong Town Corporation subsidiary) and Parameswara Holdings (the investment arm of the Singapore Indian Chamber of Commerce).

[10] The Straits Times, August 8, 1999

recreational centers. ITPL also houses the Indian Institute of Information Technology, which provides professional and skilled manpower for the Park's tenants. Operating profits have been registered, and ITPL is projected to break even within the next 4 years.

Table 3A. International Technology Park Limited - Operational Statistics (June 2003)

General Information	
Scale of Development	About 70 acres
Developed Area	1.6 million sq ft
Total Investment Value	SG$200 Million
Confirmed Tenants	100
Operating Tenants	93
Area Taken Up	1.4 million sq ft.
Park Population	8,500

Source: Ascendas International.

Table 3B. International Technology Park Limited – Tenant Profile by Country of Origin (June 2003)

Country	Percent
USA	42
India	36
Europe	16
Asia	6

Source: Ascendas International.

Table 3C. International Technology Park Limited – Tenant Profile by Sector (June 2003)

Sector	Percent	Sector	Percent
Software Development	49	IC Design	3
BPO/ITES	24	R&D	1
Biotech/Bio-Informatics	3	Educational Institutions	2
Manufacturing	10	Others	8

Source: Ascendas International.

The blend of location-specific advantages such as technology and infrastructure on one hand, and competitive skilled labor on the other led to high value added activities taking place at ITPL. ITPL's earliest clients included SAP Labs, First Ring and 24/7. As at January 2003, there are 100 confirmed tenants, of which 93 are operational with 8500 employees. More than half of these tenants are represented by wholly or partially foreign-owned firms which include some well known global players like AT&T, IBM, Motorola, Sony, Texas Instruments, Citicorp and Thomas Cook. The industries there include Software development, Business Process Outsourcing and Manufacturing.

Both BIP and ITPL reflect an "industry cluster" strategy. In BIP, this cluster is that of a concentration of electronic firms (50%) while ITPL reflects a concentration of software and e-service based firms (70%). However the difference is that while 91% of firms in BIP are engaged in manufacturing activity, the corresponding percentage in its counterpart, ITPL is only 10%. Table 3A presents ITPL's operational statistics, Table 3B shows the tenant profile by country of origin and Table 3C, the tenant profile by sector.

RESEARCH METHODOLOGY

Prior analyses on the Parks have relied primarily on secondary data from official publications, press reports, etc. To obtain primary data on the differential impact of various pull factors on firms' investment decisions, along with the differential impact of different types of constraints on their operations, we surveyed the tenants in ITPL in December 2002 and June 2003, and for BIP, in July 2003. The first set of questions sought to determine the profile of the respondents: type of ownership, nature of operations and size of establishment; and the second set was structured to gather information on the push-pull affecting the investment decisions of the tenants. Other questions pertaining to the respondents' views on the facilities and services in the Parks were culled from the open-ended questions. A total of 60 responses were collected from the two Singapore-styled investment enclaves.

Questionnaire Survey

Profile of the Respondents

There were 27 respondents in the BIP survey, of which 7 were wholly Singapore-owned, 5 were Singaporean joint ventures, and 15 were wholly foreign-owned. The respondents were mainly involved in the manufacturing of intermediate products. 7 of the respondents were involved in the manufacture of consumer products, and another 5 were providers of industrial services. There were 7 respondents with a sales turnovers

Of the 33 respondents from ITPL, 4 were wholly Singapore-owned, 6 were joint venture and 23 were wholly foreign-owned. As for the nature of operations, 16 of the respondents were involved in software development, 4 were involved in support services and 2 in research and development. 15 respondents had a sales turnover less than US$5 million and 4 respondents had sales between US$5 million and US$50 million.

Statistical Treatment of Survey Results

Apart from analyzing the descriptive statistics and popular rankings on the responses related to factors and constraints, logit analysis was used to compare the push/pull factors influencing the tenants' decision to locate in the Parks. The logit model, estimated by the maximum likelihood, takes the following form:

$P_i = \exp(Z_i) / [1 + \exp(Z_i)]$

*w*here: P_i is the probability of firm being located in the particular park
exp refers to the exponentiation operator, and
Z_i is a linear function of the push/pull factors defined as

$$Z_i = a_0 + \sum_{i=1}^{i=6} a_i F_i$$

where: F_1 = 1 if "Political commitment from the Singapore government" is selected, 0 otherwise
F_2 = 1 if "Political commitment from the host country government" is selected, 0 otherwise
F_3 = 1 if "Investment incentives" is selected, 0 otherwise
F_4 = 1 if "Competitive labor costs" is selected, 0 otherwise
F_5 = 1 if "Reliable infrastructure facilities" is selected, 0 otherwise
F_6 = 1 if "Access to domestic market" is selected, 0 otherwise
α_0 = constant term
α_i = coefficient of independent (explanatory) variable

Estimated coefficients in the logit model, if statistically significant (as indicated by the p-values), would suggest that the firm choosing that particular push/pull factor is more likely to be from BIP than from ITPL. *A* similar logit model was applied to the constraints faced by the Parks' tenants:

$P_i = \exp(Z_i) / [1 + \exp(Z_i)]$

*w*here: P_i is the probability of firm being located in the particular park
exp refers to the exponentiation operator, and
Z_i is a linear function of the constraints defined as:

$$Z_i = \beta_0 + \sum_{i=1}^{i=n} \beta_i C_i$$

In this case, estimated coefficients in the logit model, if statistically significant, would suggest that the firm choosing that particular constraint is more likely to be from BIP than from ITPL.

Analyses and Findings

Factors influencing respondents' decision to invest in BIP/ITPL (Table 4)

Singapore leverages on its infrastructure development expertise and the location-specific advantages available in the host environments to market its industrial parks. It supplements these purported advantages with its political commitment to the Parks, as demonstrated by the many bilateral agreements between the GLCs and host governments, or politically-linked business conglomerates, and a host of investment incentives to entice multinationals to locate their activities to these self-contained enclaves.

Table 4. Factors Influencing the Respondents' Decisions to Invest in BIP/ITPL

Variables	Maximum Likelihood Estimates - Binary Logits		Popular Ranking			
			BIP		ITPL	
	α_i	*p-value*	*Frequency*	*Rank*	*Frequency*	*Rank*
Political commitment from Singapore government	1.422	0.237	17	4	6	4
Political commitment from host country government	1.992	0.058**	21	3	6	4
Investment incentives	1.253	0.291	16	5	14	2
Competitive labor costs	4.274	0.003***	22	2	1	5
Availability of skilled/educated labor	-0.644	0.622	16	5	12	3
Reliable infrastructure facilities	-1.124	0.424	23	1	27	1

Note: $^{\Psi}$ Estimated values were taken from "forced entry" regression.
$^{\phi}$ p-values are for 2-tailed tests.
* Significant at 1% level
** Significant at 5% level
*** Significant at 10% level
Source: Questionnaire surveys.

Constraints on respondents' operations in BIP/ITPL (Table 5)

However, while BIP offered businesses cheap labor for their low value added activities, ITPL, with its skilled as well as cheap manpower, could facilitate activities higher up the value chain. Not unexpected, the reliable and efficient Singapore-styled infrastructure was the main draw of both BIP and ITPL. 85% and 82% of BIP and ITPL tenants surveyed cited it as the main pull factor for them to locate in the Park.

Competitive labor costs is a major pull factor for BIP tenants compared to ITPL tenants, as indicated by the positive and statistically significant α_4 (= 4.274). This is expected since BIP serves as a low-cost investment enclave, and a large proportion (71%) of the tenants in BIP engage in manufacturing activities. Manufacturing being labor intensive inherently requires low-cost labor. ITPL tenants, while valuing cheap labor as well, do not require it in the sheer amounts that manufacturing demands. 82% of ITPL survey respondents had less than 50 employees, while 52% of BIP respondents employed more than 500 people. Hence 'competitive labor costs' was a significant pull factor in the case of BIP compared to ITPL.

Table 5. Major Constraints on the Respondents' Operations in BIP/ITPL

Variables	**Maximum Likelihood Estimates - Binary Logits**	
	α_i	*p-value*
Labor Constraints		
Shortage of semi-skilled and skilled labor	2.770	0.024**
Shortage of professionals and managers	-0.182	0.865
Rising labor costs	2.283	0.021**
Industrial relations problems	3.330	0.002***
Others	1.235	0.336
Organizational/Technological Constraints		
Difficulty in obtaining capital equipment	1.246	0.226
Difficulty in introducing new technology and techniques	2.541	0.009***
Lack of good supporting services	2.504	0.007***
Difficulty in securing funds for expansion	1.699	0.135
High and/or rising overhead costs	0.914	0.303
Others	-18.831	0.999
Environmental Constraints		
Impact of host government regulations	2.312	0.018**
Competition from overseas Competitors	2.920	0.001***
Others	-2.705	0.084*

Note: $^{\Psi}$ Estimated values were taken from "forced entry" regression.
$^{\phi}$ p-values are for 2-tailed tests.
* Significant at 1% level
** Significant at 5% level
*** Significant at 10% level
Source: Questionnaire Surveys.

Political commitment from the host government is another major concern for BIP tenants compared to ITPL tenants, indicated by the positive and statistically significant α_2 (=1.992). This can be explained by the instability of Indonesia's political system. Since Soeharto was made to step down in 1998, the presidential position has changed hands several times, from Habibie, to the first democratically-elected President, Abdurrahman Wahid, and finally Megawati Sukarnoputri, on her predecessor's impeachment. Key economic positions were reshuffled and economic advisors changed frequently, as power jockeying among the parties, ministries, legislature, central bank, and other institutions continued. All these served to complicate investors' assessment of Indonesia's political outlook.

BIP is now an established industrial estate development. ITPL is relatively new. All the same, our study alludes to some emerging constraints which have undermined the attractiveness of the Parks. These constraints are categorised into three broad groups: labor-related constraints, organization and technology-related constraints, and those relating to the economic "environment", such as government policies and regulations.

Labor-related constraints

The 'cheap' labor resources which drew companies to BIP proved to be a perception rather than the reality, as "rising labor costs" was the main constraint faced by 21 (78%) of the BIP tenants surveyed. BIP tenants also found rising labor costs to be more of a concern than ITPL tenants as indicated by the positive and statistically significant β_3 (= 2.283). Other labor constraints experienced by BIP tenants (but less so by ITPL tenants) include shortage of semi-skilled and skilled labor and industrial relations problems as indicated by the positive and statistically significant β_1 (=2.770) and β_4 (= 3.330). In fact, industrial relations problems were frequently cited as being very disruptive to the operations of the tenants in BIP, as workers unhappy with labor laws often use pressure tactics such as strikes, demonstrations and work-to-rule.

Organizational and technological-related constraints

The Singapore-styled infrastructure, though reliable and efficient, also proved to be costly, as facilities such as the power plant, waste-treatment system and water supply are independently managed. This resulted in high overhead costs, especially in BIP where 74% of respondents cited it as a constraint they faced. This view was also echoed by 16 (48%) of ITPL tenants surveyed. Other organizational/ technological constraints faced by BIP tenants (but not as much by ITPL tenants) include the lack of good supporting services (β_3 = 2.504) and difficulty in introducing new technology and techniques (β_2 = 2.541), both of which are positive and significant.

Environmental' constraints

'Impact of host government regulations' and 'competition from overseas industry competitors' were constraints faced by both BIP and ITPL tenants. However, whereas 89% and 78% of BIP tenants cited the above two constraints respectively, less than one third of the ITPL tenants indicated likewise. This accounts for the positive and statistically significant β_1 (=2.312) and β_2 (=2.920). The government's control over the operating environment and the economic landscape shaped by overseas industry competitors prove to be stifling the operations of the tenants in BIP more than that of tenants in ITPL.

Case Studies (The first four companies are in BIP)

Company A (Electronics)

Company A is part of a US-based conglomerate, which operates in all 50 US states as well as over 100 countries throughout the world. The group as a whole manufactures critical infrastructure components, catering to diversified needs of businesses and governments, educational and medical institutions, and commercial industries from food to automobiles. The subsidiary in Batam is under the electronics arm of the conglomerate. The latter is a major producer of passive and active electronic components, such as complete power systems, private radio systems for governments, and undersea fiber optic telecommunications systems.

The existing Batam operations started in 1992, but belonged to a competitor German electronics components manufacturer, which located to BIP to take advantage of the stable infrastructure and low labor costs. In October 2000, Company A acquired its rival and took over all its manufacturing operations, including the facility in BIP. It has since become a leading maker of passive electronic components such as automotive relays and connectors. The BIP operations currently employ 560 workers and occupy 4,500 square meters. The company sources its inputs from around the world, and the facility in BIP is mainly for production. The final products are shipped to the US, Australia and some parts of ASEAN.

The company praises the one-stop service provided by the park's management, citing the efficient and transparent administration as a boon to its operations, by providing a more stable operating environment. However, being primarily labor-intensive, the company is feeling the impact of the rising labor and overhead costs on its operations. Specifically, it would like to see more efforts made to lower the operating overheads, such as having variable electricity rates.

Despite facing the uncertain political climate and the heightened terrorism threat, the company has intentions to expand its current operations within BIP, the key reason being that moving to other locations would be cost-prohibitive, given the huge amount of costs the company has sunk into its BIP operations.

Company B (Crystal oscillators)

Company B is a 100% owned Japanese firm which disburses in the production of crystal oscillators. Its various plants have been strategically positioned in diverse countries such as Thailand, Vietnam, USA and China. Occupying a massive space of 6,000 square meters of land, serviced by a workforce of 432 employees, the company manufactures about 100 various types of oscillators to be used in an array of products, from clocks to TGX (Mobiles). Operations and outbound logistics are administered mainly in Batam, with the parent base in Japan engaged in the development of new technology.

In 1997, economical prices on rent, utilities and labor enticed the company to invest in the Industrial Park. In surmising to locate in Batam, the company's production manager reminisce the lack of utilities in India, and BIP's competitive operational cost as compared to Thailand. Further inquiries revealed several perceived strengths that compensated the inherent weaknesses, which inveigle the company to remain. Strengths include the availability of utilities, provision of medical services and the proffer of legal documentation; poor traffic conditions, paranoia caused by SARS and banned IDD calls due to Telecom's monopoly were constituents of perceived constraints.

The company suffered losses for the fiscal year 2001-2, considering Sept 11 economy downturn and the region's instability, which further pushed down investors' confidence. Volatile mobile phone market, coupled with economic uncertainty has forced the company to reassess its investment in BIP. In a bid to maintain its cost competitiveness, the company aims to streamline its production processes, and employ advanced technology. It remains optimistic of a potential buoyant economy, fueled by the reduction of leading economies' interest rates in a bid to spur consumer spending, which bodes well for its overseas markets.

Company C (Electronic switches)

A joint venture between Singapore and Switzerland, Company C is an electronics contract manufacturer involved in printed circuit board assembly and box-build assembly. Many of its products, such as refrigerator switches, are used in industry as intermediate products. While USA was the primary market for the company's products, the events following September 11 has dealt a severe blow to demand for its products, and has led the company to restructure and diversify its markets to Europe and elsewhere in Asia. The BIP operations employs about 200 workers, and occupies one medium-sized factory. All its products are exported out of Indonesia.

The company cites the competitive costs of unskilled labor and overheads, and political commitment and incentives from the Indonesian government as pull factors which drew it to BIP. In particular, it singled out the reliable infrastructure as the park's greatest strength. It was also quite satisfied with the one-stop service provided by the park.

Granted, labor may be cheaper, but the company felt that productivity was lacking and its operations were often disrupted by industrial relations problems. There were many loopholes in labor laws which were exploited by the unions and employees. The higher overhead costs were also a concern. Though the one-stop service was commendable, the company still felt stifled by red tape as new technologies could not be easily imported.

The recent Bali bomb blasts did not have any effect on the company's plans for its Batam operations. Its operations decisions are based on demand factors outside of Indonesia. The company has plans to expand within BIP, considering the expected pick-up in demand after the current economic downturn.

Company D (Adhesives)

Company D is a manufacturer of a diverse range of adhesives for both domestic and industrial usage. It is also involved in the manufacture of the aluminum packaging for its adhesive products. The company is a wholly-owned subsidiary of a Singapore-based company, which in turn is affiliated to a larger Japanese conglomerate.

The manufacturing facility in BIP was set up in 1996, and involved the shifting of all activities purely related to manufacturing from Singapore, where labor costs were eroding their profitability. In this sense, the factory in BIP operates as an independent cost centre. All inputs for its operations are imported through Singapore. The company does not have a license to export its products, so it has to ship all final products back to Singapore for re-export. Thus, it is a purely export-oriented facility. It currently employs 150 workers and occupies 2 medium-sized factories.

Although the management acknowledges the reliable and stable infrastructure, it is generally displeased with the high cost of utilities, and feels that the premium charged is excessive compared to the benefits obtained from such basic necessities. They revealed that water and electricity were charged in Singapore dollar, rather than the Indonesian rupiah, and were in fact more expensive than in Singapore.

Another major complaint was labor. Labor costs were lower in BIP, but there had been many industrial disputes which caused much uncertainty to its operations and strained relations between the company and its workers. Unions, both registered and unregistered, wield considerable power in negotiations and even a short disruption to the company's operations could have a significant impact on the company's production schedule. Moreover, although labor costs were low, absenteeism was high and the local workers generally had poor work ethics. Labor laws were also deemed to be too protective towards workers. These laws were made known to the company only after it had established its operations. To alleviate these labor problems, the company tends to hire on a short term contract basis. While the problems it faced are significant, the company has no plans to relocate out of BIP. Neither does it have any plans to expand, or scale down its operations in BIP.

Case E (Inter-enterprise software)

Company E is a wholly-owned subsidiary of an international software giant. Its German parent is recognized as the world leader in providing collaborative business solutions for all types of industries and major markets, and enjoys the position of being the world's largest inter-enterprise software company, and the world's third largest independent software supplier overall. The parent company also employs 28,800 people in over 50 countries.

Company E was initially a German IT company, operating in Bangalore's Koramangala district. It was taken over in 1998, a move that was accompanied by a shift into ITPL. With actual operations within ITPL beginning only in 1997, the company's establishment in 1998 made it one of the first occupiers. It also boasts of being the park's largest tenant, in terms of space occupancy, covering about 9,000 m^2. The company initially had a choice of relocating itself at ITPL or at other city locations, which offered one-fourth the rent. The company chose ITPL, despite its higher rents, largely due to the following critical advantages that ITPL provided: uninterrupted power supply, state-of the-art infrastructure, ease and speed of setting up shop, and excellent communication channels. In justifying the company's relocation into ITPL, a company official had this to say: "For any company, ITPL provides excellent operating facilities, which brings about an increase in revenue. This increase in revenue is larger than the increase in costs (in terms of rent)". The company's primary operation within the park is confined to software development, and is described as a "100% export unit". All its exports go to Germany.

The company, after having completed fours years in the park, has decided to move out. The principal reason given for this is the rapid growth of the firm. In the four years since its inception, it has grown from a little over 70 employees to 500 employees today. Space constraints within the park have forced the company to look at other locations. ITPL has been unable to cater to the growing and irregular needs of the company, being a park suited for small and medium enterprises. As a fast expanding company, the company no longer views ITPL's costly rents as one that can be justified. Instead, the company has moved into an expansive new campus, 15 acres in area, where it can enjoy economies of scale. Furthermore, the company views such a shift as an opportunity to establish its own identity, which it had not fully experienced in a multi-tenanted place like ITPL. However, given ITPL's 'distinct' advantages, the company has not fully relocated. Instead it continues to retain office space in the Park's new BTS (Built-To-Suit) facilities.

Case F (Business process outsourcing)

Company F is an American-based firm undertaking e-services. It is known to provide the industry standard in customer support services and solutions to Global 500 companies. It was founded by an experienced management team with proven expertise in delivering large-scale, mission-critical customer support programs, with its corporate headquarters in Los Gatos, California, and operations at the ITPL, Bangalore.

ITPL, with its facilities best suited for small and medium enterprises engaged largely in R&D and in the service industry, has become a breeding ground, of sorts, for companies involved in Business Process Outsourcing (BPO). Located at the 'Creator' building of ITPL, company F is one of many such companies. Established in the park in April 2000, the company has over 800 employees, occupying 60,000 square feet.

Its key operations in the park include call centers, real-time customer service management and technical support to foreign firms. In fact, the facility in ITPL is the largest call centre in the state of Karnataka. Catering to customers as big as Alta Vista, the company has conducted successful programs such as outbound telemarketing, inbound phone customer service, inbound phone technical service, with service areas spanning countries worldwide, particularly, U.S and Europe.

Involved in email and telephone-based customer services targeted at customers all round the world, the company, like all others concerned with BPO operations, requires a facility that will provide the necessary round-the-clock resources. ITPL successfully makes available the same. The regular power supply, the 24-hour speedy connectivity and the plug and play services of ITPL have proven to be the distinguishing factors in luring the company. An added advantage is seen in the fact that the city of Bangalore abounds with excellent schools and universities. This coupled with the high standard of education, serves as a continuous source of skilled employment for the call centers located in the park. The company sees this pool of potential employees as an added advantage in carrying out its operations in ITPL.

Case G (Business process outsourcing)

Company G is a wholly American owned firm, with its parent company being considered a frontrunner in integrating the expanding capabilities of information technology, telecommunications and the internet. The parent company has its headquarters in Virginia, U.S.A. Its services include voice-based services, internet services, back-office functions, and interactive tele-services. Company G was incorporated in May 1999 as a 100% subsidiary. Its facility within the park spreads over 42,000 square feet and employs 12,000 employees. The company's functions within the park largely focus on Business Process Outsourcing, which include both inbound and outbound customer care.

As in the case of other companies in the same industry, Company G, too, cites the permanent power supply, 24-hour connectivity and supporting infrastructure as the vital factors that prompted it to situate in the park. The company also employs a sizeable portion of the IT graduates that Bangalore churns out every year. In addition to the above, according to a company official, the firm perceives ITPL's excellent and professional support services and maintenance programs as a huge advantage that gives it an added edge over its peers that are located elsewhere. Such benefits have been the direct result of the Singaporean-styled management. However, the company has expressed reservation over the numerous other call centers making their way into ITPL to make use of the same advantages, which escalates into other problems such as heightened competition, further sharing of resources, and the "the pool of entry level people getting smaller."

Case H (Travel and financial services)

Company H is one of the world's leading international travel and financial services groups and serves over 20 million customers a year. It provides services at 4,500 locations in more than 100 countries and employs over 20,000 people. Establishing itself in India as early as in 1881, today, the company's Indian subsidiary has a network of 54 locations in 16 cities across India and is the largest travel and financial services group in the country. Foreign exchange, corporate travel, leisure holidays, travel insurance and credit cards form the core activities of the company.

Company H is one of the very few companies that were approached by the ITPL management itself to set up shop at the park. On the management's behest, the company acquired an office within the park's premises largely to provide money-changing activity. Its core operations within the park, therefore, include ticketing and foreign exchange services. Company H is a small entity with only 5 employees. However, it has managed to secure a large customer base largely due to the fact that it is the only tenant providing such services within the park. Moreover, the company also caters to an increasing number of firms outside the park who find it convenient to visit its office in the park, which is in close proximity, instead of approaching its other branches placed in the city-center.

Discussion

Our in-depth case studies substantiate the survey results. For BIP, lower labor cost and greater availability of labor compared to Singapore were key elements in their decision to locate some of their production operations in Batam. Managers we interviewed cited labor cost and labor availability as primary reasons for relocation of labor-intensive operations, within the value chain, to Batam. However, all companies found infrastructure costs such as transport relatively uncompetitive, despite the institutional and infrastructural framework put in place in BIP. Nevertheless, each of the four companies believed that the savings in labor costs allowed them to capture competitive advantage in operations. However, these companies did not capture competitive advantage in the labor chain solely through reduced labor costs. Another, albeit related element of the functional differentiation is that, the relocation of labor-intensive operations to Batam is coupled with lower investments and therefore greater savings in production technology. This was due to a variety of factors: the difficulty in automating those processes; the use of low-cost labor as an alternative to investments in technology; the low skill of the labor force; the maintenance and upgrading of the more automated operations in Singapore. In this sense, the functional and spatial differentiation of the value chain segment `operations' was used by those companies having production operations both in Singapore and in Batam to reduce costs both in terms of labor and in technology investment. Investment in high technology was reserved for operations in Singapore. In short, the search for cost advantages has led to a spatial fragmentation of the production process, and MNCs breaking their value-added chains across national borders to maximise the competitive advantages of the contiguous economies.

The tenants at ITPL pose a stark contrast to those in BIP, which has managed to attract a significant majority of their tenants on the basis of abundant low-cost, low-skilled labor. The scenario in ITPL is decidedly different. Our study suggests that the same advantage of plentiful labor, and competitive labor costs, has not been the sole influencing factor in attracting firms to the park. The primary reason, which has encouraged firms to settle in the park, has been that of excellent infrastructural facilities and the Singapore-styled management characterized by its quintessential efficiency. Anecdotal evidence from our case studies suggests that international IT firms have relocated to ITPL from other locations for this reason. ITPL represents a modified version of the Porter-Kogut analytical framework, whereupon ITPL has witnessed the location of firms engaged in marketing and sales, and other services (viz, the primary activities), which were supported by other activities such as technological development and infrastructure within the park (viz, the secondary activities), sufficiently provided by the Singapore partner. A case in point is the rapid establishment of companies in the BPO industry, and the myriad of e-services, including telemarketing and customer sales services, by simply making utmost use of the telecommunication facilities that the park showcased, as substantiated by our case studies. This, along with the advanced technology made available at ITPL, has helped make the park the cynosure of companies engaged in the non-manufacturing industries, that is, those placed in the higher end of the value chain.

To a large extent, the case-study parks have succeeded in providing the crucial links within the value-added chain that give client firms a competitive advantage. The problem lies on the flip side of the desired strategic fit – the host country's ability to provide comparative advantages. In both scenarios, the host government has succeeded only in making available the advantages of 'basic factors of production'. Thus, while the case-study parks do provide some components of comparative advantage which the host country does not (e.g. reliable infrastructure), the strategic intent of these flagship projects remains stymied by non-economic, socio-political complexities in the larger host environment.

ISSUES AND CHALLENGES

The special privileges secured by Singapore's overseas industrial township projects share a common trait: many of the privileges obtained were unprecedented, and unique, to the case-study parks. For instance, the Singapore partners were granted licenses to build and operate their own power and water treatment plants and telecommunication facilities which, in Indonesia and India, was an exclusive concession. As such, the Parks could leverage on their reputation of reliable infrastructural facilities in areas where these facilities were an anomaly. Moreover, since local government officials were usually part of the management boards of the parks, once bureaucratic procedures, such as investment approvals, construction activities, import/export permits and immigration matters became accelerated processes. The Parks serve to attract investors with its formulaic one-stop service within a self-sufficient, self-contained environment which is unburdened by inefficient administration. Significantly, Singapore's positive reputation with multinational corporations for its stable, corrupt-free investment environment lends credibility, such that it seems privileged to be located in the Parks[11].

Influence can also be exerted through inter-governmental interaction and, where existing, through the links to influential ethnic business groups in the investment location who often rely on state patronage for their access to infrastructure development projects. The main Singapore partners involved in these projects were government-linked companies (notably, SembCorp Industries, Keppel Corp and Ascendas International), and Temasek Holdings (the Singapore government's main investment holding company). For the Indonesian parks, the main local partner was the Salim Group, which, albeit private, is nevertheless well known for its close links to senior Indonesian politicians and privileged access to major investment projects. ITPL also shares the characteristic of strong government involvement, with the Indian counterparts being the Karnataka state government and the Tata Group, which, though private, is nonetheless well connected with local authorities. The strategic alliances between Singapore's own state-owned enterprise networks, and its counterparts in the regional sites, were instrumental in mobilizing the financial resources to complete these multi-million projects and, in most cases, within a comparatively short time-frame of 18 to 24 months.

Nonetheless, as most openly admitted, the strategically `engineered', inter-government endorsement of the flagship projects, and the enormous resources mobilized through the strategic partnerships, have `failed' to shield the Parks from a gamut of problems. Issues pertaining to the scale and character of development of BIP, viz, BIP's resemblance to a Japanese investment enclave and vulnerability to a withdrawal of Japanese investments, and infrastructural dilemmas, as well as the limited impact of the Indonesia parks on the transfer of low value operations from Singapore, and the associated upgrading of linked activities in Singapore, are discussed in Peachey et al (1998), Grundy-Warr et al (1999) and Yeoh et al (*forthcoming*). Peachey et al (1998) have drawn attention to the influx of immigrants to the islands and, concomitantly, to the social problems of squatter settlements which threaten to overwhelm the investment value of the Indonesian parks. The following observations update, and offer new insights, on BIP in Indonesia, and present data on recent developments in ITPL, India.

Heightened Competition

Singapore's overseas industrial parks are increasingly facing strong mounting competition from competing parks within their vicinity. Competitor parks, some of which are backed by prominent Indonesian politicians, have mushroomed around BIP. Panbil Industrial Park, for instance, is located directly opposite BIP, and offers similar factories at competitive rentals. The premium placed on the Park's one-stop support service, and self-sufficient operating environment, is increasingly called into question. As well, competition is not limited to within Indonesia. Indonesia's minimum wage, at US$43 to US$70 a month, depending on the region, prices it out of the global competition for cheap labor. Investors can get similarly-skilled labor from Bangladesh, Vietnam, and Sri Lanka at monthly wages of US$17, US$32, and US$40 respectively. Recent press reports on Riau's investor exodus[12]

[11] This was a constant refrain throughout our interviews in ITPL.

[12] The Straits Times, 30 August 2003, The Straits Times, December 5, 2003..

cite sluggish bureaucracy, `rowdy' labor scenes, lack of legal certainty and security, and unclear investment policies as reasons for investors relocating their investments from Riau Province, and Indonesia. Populist measures such as raising the minimum wages before the general elections due in 2004, further heighten the reluctance of investors to pour money into the country.

ITPL's success hinges on the "Singapore-styled design and management" reputation. However, the premium placed on ITPL's formulaic 'one-stop' service and self-sufficient infrastructure is similarly, and increasingly, eroded by intense competition from newer, albeit, smaller parks being developed by street-savvy Indian entrepreneurs, and ITPL's capacity to provide stable electricity is the only differentiating factor from other IT parks like the Software Tech Park and Electronics City. These competitor paks market themselves aggressively on price, charging significantly lower rentals for "no-frills" factory space. A case in point, ITPL's listed lease price is Rs50 (approximately US$1) per square foot, whereas the rate in other areas, and within Electronic City itself, just outside ITPL, is less than Rs15. Our interviews with IPTL tenants have alluded to the possibility that the Park's attractiveness may, in time, be eroded, as more IT parks and companies are established within the vicinity to capitalize on the area's repute, while offering lower rentals with reliable energy, as the state develops.

Political 'Commitment'

Reliance on political patronage (and personal ties) rather than transparent contracts has had advantages and disadvantages. For BIP, the reliance on the Salim Group has been necessary in the context of the Indonesian system of 'crony capitalism' fostered by then President Soeharto. The end of the Soeharto era, and pressure from the IMF and western governments for financial transparency, has diminished Salim's political and commercial influence. Ownership changes at BIP have brought about uncertainties[13], as the Parks' privileged access to senior politicians and policy-makers in Jakarta has proved more difficult. Compounding these uncertainties, inter-governmental endorsements, post-Soeharto, no longer suffice to secure commitments at the lower tiers of government. Anecdotal evidence[14] points to a more complex regulatory environment for foreign companies, as they have to deal more intensively with the provincial and sub-provincial (district) governments. The Parks' reputation as investment enclaves has also not been left unscathed by political developments in the aftermath of the Asian financial crisis, the September 11 attacks in the United States, and more recently, the Bali and Jakarta-Merriot bomb blasts. In addition, negative press

---

13 The Indonesian Bank Restructuring Agency has reportedly offered to sell the Salim Group's stakes in all the Riau projects – estimated to be worth S$500 million – in a packaged deal (The Business Times, August 28, 2001). Further restructuring have taken place, with the three main stakeholders now being SCI, Ascendas and the Indonesian government.

14 Law No. 22/199 allows provincial, district and municipal governments to write provincial laws, some of which contradict national laws, or test the boundaries of their power. The Megawati administration is now proposing a revision of laws on regional autonomy, but the direction remains unclear. For a discussion on the problems with regional autonomy and their impact on business, see Van Zorge, Heffernan & Associates (April 2002). Interviews with BIP executives and tenants, in September 2002 and July 2003, respectively, have alluded to this changed operating environment.

reports on active terrorist cells within the region serve little to quell the innate risk-aversion of potential investors. BIP could do without these added sentiments in its larger environment.

In India, varying degrees of commitment and support by different state governments towards the country's development can affect ITPL's competitive advantage. The lack of good supporting infrastructure in the surrounding environment, and the disparity in local state-government supporting different cities, serve as a deterrent to investors, even as cities like Hyderabad, Mumbai and Chennai continue to advance technologically. On a broader front, corruption remains endemic, and bureaucratic red-tape is difficult to circumvent. These considerations are, by themselves, deterrence to potential investors, even with Singapore's presence and involvement. To hedge Singapore's strategic interests in India, Ascendas is reportedly partnering India's largest construction conglomerate, Larsen and Toubro, to build Cyber Pearl in Hyderabad's Hitec City, while plans are in place to develop similar IT parks in Chennai and other Indian cities, on a *turnkey basis*.

CONCLUDING REMARKS

Singapore's overseas parks tend to exist as investment enclaves within a disjointed economic and policy environment. They are linked to transnational investment networks, business elites and specific government commitments. The positive aspect of this is that the parks can be sites of investment privilege, in respect of their regulatory controls, infrastructure quality and status with public and private agencies. The weakness is that the privileges obtained are vulnerable to changes in political allegiances, and the infrastructure efficiency is at risk from the uncontrolled broader environment in which the park is located.

An outright assessment of failure or success may not be appropriate, given the mixed economic and political objectives[15]. However, our study suggests the economic theorization that underscores Singapore's regionalization stratagem continues to be overshadowed by the policy nuances that radiate from the host environment. The calculated, schematized efforts at trans-border industrialization, though remarkable, have been overly optimistic and have failed to engender equally compelling results, more often than not frustrated by the intricacies of

[15] Sentiments at SembCorp Industries and Ascendas International remain optimistic, as is the willingness of senior management to search for alternative strategies to re-position these flagship projects. In our discussions, the Parks' management reasons that competition is inevitable. And, rather than engaging in a price war, management has indicated a preference to adjust rates to 'better reflect market situations' while, at the same time, endeavor to differentiate the Parks from competitors by catering to higher value-added activities. For instance, in BIP, there are plans to create new initiatives for the Parks' tenants, such as offering broadband services ahead of competitors, and providing supply-chain management solutions for its tenants. Interestingly, the Parks' management view competitors as essential components of a 'living system in which all entities within the system constantly adapt to their dynamic environment and are synergistically integrated'. In the case of BIP, it is argued, co-existence must be established to augment a positive image of the Riau Islands as an investment haven, and competitors are viewed as an imperative to the long-term attractiveness of BIP. As well, Bintan Industrial Estate, in close geographical proximity to BIP, serves as a cheaper alternative for cost-conscious companies to locate their operational activities. In the case of ITPL, the project is perceived as a strategic thrust to capitalize upon first-mover advantages in a regional economy with immense market potential. ITPL, as the first entrant to successfully develop and manage a state-of-the-art technology park, has arguably enhanced Singapore's reputation for industrial-township projects. More subtly, ITPL's apparent success may leverage Singaporean companies' foray into India's aggressive infrastructure plans and commercial-residential township projects.

socio-political realities in the host economies. The limits to *'Singapore Unlimited'* have been exposed in this chapter.

REFERENCES

Asian Review .1996. Industrial parks in Asia: A special report. November.

Balakrishnan, N. 1991. Singapore: innocents abroad. *Far Eastern Economic Review*, 46.

Bellows, T. J. 1995. Globalization and regionalization in Singapore: A public policy perspective. *Asian Journal of Political Science*, 3(2): 46-65.

Blomqvist, H. 2001. State and development policy: the case of Singapore. *Asian Profile*, 29. (ERN APS 7(2): 01162002).

Blomqvist, H. 2002. Extending the second wing: the outward direct investment of Singapore, *Working Paper* No. 3, Department of Economics, University of Vaasa (ERN WPS 8(1): 01092003).

Brown, C. 1998. Overseas Chinese business in South-east Asia. In K. Sheridan (Ed.), *Emerging economic systems in Asia*. Sydney: Allen and Unwin.

Caplen, B. & Ng, L. 1990.Singapores global gamble. *Asian Business*, June, 26.

Chia, S.Y. 1986. Direct foreign investment and the industrialization process in Singapore. In C.Y. Lim and P. Lloyds (Eds.), *Resources and growth in Singapore*. Singapore: Oxford University Press.

Dunning, J.H. 1970. The multinational enterprise, *Lloyds Bank Review*, July, 19-36.

Dunning, J.H. 1980.Toward an eclectic theory of international production: some empirical tests, *Journal of International Business Studies*, 11(1): 9-31

Dunning, J.H. 1988. *Explaining international production.* London & Boston: Unwin Hyman.

Dunning, J.H. 1995. Re-appraising the eclectic paradigm in an age of alliance capitalism. *Journal of International Business Studies*, 26 (3): 461-491

Dunning, J.H. 1997. *Alliance capitalism and global business.* London & New York: Routledge.

Dunning, J.H. 1998. Location and the multinational enterprise: a neglected factor? *Journal of International Business Studies*, 29(1): 45-66.

Dunning, J.H. 2001. The eclectic (OLI) paradigm of international production: past, present, and future. *International Journal of the Economics of Business*, 8(2): 173-190

Dunning, J.H. & Narula, R (Eds.) 1996. *Foreign direct investment and governments: Catalysts for economic restructuring*. London & New York: Routledge.

Dunning, J.H. & Narula, R. 2000. Industrial development, globalization, and multinational enterprises: new realities for developing countries. *Oxford Development Studies*, 28(2): 141.

Evans, P. (1995) Embedded autonomy: States and industrial transformation. Princeton: Princeton University Press.

Goh, M.L., Sikorski, D. & Wong W.K. 2001. Government policy for outward investment by domestic firms: The case of Singapore's regionalization policy. *Singapore Management Review,* 23(2).

Grundy-Warr, C., Peachey, K. & Perry, M. 1999. Fragmented integration in the Singapore-Indonesian border zone: Southeast Asia's growth triangle against the global economy. *International Journal of Urban and Regional Research*, 23(2): 304-328.

Hill, H. 1996. *The Indonesian economy since 1966.*. Cambridge: Cambridge University Press: Cambridge.

Ho, K.C. 1994. Industrial restructuring, the Singapore city-state, and the regional division of labor. *Environment and Planning*, 26: 33-51.

Huff, W. 1995. The development state, Singapore, and Singapore's economic development since 1960. *World Development*, 23(8): 1421-1438.

Kanai, T. 1993. Singapore's new focus on regional business expansion. *NRI Quarterly*, 2(3): 18-41.

Kogut, B.1985. Designing global strategies: Corporate and competitive value added chains, *Sloan Management Review*, 25:15-28.

Kumar, S. & Siddique, S. 1994. Beyond economic reality: New thoughts on the growth triangle. In *Southeast Asian affairs 1994*. Singapore: Institute of Southeast Asian Studies, 47-56.

Kwok, K. W. 1995. Singapore: Consolidating the new political economy. *In Southeast Asian affairs 1995*, Singapore: Institute of Southeast Asian Studies, 291-308.

Lee, T.Y. 1994. *Overseas investment: Experience of Singapore's manufacturing companies.* Singapore: McGraw- Hill.

Lehman, J.P. 1998. Asian tigers make way for the bamboo network: mastering global business. *Financial Times,* October 2-4.

Liew, S.L. 1990. Charting a global strategy: Creating competitive advantage through the growth triangle. *Economic Bulletin Special Report*, November, 14-18.

Low, L. 1998. *The political economy of a city-state: Government made Singapore.* Singapore: Times Academic Press.

Mahizhnan, A. 1994. Developing Singapore's external economy. In *Southeast Asian affairs 1994.* Singapore: Institute of Southeast Asian Studies, 285-301.

Markusen, A. 1996. Sticky places in slippery space: a typology of industrial districts. *Economic Geography,* 72(3): 293-313.

Murray, G. & Pereira, A. 1995. *Singapore: The global city-state.* London: Heinemann.

Naidu, G. 1994. Johor-Singapore-Riau growth triangle: progress and prospects. In M. Thant, M. Tang & H. Kakazu (Eds.), *Growth triangles in Asia: A new approach to economic cooperation.* Hong Kong: Oxford University Press.

Ng, C.Y. & Wong P.K. 1991. The growth triangle: a market-driven response. *Asia Club Papers,* 2: 123-152.

Ng, C.Y., Sudo, S. & Crone, D. 1992. The strategic dimension of the East Asian development state. *ASEAN Economic Bulletin*, 9: 219-233

Okposin, S.M. 1999. *The extent of Singapore's investment abroad.* Aldershot: Ashgate

Parsonage, J. 1992. Southeast Asia's growth triangle: A sub-regional response to global transformation. *International Journal of Urban and Regional Research,* 16(2): 307-317.

Pang, E.F. 1987.Foreign investment and the state in Singapore. In V. Cable and B. Persaud (Eds.), *Developing with foreign investment.* London: Croom Helm, 84-100.

Peachey, K., Perry, M. & Grundy-Warr, C. 1998. The Riau islands and economic cooperation in the Singapore-Indonesian border zone. *Boundary and Territory Briefing*, 2(3).

Peck, F.W. 1996. Regional development and the production of space: the role of infrastructure in the attraction of new inward investment, *Environment and Planning*, 28: 327-329.

Pereira, A.2001. Revitalizing national competitiveness: The transnational aspects of Singapores regionalization strategy (1990-2000), *Working Paper No.161,* National University of Singapore.

Perry, M. 1991. The Singapore growth triangle: State, capital and labor at a new frontier in the world economy. *Singapore Journal of Tropical Geography*, 12(2): 138-151.

Perry, M. 1995. New corporate structures, regional offices and Singapore's new economic directions. *Singapore Journal of Tropical Geography*, 16(2): 181-196.

Perry, M. & Yeoh, C. 2000. Asia's transborder industrialization and Singapore's overseas industrial parks. *Regional Studies*, 4(2): 199-206.

Porter, M.E. 1986. Changing patterns of international production. *California Management Review,* XXVIII (2): 9-40.

Porter, M.E. 1990. *The competitive advantage of nations*. New York: The Free Press.

Porter, M.E. 1994. The role of location in competition. *Journal of Economics of Business*, 1(1):35-39.

Porter, M.E. 1996. Competitive advantage, agglomeration economies and regional policy. *International Regional Science Review*, 19(1& 2): 85-94.

Redding, G. 1990. *The spirit of Chinese capitalism*. Berlin: de Gruyter.

Regnier, P. 1991. *Singapore: City-state in Southeast Asia*. London: Hurst and Company.

Regnier, P. 1993. Spreading Singapore's wings worldwide: a review of traditional investment strategies. *The Pacific Review*, 6, 305-312.

Rodan, G. 1989. The political economy of Singapore's industrialization. London: Penguin.

Sato, T. 1993. The Salim group in Indonesia: The development and behaviour of the largest conglomerate in Southeast Asia. *The Developing Economies*, 31(4): 408-441.

Singapore Economic Development Board. 1988. *Global Strategies - The Singapore Partnership* (Conference Proceedings), October 24-26.

Singapore Economic Development Board. 1990. *Global Strategies - World Class Partnership* (Conference Proceedings), June 4-6.

Singapore Economic Development Board. 1993a. *Regionalization Forum* (Conference Proceedings), May 21-23.

Singapore Economic Development Board. 1993b. *Singapore Investment News, Regionalization Supplement*, May.

Singapore Economic Development Board. 1993c. *Growing with Enterprise: A National Effort.*

Singapore Economic Development Board. 1995a. *Singapore Unlimited.*

Singapore Economic Development Board. 1995b. *Regionalization 2000.*

Singapore Ministry of Finance. 1993. *Final Report of the Committee to Promote Enterprise Overseas.*

Sitathan, T. 2002. Singapores regionalisation challenge. *Asia Times* (online edition), July 26.

Stoever, W.A. 1985. The stages of development policy towards foreign direct investment. *The Columbia Journal of World Business,* XX (3): 3-9.

Tan, C.H. 1995. *Venturing overseas: Singapore's external wing*. Singapore: McGraw-Hill.

Van Zorge, Heffernan & Associates. 2002. Re-centralization, guided decentralization, or chaos? *Van Zorge Report on Indonesia* (online edition), April.

Yeoh, C. 1990. The Batam-Singapore-Johor growth triangle: a new dimension in ASEAN economic co-operation. *Asia-Oceania Report*, 18: 4-7.

Yeoh, C., Lau G.T., Goh M. & Richardson, J. 1992. *Strategic business opportunities in the growth triangle.* Singapore: Longman.

Yeoh, C., Perry, M., & Lim, M.L. 2000. Profile of a low cost manufacturing enclave: the case of Batamindo industrial park, Indonesia. In R. Edwards, C. Nyland and M. Coulthard (Eds.), *Readings in International Business.* New South Wales: Pearson Education Australia, 193-212.

Yeoh, C., Lim, D. & Kwan, A. 2004. Regional Co-operation and low-cost investment enclaves: An empirical study of Singapore's industrial parks in Riau, Indonesia. *Journal of Asia-Pacific Business,* forthcoming.

Yeung, H. 1997. Cooperative strategies and Chinese business networks. In P. Beamish and J. Killing (Eds.), *Cooperative strategies: Asian perspective.* San Francisco: The New Lexington Press.

Yeung, H. 1998. The political economy of transnational corporations: a study of the regionalization of Singaporean firms. *Political Geography*, 17(4): 389-416.

Yeung, H. 2001. Towards a regional strategy: The role of regional headquarters of foreign firms in Singapore. *Urban Studies,* 38: 157-183.

Zutshi, R. & Gibbons, P. 1998. The internationalization process of Singapore government-linked companies: A contextual view, *Asia-Pacific Journal of Management,* October, 15(2).

In: Focus on Urban and Regional Economics
Editor: Lawrence Yee, pp. 133-153
ISBN 1-59454-740-8

Chapter 7

IS AN INCREASING WAGE INEQUALITY BENEFICIAL OR DETRIMENTAL TO THE POOR?[1]

Youngsun Kwon and Changi Nam
School of Management, Information and Communications University, South Korea

ABSTRACT

This chapter uses comparative statics to derive the effects of a median preserving increase in wage inequality on the welfare of households. It assumes that the commuting cost is a function of distance and income and that two income classes are living in a city. An increase in income of the wealthy living in the suburban area can either improve or hurt the welfare of the poor depending on the relative magnitudes of operating cost and time cost. If technology development, driving wage inequality, reduces time cost of commuting of the rich, it may increase the welfare of the poor.

INTRODUCTION

During the 1990s, an ardent debate over what causes the widening wage inequality in the U.S. has continued between trade and labor economists.[2] Most trade economists support the view that technology development is the driving force of wage inequality. The point is that technology development improves the productivity of skilled workers and reduces job opportunities of low skilled workers because technology development results in labor saving in many industries.[3] Contrary to the views of trade economists, labor economists find a cause

---

[1] The comparative statics analysis shown at the fifth section of this chapter was published in Youngsun Kwon's paper, "the effect of a change in wages on welfare in a two-class monocentric city," *Journal of Regional Science* (Blackwell Publishing Ltd.), *43*(1), 2003, pp. 63–72.

[2] The *Journal of Economic Perspectives*, *9*(3), in 1995, published papers representing different views of both sides. Lawrence [169] discussed in detail the relationship between technology and wage inequality.

[3] See Autor, Katz and Krueger [157] for an empirical study on changes in demand for more skilled and less skilled workers.

of wage inequality from trade. Labor economists claim that trade with developing countries shrinks the U.S.' labor intensive industries and in turn reduces job opportunities of low skilled workers.[4] Even though economists of both sides still do not fully agree on what causes the growing wage inequality in the U.S., they do agree that technology development is a major source of wage inequality.

Even though there has been much debate on what has caused rising wage inequality in the U.S., there has been virtually no study on the effects of an increasing wage inequality on the welfare of the poor. This chapter has two purposes. One is to find the welfare implication of increasing wage inequality and the other is to explain analytically the role of time cost of commuting. This chapter finds a somewhat counter intuitive result that a rising wage inequality does not always mean a fall in the welfare of the poor. Furthermore, an increasing wage inequality can increase the welfare of the poor if the time cost of commuting of the rich falls enough to be less than the operating cost of commuting as a result of technology development.

Next section overviews approaches taken by previous studies on the relationship between wage (or income) inequality and welfare (or growth) and introduces the intuition behind the approach used in this chapter. The third section compares the residential distribution by income[5] level and that by skill level. The fourth section introduces the model and the fifth section performs a comparative static analysis to derive the effect of rising wage inequality on welfare. Finally, conclusion follows.

APPROACHES OF PREVIOUS RESEARCH AND THIS CHAPTER

It is hardly possible to find a common approach from the literatures on the relationship between welfare and wage (or income) inequality. Burtless [159] finds that rising wage inequality has had a minimal impact on family income inequality because family size headed by men in the lowest earnings quintile has decreased.[6] Welch [178] reports a similar observation and discusses the positive side of rising wage inequality. Welch [178] defends rising wage inequality on the ground that wage inequality is a reflection of the growing opportunity for specialization, but in defending rising inequality, he does not directly discuss the effect on welfare of rising wage inequality. Frank and Cook [164] and Frank [163] analyze the problem of rising wage inequality in terms of the resource allocation of a whole society. They point out wasteful resource allocation due to the conspicuous consumption behavior of high wage earners, a so-called small group of winners, and advocate a progressive consumption tax. However, their analysis has not been based on a formal economic model and has not directly dealt with the effect on welfare. A group of economists studied the effect of income inequality on the aggregate saving of a country. According to Schmidt-Hebbel and Serven [175], it is fair to conclude that the effect of income inequality on aggregate saving is ambiguous.

---

[4] Wood [180] presents well the views of labor economists.

[5] Income is used as a proxy for wage.

[6] The marriage rate of men in the lowest earnings quintile dropped by about 14 percentage points from 57% to 43% between 1979 and 1996 (Burtless [159]).

Welfare (utility) is a function of a consumer's own income and prices in models of microeconomics.[7] Therefore, an increase in income of the wealthy does not affect the welfare of the poor unless it alters relative prices of goods that the poor consume.[8] Surely, in a general equilibrium model, there is a certain linkage between income (wage) of the poor and income (wage) of the rich due to the substitutability between both factors.[9] This chapter does not consider this possibility for two reasons. First, it is possible to assume that the effect of factor substitution on relative wage rate may be nil since changes in relative wage rates due to factor substitution is a secondary effect of a change in relative wage rate initially stemming from technology development. Second, rising wage inequality is a fact that has been observed for a long period of time in the U.S. economy. This indirectly supports the view that reshuffling of factor use in production does not stop rising wage inequality. Therefore, reshuffling of factor use can be ignored and this ignorance does not lead to an oversimplification of the model.

The intuition behind this chapter is based on the points discussed above. Roughly speaking, the effect of rising wage inequality on welfare can be studied by analyzing how wage inequality affects competition in various commodity markets. Welch [178] mentioned this possibility implicitly in his article. However, Welch [178] seems to believe that wage inequality is not directly related to welfare by writing:

> ... [W]elfare statements regarding consumer unit access to goods and services are only remotely related to wages at the extremes of the wage distributions (p. 6).

In many cases, commodities are differentiated based on either quality or commodity types, and low-income households spend a lion's share of income on low quality and cheap products. Also, some commodities, such as necessities, have an inelastic income elasticity of demand. Thus, if commodity markets are segmented based on differences in quality or type, rising inequality may not intensify competition between low-income and high-income households in many commodity markets.

Contrary to usual commodity markets, in the land market (or the housing market) the spatial (locational) competition between two (or multiple) income groups is directly affected by changes in wage inequality between household types. This is because land is homogenous, its supply is limited, and a parcel of land is distinguished by its location. Thus, the market for land provides one feasible way to examine the effect of rising wage inequality on welfare. Consumers (residents) compete for a location with one another to economize on commuting cost because commuting cost to work places is directly related to households' location and wage rate. Rising wage inequality disproportionately affects different income group's land consumption and commuting costs, especially time costs. This chapter derives the effect of rising wage inequality on the welfare of the poor and the rich by investigating changes in competition for land between two income classes. Rising wage inequality can either reinforce or dampen competition between income groups in land market depending on the type of commuting cost function.

---

[7] This statement is based on an indirect utility function.

[8] As Frank [162] explains at chapter 7, a consumer's utility can depend of others' income, but this chapter assumes that a consumer's utility is a function of only own income and prices.

[9] An anonymous referee who recommends including production sector in the model raises this point.

LOCATIONAL COMPETITION BETWEEN LOW SKILLED AND HIGH SKILLED WORKERS

Currently, rising wage inequality occurs between the low skilled and the high skilled, not between low-income and high-income households. Therefore, if residential distribution based on skill level is different from that based on wage rate (income level), welfare analysis using standard urban models assuming two income classes may not be appropriate. In other words, if each residential area is homogeneous in income level but heterogeneous in skill level, it is not possible to analyze locational competition between the two groups differentiated by skill levels using standard urban models.[10] However, since wage rate (or income) has a positive correlation with skill level, high skilled workers are likely to live in the suburbs.

According to 1990 Census data, the residential distribution by income is closely related to the residential distribution by skill level. Correlation coefficients are calculated with two variables: household median income by tract and percentage of population who have a bachelor's degree or higher by tract. Correlation coefficients of five metropolitan statistical areas (MSAs) shown in Table 1 are all positive and highly significant. This result is not unusual at all because skill levels are correlated with income levels. Therefore, it can be noticed that locational distribution of households by income level will be similar to that of households by skill level.

Table 1. Correlation between Residential Location by Income and Skill Level

	Correlation Coefficient	Number of tracts
Atlanta MSA	0.66*	477
Washington DC. MSA	0.64*	909
Chicago CMSA	0.69*	1,887
Los Angeles CMSA	0.73*	2,540
New York CMSA	0.72*	5,010

* Significant at the 0.01 level. Raw data source: CensusCD+Maps (GioLytics, Inc.)

Figure 1 and 2 for the Chicago consolidated metropolitan statistical area (CMSA) and Figure 3 and 4 for the Los Angeles CMSA present maps showing a close relationship between residential sorting by income and by skill level.[11] The grids in the figures are Census tracts. The size of the population in tracts varies tract by tract, but tracts are defined based on population size.[12] Thus, on average a bigger tract means less population density, and the central areas of each CMSA can be recognized by the size of tracts. Two income groups are distinguished based on the median income of each CMSA. White tracts are those where median income is lower than CMSA median income, while blue tracts are those where median income is higher than CMSA median income. Based on median skill level, all tracts

[10] Skill level is defined by educational level, so high skilled workers are those who have a bachelor's or higher degree. Sachs and Shatz [173] used a similar criterion based on whether workers had high school diplomas.

[11] Figures of Atlanta MSA, New York CMSA and Washington D.C. MSA are omitted here to save space, but they are available upon request from the author or see Kwon [168].

[12] Census tracts have between 2,500 and 8,000 persons. Retrieved December 23, 1999 from the World Wide Web: http://www.census.gov/td/stf3/append_a.html#CENSUS TRACT.

are also classified into two groups. White tracts represent tracts whose percentage of persons with bachelor's degree or more education is lower than the median level of each CMSA. Blue tracts represent tracts whose percentage of persons with bachelor's or more education is higher than the median level.

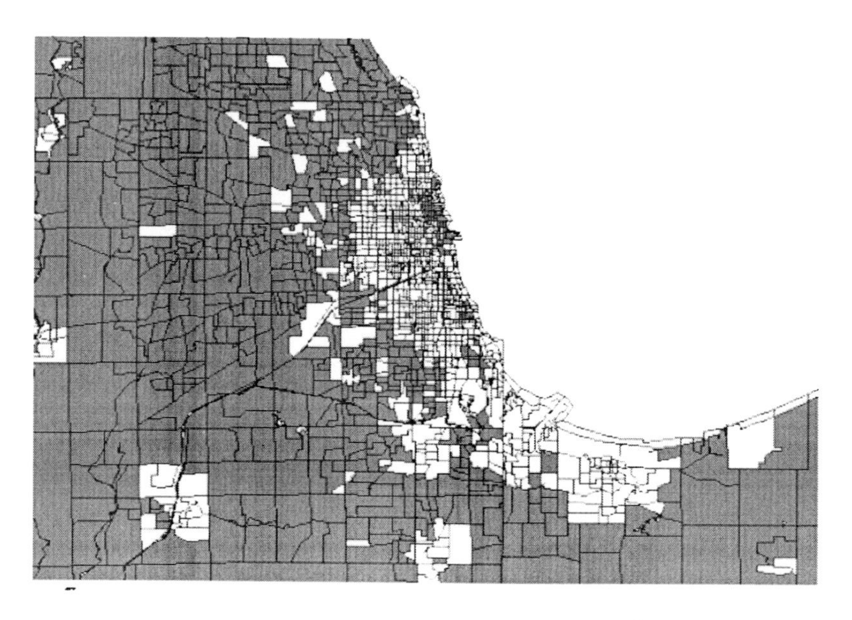

Figure 1. Chicago: Two Income Classes (based on median household income)[13]

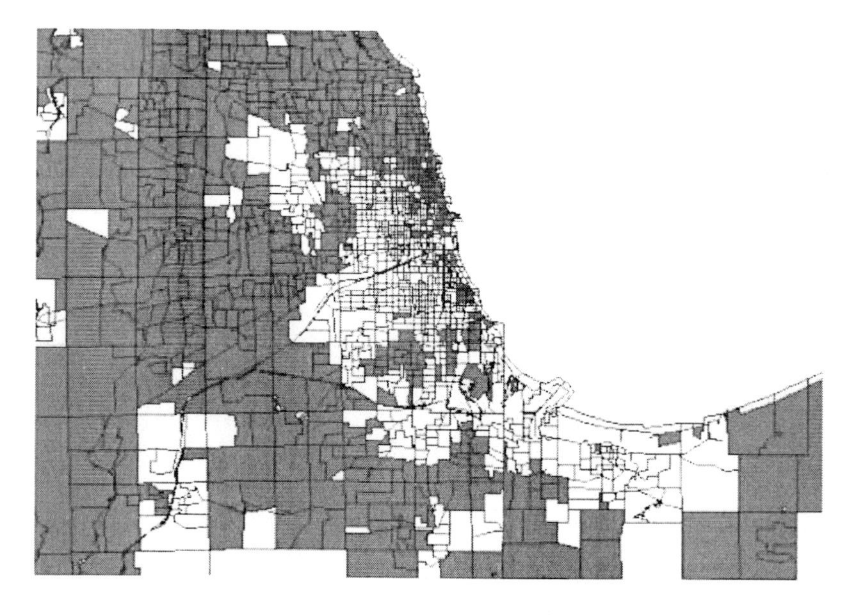

Figure 2. Chicago: Percentage of Persons who have Bachelor's Degree or Higher[14]

[13] Maps are created by the program in the Census CD+Maps CD (Manufactured by GeoLytics, Inc. [166])

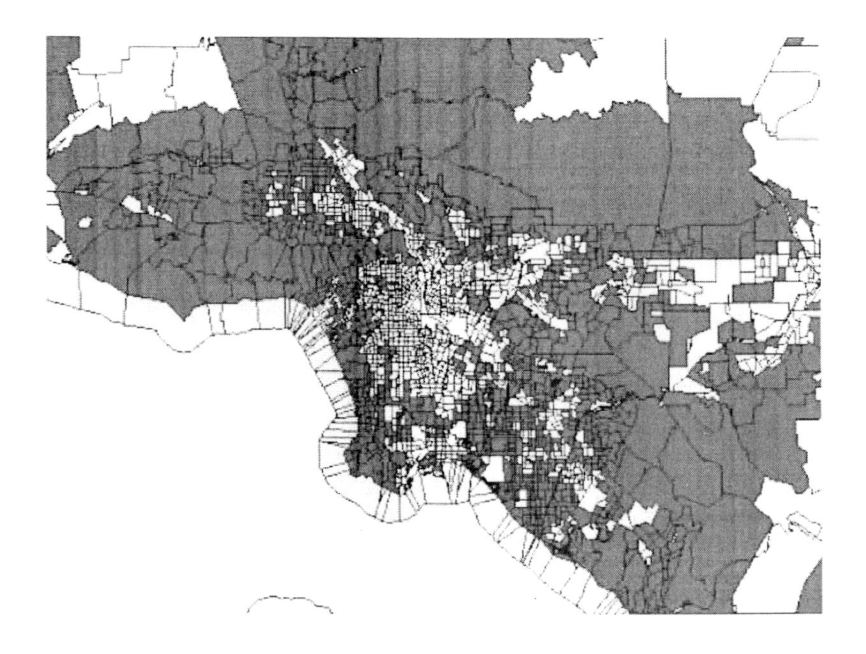

Figure 3. Los Angeles: Two Income Classes (based on median household income)

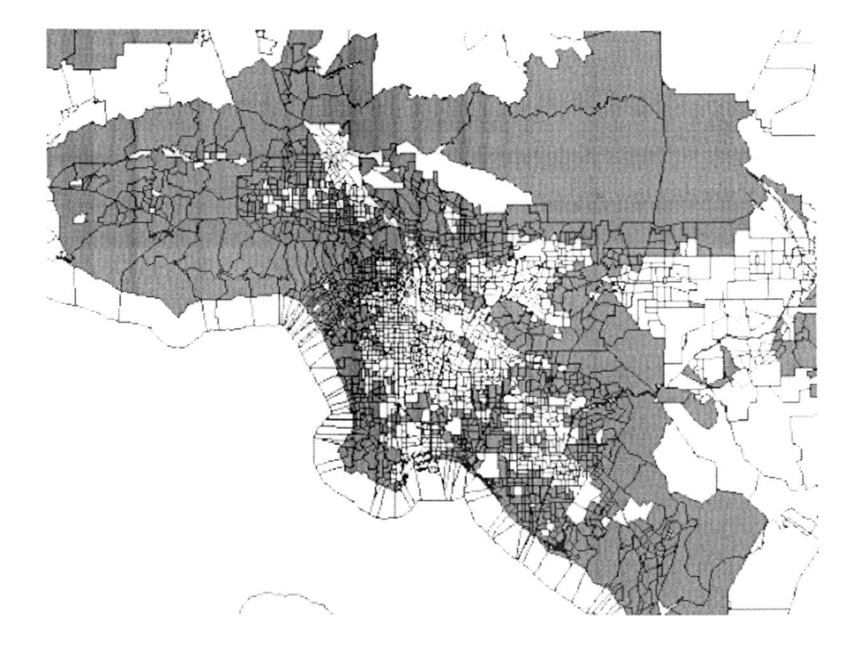

Figure 4. Los Angeles: Percentage of Persons who have Bachelor's Degree or Higher

[14] Universe: 25 years and over. Retrieved December 21, 1999, from the World Wide Web: http://www.census.gov/td/stf3/tableddf.txt.

Figures 1 to 4 confirm that low-income and low-skilled households occupy the central area of the city, and high-income and high-skilled households live in the suburban areas. This implies the pattern of locational competition between two income classes coincides with the pattern of locational competition between low-skilled and high-skilled households. Therefore, a standard closed urban model with two-income classes can be utilized to study how the rising wage inequality between low-skilled and high-skilled households will affect the welfare of the two household groups.

THE MODEL

In setting up the model, two things are considered. First, technology development is not only driving wage inequality but also reducing commuting time for business and shopping.[15] That is, technology development is an exogenous shock that alters both relative wage rates and commuting cost. Therefore, the model should be able to handle both endogenous changes due to technology development, i.e., the model should have at least two income classes and a commuting cost function that is a function of distance and time. Second, it is well known that income affects commuting cost and land demand, but there have been virtually no studies that elucidate the effect of time cost on locational competition when income of a class increases in a multiple class urban model. Two exceptions are Sasaki [174] and Arnott, MacKinnon and Wheaton [158] (hereafter AMW). Sasaki [174] investigates the effect of income on welfare and identifies that an increase in income of the rich living in the suburban area can increase the welfare of the poor living in the central area. However, he does not explain under what conditions it happens.[16] In this chapter, however, it is clearly shown when it happens. In other words, as shown later, if time cost is greater than operating cost, an increase in income of the rich always lowers the welfare of the poor. AMW also found that when the income of the household living in the suburban area rises, the welfare of the household living in the central area depends on competition for land at the boundary between two income classes. One flaw of their simulation study is that their commuting cost function is rather specific.[17]

The model used in this chapter is similar to that of Wheaton [179] except that the commuting cost is a function of both distance and income. The city is featureless and the commuting network is a dense hub-and-spoke type, resulting in a circular monocentric city. Two income classes, denoted by subscript 1 and 2, share the same preferences. Subscript 1 is used for the variables of the low-income class, and subscript 2 for the high-income class. The model assumes that the households of the two income classes are sorted by income level, and that the low-income households live in the central area of the city, and the high-income

---

[15] Ernst & Young [160] reports that over half of online shoppers visit stores less often due to shopping online (p. 8).

[16] Sasaki [174] focuses on the effect of income on the boundary (z) between two income classes. From the ambiguous effect of income on the boundary, he deduces changes in endogenous variables due to an increase in household income.

[17] Commuting costs: $k(t, y) = 100t$, if $y \leq 14{,}000$,
$= (100+(y\text{-}14{,}000)/30)t$, if $14{,}000 < y < 20{,}000$,
$= 300t$, if $y \geq 20{,}000$, where t is distance and y income.

households live in the suburban area.[18] Utility functions in (1) are assumed to be concave and have two normal goods as their arguments. All wages are assumed to be used for the consumption of the two goods and commuting as shown in (2)

$$u_1 = u(z_1, l_1) \text{ and } u_2 = u(z_2, l_2) \tag{1}$$

$$y_1 = z_1 + r_1(x)l_1 + k_1 x \text{ and } y_2 = z_2 + r_2(x)l_2 + k_2 x \tag{2}$$

$$k_1 = k_{o_1} + k_{y_1} y_1 \text{ and } k_2 = k_{o_2} + k_{y_2} y_2$$

$$N_1(x)l_1(x) = 2\pi x \text{ and } N_2(x)l_2(x) = 2\pi x, \tag{3}$$

where u is utility, z is composite good, l is land, y is earned income (wage), r is land rent, k is the marginal commuting cost, x is the commuting distance, k_o is the operating cost of commuting, $k_y y$ is the time cost of commuting, $N(x)$ is the population at x, and $2\pi x$ is the land supply at x.[19] Total commuting cost is composed of the monetary cost of commuting (operating cost) and the time cost $k_y y x$, where $k_y y$ is the opportunity cost of the time spent on commuting. The marginal commuting costs, k_1 or k_2, do not vary with distance of travel.[20] Equation (3) is the land market-clearing condition at a distance x from the central business district (CBD) of the city.

The following four equations, (4)-(7), attain the equilibrium of a closed urban model.[21] Equation (4) is the condition that the bid-rent at the boundary (b_1) of the two classes be the same because of competition for cheaper land between the two income classes. Technically, equation (4) attains a continuous rent distance function even though there is a kink at b_1. Equation (5) requires that, at the border of the city, land rent paid for residential use should be the same as the rent s for alternative uses. Equations (6) and (7) denote the conditions that populations of each household type, N_1 and N_2, should be housed in the city. The second equations in (6) and (7) can be obtained from the first equations by using the rent gradient and then integrating by parts.[22]

$$r_1(u_1, b_1, y_1, k_{o_1}, k_{y_1}) = r_2(u_2, b_1, y_2, k_{o_2}, k_{y_2}) \tag{4}$$

$$r_2(u_2, b_2, y_2, k_{o_2}, k_{y_2}) = s \tag{5}$$

[18] For multiple income class models, see Miyao [171] and Hartwick, Schweizer and Varaiya [167]. In the models of two papers, commuting cost is a function of distance.

[19] Mills and Hamilton [170] (p. 393) provided examples of specific values for parameters in equation (2).

[20] For the strengths and weaknesses of the commuting cost function used in this chapter, see Chapter III of Kwon [168].

[21] The model can be considered as a semi-closed model in the sense that the land rent goes to absentee landlords (See Pines and Sadka [172] for further explanation).

[22] $\frac{\partial r_i}{\partial x} = \frac{-k_i}{l_i}$, where $i = 1, 2$.

$$N_1 = 2\pi \int_0^{b_1} \frac{x}{l_1} dx \text{ or}$$
$$b_1 r_1(u_1, b_1, y_1, k_{o_1}, k_{y_1}) - \int_0^{b_1} r_1(u_1, x, y_1, k_{o_1}, k_{y_1}) dx = \frac{-k_1 N_1}{2\pi} \quad (6)$$

$$N_2 = 2\pi \int_{b_1}^{b_2} \frac{x}{l_2} dx \text{ or}$$
$$b_2 s - b_1 r_2(u_2, b_1, y_2, k_{o_2}, k_{y_2}) - \int_{b_1}^{b_2} r_2(u_2, x, y_2, k_{o_2}, k_{y_2}) dx = \frac{-k_2 N_2}{2\pi} \quad (7)$$

THE EFFECT OF CHANGES IN WAGES ON WELFARE

As observed in section 3, it is assumed that high skilled and high wage households live in the suburban area, and low skilled and low wage households live in the central area of the city. Given this condition, this section analyzes how a median preserving increase in wage inequality affects the welfare of the poor.[23]

In a closed urban model, an increase in the wage of the rich can be viewed as a median preserving increase in wage inequality if the population of two household types is equal. Thus, it is possible to experiment with a median preserving increase in wage inequality by fixing the wage of the poor and increasing the wage of the rich.[24] When commuting costs are only a function of distance and the rich occupy the suburban areas of a city, Wheaton [179] finds that an increase in the income of the rich always enhances the welfare of the poor living in the central area. As discussed later, however, if commuting costs are a function of distance and income, a median preserving increase in wage inequality can either improve or hurt the welfare of the poor depending on the relative size of operating and time costs of the rich.

Case I: Effects of an Increase in the Wages of the Rich: A Case of Median Preserving Increase in Wage Inequality

This section derives the effect of an increase in the wages of the rich y_2 on the welfare of the poor u_1.[25] It is not possible to completely solve for $\frac{du_1}{dy_2}$, and, as it was in Wheaton [179],

[23] Welch [178] and Weinberg [177] describe a median preserving increase in wage inequality as a phenomenon of ongoing wage inequality in the U.S. Welch [178] (p. 14) wrote that "[t]he period of growing wage dispersion was one during which, judged by the personal consumption expenditures (PCE) (the implicit deflator for consumer goods), median real wages were roughly constant".

[24] This is an incomplete experiment because a change in income yields a change in land rent. Therefore, before and after experimentation, the real income of the poor may rise or fall.

[25] The comparative static analysis in this section is based on the solution technique developed by Wheaton [179]. Due to the complexity of differentiated equations with respect to wage y, we make use of a graphical presentation as Wheaton [179] did.

the sign of $\frac{du_1}{dy_2}$ is derived from the functional relationship between $\frac{du_1}{dy_2}$ and $\frac{du_2}{dy_2}$. Equation (8) is obtained by differentiating equation (6) with respect to y_2. In equation (8), $-b_1 \frac{\partial r_1}{\partial x}\Big|_{b_1}$ is positive, and $b_1 \frac{\partial r_1}{\partial u_1}\Big|_{b_1} - \int_0^{b_1} \frac{\partial r_1}{\partial u_1} dx$ is also positive because two goods are assumed to be normal goods.[26] Thus, $\frac{du_1}{dy_2}$ and $\frac{db_1}{dy_2}$ have the same sign. After differentiating equation (4) with respect to y_2 and rearranging, we obtain equation (9).

$$\frac{du_1}{dy_2} = \frac{-b_1 \frac{\partial r_1}{\partial x}\Big|_{b_1} \frac{db_1}{dy_2}}{b_1 \frac{\partial r_1}{\partial u_1}\Big|_{b_1} - \int_0^{b_1} \frac{\partial r_1}{\partial u_1} dx} \tag{8}$$

$$\frac{db_1}{dy_2} = \frac{\frac{\partial r_2}{\partial u_2}\Big|_{b_1} \frac{du_2}{dy_2} - \frac{\partial r_1}{\partial u_1}\Big|_{b_1} \frac{du_1}{dy_2} + \frac{\partial r_2}{\partial y_2}\Big|_{b_1}}{\frac{\partial r_1}{\partial x}\Big|_{b_1} - \frac{\partial r_2}{\partial x}\Big|_{b_1}} = \frac{\frac{\partial r_2}{\partial u_2}\Big|_{b_1} \frac{du_2}{dy_2} - \frac{\partial r_1}{\partial u_1}\Big|_{b_1} \frac{du_1}{dy_2} + \frac{\partial r_2}{\partial y_2}\Big|_{b_1}}{D} \tag{9}$$

where, $D = \frac{\partial r_1}{\partial x}\Big|_{b_1} - \frac{\partial r_2}{\partial x}\Big|_{b_1}$ is negative because household type 1 lives in the central area of the city and household type 2 in the suburban area. In order for household type 1 to live in the central area of the city, at b_1, the rent gradient of household type 1 should be greater, in absolute value, than that of household type 2.

$$\frac{du_2}{dy_2} = \frac{\frac{\partial r_2}{\partial y_2}\Big|_{b_1}}{-\frac{\partial r_2}{\partial u_2}\Big|_{b_1}} + \frac{\left. \int_0^{b_1} \frac{\partial r_1}{\partial u_1} dx + b_1 \frac{\partial r_2}{\partial x}\Big|_{b_1} \frac{\partial r_1}{\partial u_1}\Big|_{b_1} \middle/ D \right.}{\left. b_1 \frac{\partial r_1}{\partial x}\Big|_{b_1} \frac{\partial r_2}{\partial u_2}\Big|_{b_1} \middle/ D \right.} \frac{du_1}{dy_2} = a + c\frac{du_1}{dy_2} \tag{10}$$

---

[26] $\frac{\partial r_1}{\partial u_1} = -\frac{1}{l_1 u_{z_1}}$ has the highest absolute value at $x = 0$ and the lowest absolute value at $x = b_1$ because the utility function of the residents is convex and land is a normal good. Hence, $b_1 \frac{\partial r_1}{\partial u_1}\Big|_{b_1} - \int_0^{b_1} \frac{\partial r_1}{\partial u_1} dx$ is positive.

Substituting equation (9) into equation (8) leads to equation (10), and a functional relationship between $\frac{du_2}{dy_2}$ and $\frac{du_1}{dy_2}$ is derived. In equation (10), a and c are positive (see Appendix A). From equation (10), an upward sloping line having a positive intercept in $\frac{du_2}{dy_2}$ and $\frac{du_1}{dy_2}$ space is drawn in Figure 5, even though its exact curvature is not known.

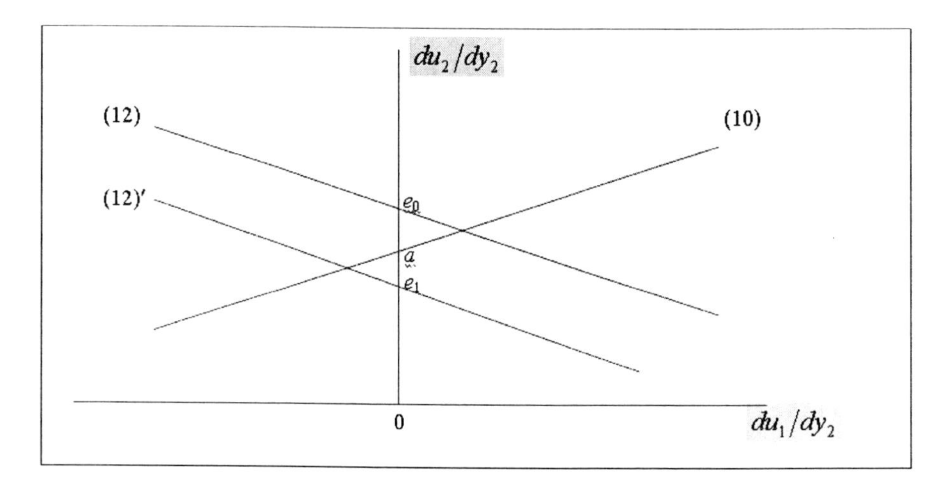

Figure 5. Effects on Welfare of a Median Preserving Increase in Wage Inequality

Another functional relationship between $\frac{du_2}{dy_2}$ and $\frac{du_1}{dy_2}$, equation (12), can be found from equation (11), which is obtained by adding two population conditions, equations (6) and (7). At the boundary b_1, bid-rents by two household types are the same, so equation (11) can be obtained by canceling the land rents of the two household types at b_1.

$$b_2 s - \int_0^{b_1} r_1(u_1, x, y_1, k_{o_1}, k_{y_1})dx - \int_{b_1}^{b_2} r_2(u_2, x, y_2, k_{o_2}, k_{y_2})dx = \frac{-k_1 N_1}{2\pi} - \frac{k_2 N_2}{2\pi} \tag{11}$$

$$\frac{du_2}{dy_2} = \frac{\int_{b_1}^{b_2} \frac{\partial r_2}{\partial y_2} dx - \frac{k_{y_2} N_2}{2\pi}}{-\int_{b_1}^{b_2} \frac{\partial r_2}{\partial u_2} dx} - \frac{\int_0^{b_1} \frac{\partial r_1}{\partial u_1} dx}{\int_{b_1}^{b_2} \frac{\partial r_2}{\partial u_2} dx} \frac{du_1}{dy_2} = e + f \frac{du_1}{dy_2} \tag{12}$$

Differentiating equation (11) with respect to y_2 leads to equation (12). In equation (12), e is positive and f is negative (see Appendix A), so the line derived from equation (12) is downward sloping and has a positive intercept, as shown in Figure 5.[27] The effect of an increase in the wages of the rich on the utility levels of the two household types is determined at the point where the two lines from equations (10) and (12) cross. If two lines cross on the right-hand side quadrant (line (12) in Figure 5), both types of households are better off. If they cross on the left-hand side quadrant (line (12)′ in Figure 5), household type 1 is worse off and household type 2 is better off. An increase in the wages of the rich always improves their own utility as shown in Figure 5, because the two lines have positive intercepts. This means that the whole amount of increased wages cannot be absorbed by increased commuting costs. Put differently, some amounts of increased income are spent on consumption because the two goods are normal goods.

Note from Figure 5 that the relative magnitude of the intercepts a and e determines the effect of median preserving wage inequality on the welfare of the poor, du_1/dy_2. If $e = e_0$, a is less than e and an increase in the wages of the rich entails an increase in the welfare of all residents. If $e = e_1$, poor households become worse off, whereas rich households are made better off. Equation (13) presents the relative magnitude of e and a (see Appendix A for derivation). Therefore, the effect of a median preserving wage inequality on the welfare of the poor depends on the sign of equation (13).

$$\frac{e}{a} = \frac{\int_{b_1}^{b_2} \frac{1}{l_2 u_{z_2(x)}} \left[\frac{(1-2xk_{y_2})u_{z_2(x)}}{(1-b_1 k_{y_2})u_{z_2(b_1)}} \right] dx}{\int_{b_1}^{b_2} \frac{1}{l_2 u_{z_2(x)}} dx} \tag{13}$$

Let $\frac{(1-2xk_{y_2})u_{z_2(x)}}{(1-b_1 k_{y_2})u_{z_2(b_1)}}$ be $\Omega(x)$. The numerator and the denominator in equation (13) are exactly the same except for $\Omega(x)$, which is a scaling factor over the range of x between b_1 and b_2. In Wheaton [179], the commuting cost function does not have a time cost component that is related to income, so k_{y_2} is zero and $\Omega(x) = \frac{u_{z_2(x)}}{u_{z_2(b_1)}}$. Since $u_{z_2(b_1)}$ is less than $u_{z_2(x)}$ in the range of x between b_1 and b_2 if preferences of households are convex, $\frac{u_{z_2(x)}}{u_{z_2(b_1)}}$ is always greater than unity for $x \in [b_1, b_2]$ and so is e/a. Therefore, in Wheaton [179], a median preserving increase in wage inequality always enhances the welfare of the poor. However, if $k_{y_2} \neq 0$, $\frac{1-2xk_{y_2}}{1-b_1 k_{y_2}} < 1$ for $x \in [b_1, b_2]$, and, contrary to Wheaton [179], e/a can be either

[27] In equation (12), the numerator of e (see Appendix A) $\int_{b_1}^{b_2} \frac{1-2xk_{y_2}}{l_2} dx$ is positive. For proof, refer to Kwon [168] or the proof is available from the authors upon request.

greater or less than unity depending on the relative size of $\frac{1-2xk_{y_2}}{1-b_1k_{y_2}}$ and $\frac{u_{z_2(x)}}{u_{z_2(b_1)}}$. In other words, $\Omega(x)$ can have three values. Put differently, if it is unity, then $e = a$. In this case, as shown in Figure 6, a median preserving increase in wage inequality improves the welfare of the rich but does not reduce the welfare of the poor.[28] In addition, if $\Omega(x) = 1$, at b_1 land rent does not change after y_2 increases and nothing happens to the rent-distance function of the poor. Locational competition at b_1 remains the same, while the border of the city elongates from b_2 to b_2'.

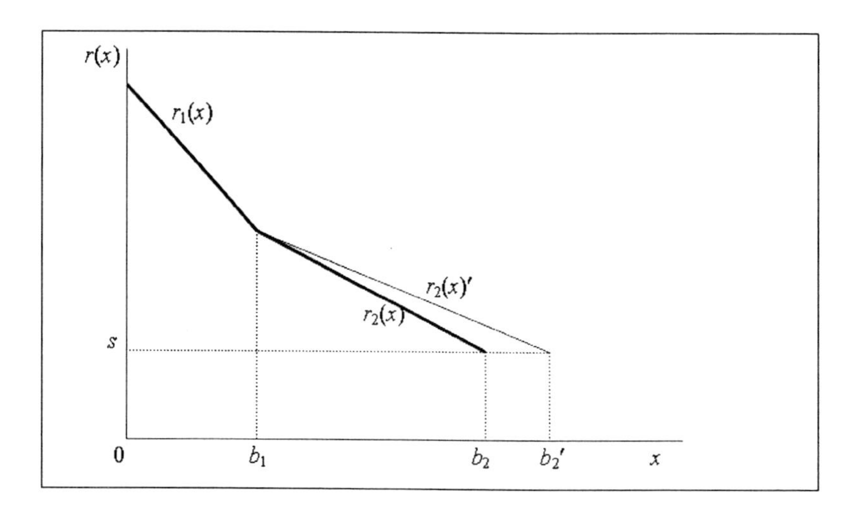

Figure 6. Rent-distance Functions when $e = a$

If $\Omega(x)$ is greater than unity as it is in the case of Wheaton [179], e is greater than a and a median preserving increase in wage inequality results in an increase in the welfare of the poor. Figure 7 illustrates this mutually beneficial case. At the boundary between two classes b_1, land rent falls and b_1 gets longer. The border of the city b_2 also increases because as the income of the rich grows b_1 increases and household type 2 consumes more land. These results are not derived formally but are true because in terms of the poor a decrease in $r_1(b_1)$ is the same as a fall in land rent for an alternative use in one income class model.

It is not clear how the scaling factor, $\Omega(x)$, changes over x between b_1 and b_2. It is clear, however, that at $x = b_1$, $\Omega(x) < 1$. This means that the function in the integral of the numerator in equation (13) locates below the function in the integral of the denominator, at least in some range from b_1 to b_2. In other words, e/a is likely to be smaller than unity, and the welfare of the poor living in the central area of the city is prone to be decreased by an increase in the wages of the rich.

---

[28] The rent-distance functions in Figures 6, 7 and 8 should be curved, but for expositional purposes they are drawn as straight lines. The thick lines represent the initial rent-distance curves and the thin lines new rent-distance curves.

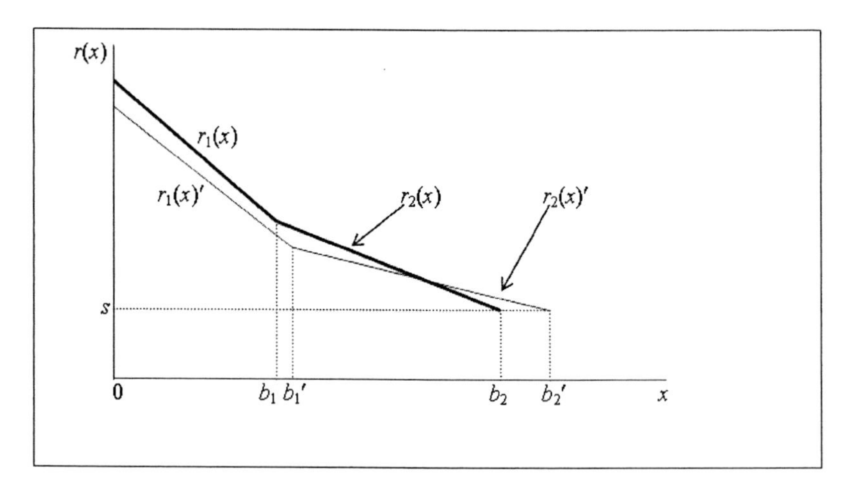

Figure 7. Rent-distance Functions when $e > a$.

By specifying the type of utility function, it is possible for us to see clearly how $\Omega(x)$ changes over x in the range between b_1 and b_2, and to see the effect of an increase in the wages of the rich on the welfare of the poor. For example, when the preferences of residents are CES preferences, $\Omega(x)$ becomes equation (14).[29]

$$\Omega(x) = \frac{(1 - 2xk_{y_2})(y_2 - k_2 b_1)}{(1 - b_1 k_{y_2})(y_2 - k_2 x)} \tag{14}$$

Proposition

If the preferences of residents are CES and the time cost of commuting is greater than the operating cost of commuting, an increase in the wages of the rich with holding the wages of the poor always harms the welfare of the poor, i.e., $k_{y_2} y_2 > k_{o_2}$ is a sufficient condition for an increase in y_2 to reduce u_1.

Proof:

Already, we know that at b_1, $\Omega(x) < 1$. $\frac{\partial \Omega(x)}{\partial x} = \frac{(y_2 - k_2 b_1)(k_{o_2} - k_{y_2} y_2)}{(1 - b_1 k_{y_2})(y_2 - k_2 x)^2}$. Thus, if $k_{y_2} y_2 > k_{o_2}$, $\partial \Omega(x) / \partial x < 0$. In other words, if $k_{y_2} y_2 > k_{o_2}$, then the scaling factor, $\Omega(x)$, is less than unity over x in the range between b_1 and b_2 and $e/a < 1$.

If the time cost of commuting is greater than the operating cost of commuting, land rent at b_1 increases and the boundary between the two classes decreases as shown in Figure 8. This coincides with the case where land rent for an alternative use rises in a model with one income class. If the time cost component is greater than the operating cost component, competition for land at b_1 becomes intensified and land rent at b_1 rises. The border of the city b_2 can either grow or shrink after y_2 increases as shown in Figure 8.[30] It depends on how much b_1 decreases and the amount of increase in land demand by the rich.

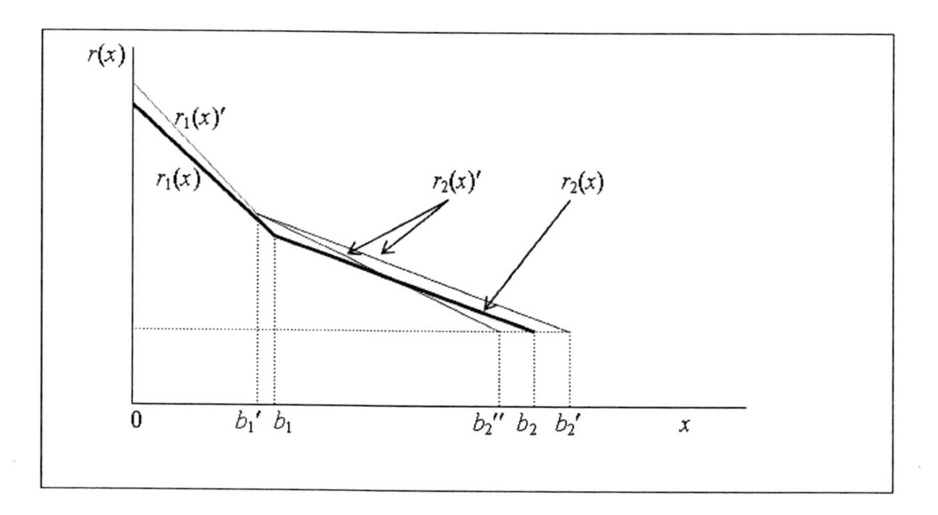

Figure 8. Rent-distance Functions when $e < a$.

To sum up, when the income of the rich rises with holding the income of the poor constant, the welfare of the poor hinges on whether the time cost of commuting of the rich is greater than their operating cost of commuting. More precisely, the welfare of the poor in the model depends on whether land rent rises or falls at the boundary of the two classes. If land rent at b_1 rises, a median preserving increase in wage inequality decreases the welfare of the poor, but if it falls, the welfare of the poor is improved.

Case II: Effect of an Increase in Income of the Poor

The solution begins with differentiating equation (4) with respect to y_1. This leads to equation (15). Differentiating equation (6) with respect to y_1 and rearranging result in equation (16). Substituting equation (15) into equation (16) and rearranging yield equation (17).

$$\frac{db_1}{dy_1} = \left(\left.\frac{\partial r_2}{\partial u_2}\right|_{b_1} \frac{du_2}{dy_1} - \left.\frac{\partial r_1}{\partial u_1}\right|_{b_1} \frac{du_1}{dy_1} - \left.\frac{\partial r_1}{\partial y_1}\right|_{b_1} \right) \Big/ D \qquad (15)$$

---

[29] If the utility function is the CES function, then $\frac{u_{z_2(x)}}{u_{z_2(b_1)}} = \frac{\frac{u_2}{(y_2 - k_2 x)}}{\frac{u_2}{(y_2 - k_2 b_1)}} = \frac{y_2 - k_2 b_1}{y_2 - k_2 x}$. For derivation, see Appendix B.

[30] As pointed by an anonymous referee, if the income elasticity of demand for land is greater than unity (or the income elasticity of marginal commuting cost), the border of the city grows since the gradient of the rent distance function of the rich gets flatter.

$$\left(b_1 \frac{\partial r_1}{\partial u_1}\bigg|_{b_1} - \int_0^{b_1} \frac{\partial r_1}{\partial u_1} dx \right) \frac{du_1}{dy_1} = \int_0^{b_1} \frac{\partial r_1}{\partial y_1} dx - \frac{k_{y_1} N_1}{2\pi} - b_1 \frac{\partial r_1}{\partial y_1}\bigg|_{b_1} - b_1 \frac{\partial r_1}{\partial b_1}\bigg|_{b_1} \frac{db_1}{dy_1} \tag{16}$$

$$\frac{du_1}{dy_1} = \frac{\left(\int_0^{b_1} \frac{\partial r_1}{\partial y_1} dx + b_1 \frac{\partial r_1}{\partial y_1}\bigg|_{b_1} \frac{\partial r_2}{\partial b_1}\bigg|_{b_1} \Big/ D - \frac{k_{y_1} N_1}{2\pi} \right)}{- \int_0^{b_1} \frac{\partial r_1}{\partial u_1} dx - b_1 \frac{\partial r_2}{\partial b_1}\bigg|_{b_1} \frac{\partial r_1}{\partial u_1}\bigg|_{b_1} \Big/ D} -$$

$$\frac{\left(b_1 \frac{\partial r_1}{\partial b_1}\bigg|_{b_1} \frac{\partial r_2}{\partial u_2}\bigg|_{b_1} \Big/ D \right) \frac{du_2}{dy_1}}{- \int_0^{b_1} \frac{\partial r_1}{\partial u_1} dt - b_1 \frac{\partial r_2}{\partial b_1}\bigg|_{b_1} \frac{\partial r_1}{\partial u_1}\bigg|_{b_1} \Big/ D} = g + h \frac{du_2}{dy_1} \tag{17}$$

In equation (17), g and h are positive (for proofs see Appendix 1 of Kwon [168]), so equation (17) represents a line that is upward sloping with a positive intercept in $\frac{du_1}{dy_1}$ and $\frac{du_2}{dy_1}$ space. Figure 9 shows an example of the line from equation (17). Differentiating equation (11) with respect to y_1 yields equation (18).

$$\frac{du_1}{dy_1} = \frac{\int_0^{b_1} \frac{\partial r_1}{\partial y_1} dx - \frac{k_{y_1} N_1}{2\pi}}{- \int_0^{b_1} \frac{\partial r_1}{\partial u_1} dx} - \frac{\int_{b_1}^{b_2} \frac{\partial r_2}{\partial u_2} dx}{\int_0^{b_1} \frac{\partial r_1}{\partial u_1} dx} \frac{du_2}{dy_1} = m + n \frac{du_2}{dy_1} \tag{18}$$

In equation (18), m is positive but n is negative (for proofs see Appendix 1 of Kwon [168]). From equation (18), a downward sloping line with a positive intercept is also drawn in Figure 9. As in the previous case, the effect of an increase in the income of household type 1 on the utility of both groups depends on the relative magnitudes of the intercepts, g and m.

In contrast to the case where the income of the rich increases, when the income of the poor increases, the rich are always hurt. Equations (19) and (20) are derived by replacing the partial derivatives of g and m with their values.

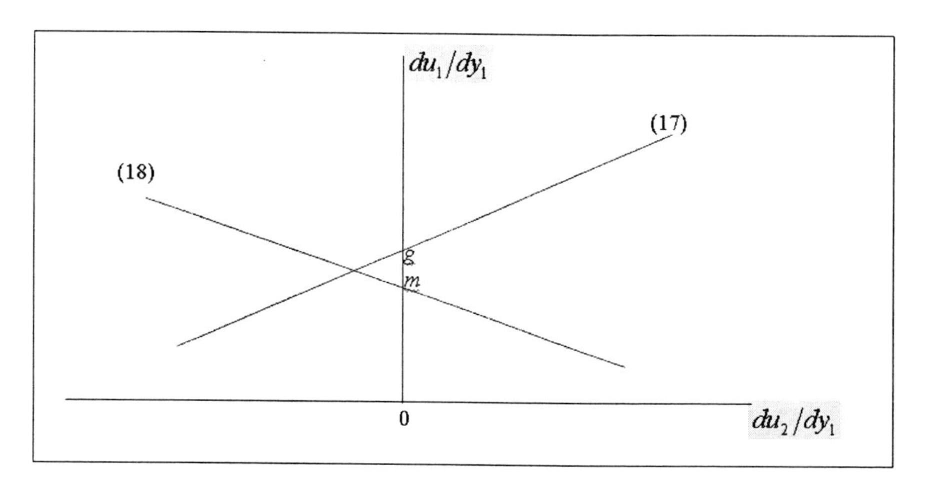

Figure 9. Effects on Welfare of an Increase in Income of the Poor.

$$g=\frac{u_{z_1(b_1)}(1-b_1k_{y_1})\left[\frac{1}{(1-b_1k_{y_1})}\int_0^{b_1}\frac{1-2xk_{y_1}}{l_1}dx-\left(\frac{b_1k_2}{l_1|_{b_1}l_2|_{b_1}}\right)\Big/D\right]}{u_{z_1(b_1)}\int_0^{b_1}\frac{1}{l_1u_{z_1}}dx-\left(\frac{b_1k_2}{l_2|_{b_1}l_1|_{b_1}}\right)\Big/D} \tag{19}$$

$$m=\frac{u_{z_1(b_1)}(1-b_1k_{y_1})\left[\frac{1}{1-b_1k_{y_1}}\int_0^{b_1}\frac{1-2xk_{y_1}}{l_1}dx\right]}{u_{z_1(b_1)}\int_0^{b_1}\frac{1}{l_1u_{z_1}}dx} \tag{20}$$

As Wheaton [179] did, let $A_1=\frac{1}{(1-b_1k_{y_1})}\int_0^{b_1}\frac{1-2xk_{y_1}}{l_1}dx$, $A_2=u_{z_1(b_1)}\int_0^{b_1}\frac{1}{l_1u_{z_1}}dx$, and $B=-\left(\frac{b_1k_2}{l_2|_{b_1}l_1|_{b_1}}\right)\Big/D$. Given that A_1, A_2, and B are positive and $A_2 > A_1$, equation (21) is derived. This reveals that g is greater than m and the two lines (17) and (18) cross in the left quadrant as shown in Figure 9. As a result, an increase in income of the poor with holding the income of the rich constant reduces the welfare of the rich and improves the welfare of the poor.

$$\frac{g}{m}=\frac{(A_1+B)A_2}{(A_2+B)A_1}>1 \tag{21}$$

Summary and Discussion

The analytical results derived in this chapter coincide with those derived through simulation by AMW. When the income of one household type rises, the effect on the utility level of the other class depends on whether an increase in income of one group intensifies locational competition between the two classes at the boundary, b_1. This type of general explanation is not new since it appeared in Wheaton [179] and Sasaki [174]. Sasaki [174] shows that an increase in the income of the rich improves the welfare of the poor, but Sasaki does not show what caused the result. However, we explicitly derive a determinant of competition at the boundary of the two classes, which is unexplained by previous research.

An increase in the income of the rich living in the outskirts of the city can either reduce locational competition at b_1 or increase it. In addition, locational competition depends on the relative magnitudes of the operating cost of commuting and the time cost of commuting. This result parallels the condition that determines land rent at the center of the city in one income class model.[31] As the income of the rich increases, if the time cost of commuting is greater than the operating cost, the land rent at the boundary between the two classes rises. This reflects increased competition at b_1 and leads to a decrease in the welfare of the poor.

An increase in the income of the poor living in the central area of the city always lowers the welfare of the rich. This is because land is a normal good by assumption, and as the income of the poor increases, their total consumption of land increases as well. As a result, at the boundary of the two classes, competition for land will be strengthened. The exchange of initial locations of the two classes does not alter the analytical results because of the symmetry of the model. An increase in the income of the poor living in the suburban area can either reduce or enhance the welfare of the rich, but an increase in the income of the rich living in the central area of the city always reduces the welfare of the poor.

CONCLUSION

This chapter sheds light on the effect of a median preserving increase in wage inequality on the welfare of the poor and the rich using a closed urban spatial competition model. In the U.S., on average the wealthy and high skilled live in suburban areas and the poor and low skilled in the central areas of the city. An increase in the income of the class living in the central area always lowers the welfare of the class living in the suburban area. However, an increase in the income of the class living in the suburban area can either increase or decrease the welfare of the class living in the central area of the city. Therefore, the growing wage inequality in the U.S. may not reduce the welfare of the poor.

A priori, it is unclear if the median preserving wage inequality lowers or improves the welfare of the poor because there is no information on the relative size of the two costs of commuting. Nowadays, new computer based information technology tends to not only enlarge the wage inequality but also reduce the time cost of commuting for work and/or shopping. However, computer based information technology may increase high skilled workers' time cost of commuting by increasing their wage rate, inducing them to move closer

[31] See Chapter III of Kwon [168].

to the CBD of a city. If the time cost falls enough to reduce the competition for land at the boundary of the two classes, all households in the city may be better off from the rise in wage equality. Even though there are some evidences[32] supporting this win-win possibility, currently it is unsure if the use of computer and the Internet reduces commuting cost of the rich large enough to dampen the locational competition between the two household types.

APPENDIX A

Partial derivatives are $\frac{\partial r_1}{\partial x} = \frac{-k_1}{l_1}$ and $\frac{\partial r_2}{\partial x} = \frac{-k_2}{l_2}$, $\frac{\partial r_1}{\partial y_1} = \frac{1 - xk_{y_1}}{l_1}$ and $\frac{\partial r_2}{\partial y_2} = \frac{1 - xk_{y_2}}{l_2}$ and $\frac{\partial r_1}{\partial u_1} = \frac{-1}{l_1 u_{z_1}}$ and $\frac{\partial r_2}{\partial u_2} = \frac{-1}{l_2 u_{z_2}}$. Let $D = \frac{\partial r_1}{\partial x}\Big|_{b_1} - \frac{\partial r_2}{\partial x}\Big|_{b_1} < 0$ be assumed for a normal sorting. In equation (10), c is negative because all partial derivatives in c are negative, and D is negative. $a = \frac{\partial r_2 / \partial y_2}{-\partial r_2 / \partial u_2} = \frac{1 - b_1 k_{y_2}}{l_2|_{b_1}} \Big/ \frac{1}{l_2|_{b_1} u_{z_2(b_1)}}$ $= (1 - b_1 k_{y_2}) u_{z_2(b_1)} > 0$.

In Equation (12), f is negative since two partial derivatives in f are negative, and e is positive because

$$e = \frac{\int_{b_1}^{b_2} \frac{\partial r_2}{\partial y_2} dx - \frac{k_{y_2} N_2}{2\pi}}{-\int_{b_1}^{b_2} \frac{\partial r_2}{\partial u_2} dx} = \frac{\int_{b_1}^{b_2} \frac{1 - xk_{y_2}}{l_2} dx - \frac{k_{y_2} N_2}{2\pi}}{\int_{b_1}^{b_2} \frac{1}{l_2 u_{z_2}} dx} = \frac{\int_{b_1}^{b_2} \frac{1 - 2xk_{y_2}}{l_2} dx}{\int_{b_1}^{b_2} \frac{1}{l_2 u_{z_2}} dx} > 0.$$

$$\frac{e}{a} = \frac{\int_{b_1}^{b_2} \frac{1 - 2xk_{y_2}}{l_2} dx \Big/ \int_{b_1}^{b_2} \frac{1}{l_2 u_{z_2(x)}} dx}{(1 - b_1 k_{y_2}) u_{z_2(b_1)}} = \frac{\frac{1}{(1 - b_1 k_{y_2}) u_{z_2(b_1)}} \int_{b_1}^{b_2} \frac{1 - 2xk_{y_2}}{l_2} dx}{\int_{b_1}^{b_2} \frac{1}{l_2 u_{z_2(x)}} dx}$$

---

[32] Gaspar and Glaeser [165] discusses how new information technology (IT) can be either substitute or complement face to face contact. If IT is complementary to face to face contact, the time cost of commuting will not fall as IT develops. Fogel [161] predicted that commuting time to and from work would decrease from 1 hour in 1995 to half an hour in 2040 without explaining why. According to the Department of Commerce [176], 41.5% of American households are using the Internet and 51% have a computer as of August 2000. 37.7% of central city households have Internet access, while 42.3% of urban households do. Also, it is well known that household Internet access is closely correlated with household income. Furthermore, higher education increases the use of the Internet with holding income level. Among households belonging to the income level between \$15,000 and \$34,999, 46% of households headed by those with college degree or higher use the Internet, where as 11% of households headed by those with less than high school degree do.

By rearranging, the equation (13) is derived.

$$\frac{e}{a} = \frac{\int_{b_1}^{b_2} \frac{1}{l_2 u_{z_2(x)}} \left(\frac{(1-2xk_{y_2})u_{z_2(x)}}{(1-b_1 k_{y_2})u_{z_2(b_1)}} \right) dx}{\int_{b_1}^{b_2} \frac{1}{l_2 u_{z_2(x)}} dx}$$

APPENDIX B

The Cobb-Douglas utility function is a special case of the CES utility function, so $\Omega(x)$ is derived for the CES utility function in here. The CES utility function is denoted as $u = \left[(1-\beta)z^{\rho} + \beta l^{\rho}\right]^{1/\rho}$, where β and ρ are parameters and $u_{z(x)} = \frac{u(1-\beta)z^{\rho-1}}{(1-\beta)z^{\rho} + \beta l^{\rho}}$.

From the first-order conditions, it follows that $r = \frac{\beta l^{\rho-1}}{(1-\beta)z^{\rho-1}}$. Substituting this into the budget constraint, equation (2), leads to $z + \frac{\beta l^{\rho}}{(1-\beta)z^{\rho-1}} = y - kx$. By rearranging, $z^{\rho}(1-\beta) + \beta l^{\rho} = (y-kx)(1-\beta)z^{\rho-1}$ results. Finally, $u_{z(x)} = \frac{u}{y-kx}$.

REFERENCES

Autor, D.H., Katz, L.K., & Krueger, A.B. (1997). Computing inequality: have computers changed the labor market? *NBER Working Paper, 5956.*

Arnott, R.J., MacKinnon, J.G., & Wheaton, W.C. (1978). The welfare implications of spatial interdependence: an extension of Wheaton's "Optimal distribution of income among cities." *Journal of Urban Economics, 5*, 131-136.

Burtless, G. (1999). Effects of growing wage disparities and changing family composition on the U.S. income distribution. *European Economic Review, 43*, 853-865.

Ernst & Young. (2001). *Global online retailing: an Ernst & Young special report.* Retrieved January 18, 2002, from http://www.ey.com/GLOBAL/gcr.nsf/US /Online_Retailing_-_Thought_Center_-_Ernst_&_Young_LLP).

Fogel, R.W. (1999). Catching up with the economy. *American Economic Review, 89*, 1-21.

Frank, R.H. (1997). *Microeconomics and behavior.* (3rd ed.). New York: McGraw-Hill.

Frank, R.H. (1999). Luxury fever: why money fails to satisfy in an area of excess. New York: The Free Press.

Frank, R.H., & Cook, P.J. (1995). *The Winner-Take-All society.* New York: The Free Press.

Gaspar, J., & Glaeser, E.L. (1998). Information technology and the future of cities. *Journal of Urban Economics*, *43*, 136-156.

GeoLytics, Inc. (1999). CensusCD+Maps: the complete Census reference plus maps on a single CD. East Brunswick, NJ.

Hartwick, J., Schweizer, U., & Varaiya, P. (1976). Comparative statics of a residential economy with several classes. *Journal of Economic Theory*, *13*, 396-413.

Kwon, Y. (2000). *Income, spatial competition and welfare*. Unpublished doctoral dissertation, Syracuse University.

Lawrence, R.Z. (1996). Single world, divided nations? : international trade and OECD labor markets. Washington, D.C.: Brookings Institution Press.

Mills, E.S., & Hamilton, B.W. (1984). *Urban economics*. (3rd ed.). Glenview, IL: Scott, Foresman and Company.

Miyao, T. (1975). Dynamics and comparative statics in the theory of residential location. *Journal of Economic Theory*, *11*, 133-146.

Pines, D., & Sadka, E. (1986). Comparative statics analysis of a fully closed city. *Journal of Urban Economics*, *20*, 1–20.

Sachs, J.D., & Shatz, H.J. (1996). U.S. trade with developing countries and wage inequality. *American Economic Review*, *86*, 234-239.

Sasaki, K. (1990). Income class, modal choice, and urban spatial structure. *Journal of Urban Economics*, *27*, 322-343.

Schmidt-Hebbel, K., & Serven, L. (2000). Does income inequality raise aggregate saving? *Journal of Development Economics*, *61*, 417-446.

U.S. Department of Commerce. (2000). *Falling through the net: Toward digital inclusion.* Washington, D.C.

Weinberg, D.H. (1996). A brief look at postwar U.S. income inequality. *Current Population Report*, P60-191, 1-4.

Welch, F. (1999). In defense of inequality. *American Economic Review*, *89*, 1-17.

Wheaton, W.C. (1976). On the optimal distribution of income among cities. *Journal of Urban Economics*, *3*, 31-44.

Wood, A. (1995). How trade hurt unskilled workers. *Journal of Economic Perspectives*, *9*, 57-80

In: Focus on Urban and Regional Economics
Editor: Lawrence Yee, pp. 155-171
ISBN 1-59454-740-8

Chapter 8

AGENT-BASED MODELS OF INDUSTRIAL CLUSTERS AND DISTRICTS

Guido Fioretti [1, 2]
University of Bologna

ABSTRACT

Agent-based models, an instance of the wider class of connectionist models, allow bottom-up simulations of organizations constituted by a large number of interacting parts. Thus, geographical clusters of competing or complementary firms constitute an obvious field of application. This contribution explains what agent-based models are, reviews applications in the field of industrial clusters and focuses on a simulator of infra- and inter-firm communications.

Keywords: Agent-Based Models, Industrial Clusters, Industrial Districts

INTRODUCTION

In the nineteenth century, Alfred Marshall used the expression "industrial districts" while remarking that industries tend to concentrate in specific geographical areas [28]. Marshall mentioned straw plaiting in Bedfordshire or cutlery in Sheffield, pointing out that geographical proximity provides specialized labor, nurtures subsidiary industries, stimulates innovative activity and enables technological spillovers.

Although contemporary industries are often oligopolistic and technologically sophisticated, geographical proximity is no less important today than a century ago. Indeed, a popular writer such as Michael Porter ascribed the dynamics of national competitive advantage to the ability to create, sustain and develop clusters of firms that attain world

---

[1] E-mail: fioretti@cs.unibo.it
[2] I wish to thank David Hales and Leigh Tesfatsion for generous help and suggestions.

excellence in specific industries [32]. Writing from the perspective of a business economist, Porter stressed that competition between neighboring rivals and availability of sophisticated customers stimulates innovation and engenders positive feed-backs for all firms in a cluster.

Are "districts" the same thing as "clusters"? Definitely yes, if we look at the original writings of both Alfred Marshall and Michael Porter. However, some authors have presented industrial districts as a peculiar path of economic development based on small family businesses that would preserve community values [7]. By reaction, the word "clusters" is eventually preferred by those who focus on the more general phenomenon of firms agglomeration. Since this review is not focused on the aspects that distinguish "clusters" from "districts", these two terms will be used as synonyms. In other contexts, they are not.

A feature that attracted the attention of Marshall, Porter and many other authors who wrote on this subject, is that industrial districts are an instance of the dictum that "the whole is more than the sum of its parts". Apparently, a cluster of competing and complementary firms, local institutions and shared values has more to offer on the international arena than the very same firms taken in isolation fron one another.

Economic theory accounts for this sort of phenomena by means of positive externalities. Since economics wants to describe competitive equilibria, but since competitive equilibria do not exist unless returns decrease with the scale of activity, the following trick has been devised: returns decrease for single firms but increase with the scale of activity of the whole cluster of firms. In this way, an empirical fact such as the existence of industrial districts can be accomodated with economic theory [25] [21].

However, one may be interested in out-of-equilibrium dynamics of industrial clusters. Economic equilibrium may not exist, for instance because competitive industries may be constituted by firms that experience increasing returns but whose growth is limited by the innovations introduced by their competitors. Or, it may exist because of reasons other than decreasing returns, such as a desire to keep a family firm at family size or a search for excellence in a minuscule market niche.

Most importantly, one may be interested in grasping the structures and contents of interactions that make a district "more" than the sum of its parts. What do these "positive externalities" between firms consist of? Qualitative accounts of industrial districts mention specific "atmospheres" conducive of innovation, entrepreneurship, collaborative efforts, shared values and institutions. How do we model these aspects?

The issue is one where structures of microscopic interactions generate a coherent whole. Typically, this is the sort of problems addressed by the sciences of complexity. Thus, one would expect that agent-based and other connectionist models have enormous potentialities for industrial clusters [27]. This review wants to summarize to what extent this possibility has been exploited hitherto.

It may be wise to be clear regarding which topics this review does *not* cover:

- Cellular automata models of surface occupation, e.g. models of the growth of urban areas;
- Prisoner's dilemma and other pure models of competition, cooperation and collaboration;
- System dynamics models of inter-firm or inter-industry relations;
- Economic models of perfect vs. oligopolistic competition;
- Models of the distribution of the size of firms.

These exclusions are merely due to the need to keep the scope of this review within manageable bounds. It is obvious that the aforementioned research areas do have some connection with industrial districts.

The rest of this review is organized as follows. The ensuing section explains the functioning of connectionist models, particularly of agent-based models. It is followed by a section that illustrates a series of connectionist models of clustered firms. This section articulates in three subsections, depending on the questions addressed by particular models. The models of the first subsection are concerned with the relative advantage of clustered firms with respect to isolated firms. The models of the second subsection deal with issues of competition, collaboration and cooperation in industrial districts. The models of the third subsection investigate the evolutionary paths of clusters and districts. Those of the fourth subsection focus on their innovative activity. Finally, the models of the fifth subsection evaluate the impact of institutional policies on clusters of firms. Thereafter comes a section with a more practical flavor. In fact, it illustrates an agent-based platform that may support inter-firm relationships. Finally, the last section concludes with an evaluation of what is still to be done and which may be the most promising research fields.

CONNECTIONIST AND AGENT-BASED MODELS

Agent-based models constitute the bulk of connectionist models of clusters of firms. In their turn, agent-based models rest on object-oriented programming.

Since practical concepts may be easier to grasp than abstract concepts, this section proceeds from the particular to the general. First, it explains the idea of object-oriented programming. Subsequently, it arrives at the concept of agent-based models. Finally, it generalizes to the class of connectionist models.

Traditional programming, now sometimes called procedural programming, consists of:

- Instructions, such as value assignents and arithmetical operations of any kind;
- Conditions that command branching or looping over a set of instructions.

Figure 1 illustrates a possible structure of a piece of code. Programs may involve functions, i.e. pieces of code that are written separately and called at need, but this does alter their logical structure.

Flow charts may become very complicated as programs become very large. Since a programmer must overview all logical relations in a program, the cognitive burden may become unbearable.

Object-oriented programming consists of subdividing a computer program into relatively independent modules, called *objects*. Each object has the structure of a procedural program. Objects interact with one another by means of *methods*, which take the role of questions, answers or orders in the real life. Figure 2 illustrates a typical structure.

Objects may entail different algorithms, in which case they are qualitatively different from one another. Or they may all entail the same algorithm, in which case they are said to be instances of a class of objects. However, even objects entailing the same algorithms may behave differently from one another if their parameters have taken different values depending on the history that they experienced. Since it is very easy to replicate instances of a class, objects may be very many.

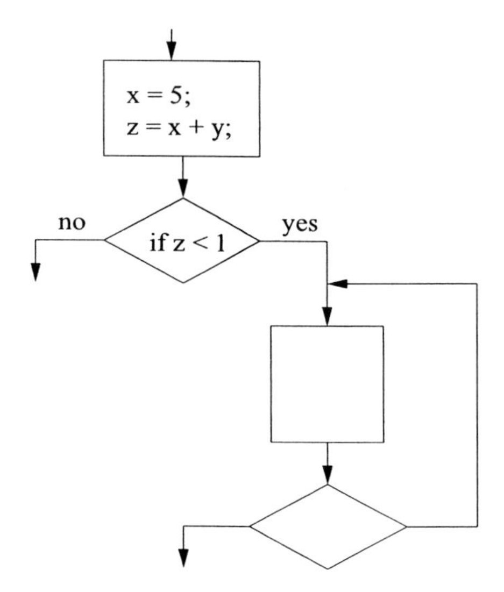

Figure 1. A typical flow chart of a procedural program. Instructions and conditions, where made explicit, should be meant as generic examples.

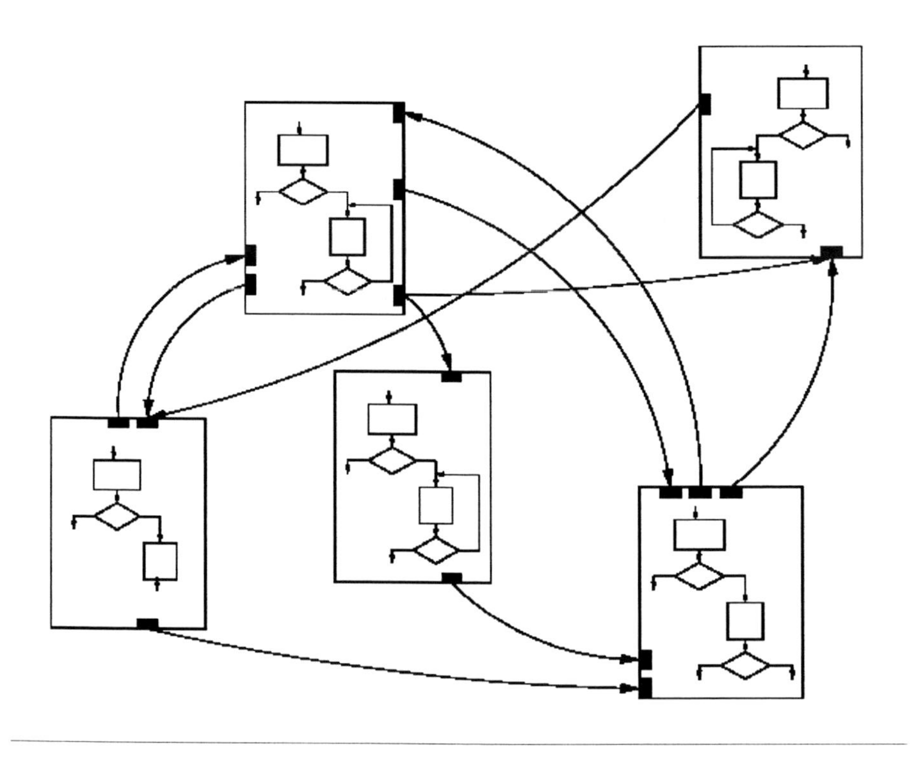

Figure 2. Computational objects (squares) and their relationships (arrows). Methods are denoted by black areas at the borders of objects. At any point in time, the objects are in a certain state of their flow diagram and only some of the depicted relations are taking place. Note that a method may issue/receive a communication to/from several other methods located in different objects.

A parallel may be traced with the behavior of natural beings. The DNA is the analogous of the algorithm that is inside an object. The DNA specifies a substantial part of the behavior of an animal, but not all of it. Even animals with the same DNA such as omozygote twins — natural clones — may behave differently because they make different experiences so their basic algorithm specializes into different responses. In humans, this effect is paramount: Everyone knows that omozygote twins, though identical in appearance, may have very different characters and personalities. Coming back to the context of object-oriented programming, objects with the same algorithm may behave very differently depending on the parameters with which they are initialized and the communications they entertain with other objects.

Object-oriented programming lends itself very naturally to social simulation. In fact, it is straightforward to think of social actors as computational objects. Since computational objects that represent social actors are generally endowed with a substantial degree of autonomy and with sophisticated cognitive abilities, they are generally called *agents*. Hence the expression "agent-based models".

Agent-based models are good at generating emergent macroscopic behavior. Of course, a necessary condition is that microscopic agent behavior is known reasonably well.

Agent-based models are appropriate when aggregate behavior depends on structures of relations, so it cannot be ascribed to a fictitious "representative agent" [26]. Indeed, simple agent-based models have been able to account for the emergence of social phenomena ranging from wealth distribution to the development of national cultures [19]. More flexible than differential equations and yet more precise than verbal descriptions, agent-based models offer to the social sciences a descriptive language that attains sharpness retaining the richness of verbal accounts [24].

Note that, in principle, any agent-based model could be written as a set of differential equations. However, when a system is composed by very many interacting parts, as social systems are, it is extremely difficult for a modeler to oversee all combinations of their dynamics. Agent-based models constitute a bottom-up approach that allows to reconstruct structures of interactions that would not be envisioned otherwise. Thus, the real difference in not in the tool *per se*, but in the psychology of the modeler when using it.

Ultimately, agent-based modelling consists of the idea of a bottom-up description of systems composed by many active and autonomous interacting parts, which is opposite to more traditional top-down descriptions. It is not necessarily linked to the technique of agent-based programming. And as a matter of fact, any model that is written with the idea of describing intelligent agents and letting them interact, rather than describing the macroscopic outcome of their interactions from the outset, may be called an agent-based model. Even if the modeller prefers to describe agent behavior by means of equations rather than by writing computer code.

Agent-based is a modelling philosophy. Object-oriented programming is a technique. It is the technique that best suits the agent-based modelling philosophy, but it is not the only one.

Agent-based models are an instance of the wider class of *connectionist* models. This class includes such diverse models as classifier systems, cellular automata, hypercycle models and neural networks.

All connectionist models share the idea that the interactions between a large number of micro-elements gives rise to complex macro-phenomena. In particular, the elements of agent-based models may be quite complex and "intelligent" on their own. On the contrary, other connectionist models tend to make use of simpler elements and to constrain their interactions to a greater extent.

The vast majority of connectionist models of industrial districts are agent-based models. However, there are also a few models based on cellular automata (2 models), hypercycles (1 model) and neural networks (1 model). Thus, a brief introduction to these branches of the connectionist family may be in order.

Nevertheless, agent-based models are expected to monopolize the scene of connectionist models of industrial districts. Thus, the following scheme illustrates cellular automata, hypercycles and neural networks by means of their differences with respect toagent-based models. Classifier systems have not been included because they have never been used in models of clustered firms.

- Cellular automata are composed by a set of elements in a ordered space, usually a plane, that change their state according to the state attained by the elements in their neighborhood. In general, the neighborhood is either defined as the four or the eight closest neighbors. Roughly speaking, cellular automata may be seen as agent-based models whose agents are constrained to communicate with a fixed subset of other agents and, most importantly, the state of whose agents does not depend on their own past state. Typically, cellular automata are good at describing diffusion phenomena such as growth of cities, herding behavior and sandpiles cascades.
- Hypercycle models are used to model the origin of life. The idea is that a set of chemicals may start a series of reactions that may eventually close in a loop and repeat themselves. If this happens, the process may continue for ever and constitute what we call "life". Hypercycle models may be seen as agent-based models whose agents – the chemicals – have rules of behavior that are extremely simple and sufficiently compatible with one another to form stable loops. Indeed, nothing prevents agent-based models to form hypercycles.
- Neural networks are composed of elements — called neurons — which sum a certain number of inputs by means of proper weights. Eventually, the outputs of some neurons may feed the inputs of other neurons. Some neurons receive exogenous inputs, and some other neurons provide the outputs of the network. Since summation is a many-to-one function (e.g. 5 + 2 = 7 but also 3 + 4 = 7), neural networks provide the same outputs for whole classes of inputs. In other words, they classify exogenous inputs in a certain number of classes. Thus, they can be used to model the classification of stimuli into categories operated by our brains. Since the shape of these artificial mental categories depends on the weights of the neurons, various methods have been developed in order to make them evolve with time. For our purposes, neural networks may be considered as agent-based models where the agents' algorithms consist of summing inputs by means of weights that are either fixed once and for all, or updated depending on communications with other agents and past states.

Axelrod and Tesfatsion [6] is a key reference for readers interested in the wider topic of agent-based modeling in social science. The rest of this review is focused on applications to industrial clusters and districts.

Models of Clusters and Districts

This section reviews the connectionist models of industrial clusters that have been made hitherto. They are few, but they cover most of the issues that are generally associated with clusters and districts. The rest of this section groups them in a few subsections.

The Advantages of Agglomeration

What is the competitive advantage of industrial districts with respect to isolated, vertically integrated firms? How can clusters be economically feasible and even more successful than large firms that exploit economies of scale? This is, obviously, a very basic question.

Brusco, Minerva, Poli and Solinas built a model based on cellular automata loosely inspired by the Carpi (Modena, Italy) apparel cluster [13]. This industrial district is characterized by a large number of very small family firms which can survive periods of low demand incurring a very small loss because most of their workers are the owners themselves. However, the district as a whole is able to mobilize a large productive capacity when demand is high for a particular item. Thus, its competitive advantage lies in its high flexibility with respect to oscillations and shifts of demand with respect to both quantity and features of the goods requested. Cellular automata are good at reproducing the avalanches triggered by a firm that discovered a profitable market niche. Essentially, this model rests on the fact that small flexible firms may be more profitable than large integrated firms if demand is variable enough, particularly in industries where returns to scale do not increase very rapidly with the scale of activity.

Fioretti built an agent-based model of the Prato (Italy) textile district [20]. This district is characterized by fragmentation of the production process, with each firm typically carrying out only one production phase. By making use of data on the number of firms for each production phase, the model reconstructs the structure of interactions that took place in the period 1947-1993. This highlights that while in the 1950s and 1960s the district based its competitive advantage on price competition between a large number of firms, through the 1970s, the 1980s and the 1990s a new structure emerged. A steep increase of the number of firms doing a variety of finishing operations caused the number of qualitatively different cloths to explode. As a consequence of this structural transformation, the Prato district re-directed its competitive advantage on the ability to offer an immense variety of products in a short time and small lots.

Chang and Harrington built an agent-based model of multiunit firms which may either centralize decision-making as traditional hierarchical firms, or decentralize to single units [14] [15]. Though this model has not been designed in order to represent clusters of independent firms, it does deal with the alternative between a large integrated firm and a many small and proximate firms that imitate one another. Chang and Harrington find that centralized decision-making is superior in the short run, particularly if the units operate in similar markets, because best practices are immediately adopted. However, if the units operate in qualitatively different markets a decentralised structure may be superior because it fosters a higher degree of exploration.

Competition, Collaboration and Cooperation

Issues of competition, collaboration and cooperation are key in the debates surrounding industrial districts. Whilst the meaning of "competition" is obvious, the distinction between "collaboration" and "cooperation" is not always clear. Essentially, the expression "collaboration" should be used for all situations where agents do something together and have a material and immediate incentive to do it. For instance, competitors may collaborate within an industrialists union in order to improve the infrastructure of a region. On the contrary, "cooperation" should be used in situations where the prisoner's dilemma applies, i.e. where agents do things together even if they lack an immediate material incentive. For instance, small competing firms may alternatively subcontract one another rather exploiting the whole order. As in the classical prisoner's dilemma, the key to cooperation is repetition of interactions: because both firms repeatedly subcontract one another, if one of them exits the agreement, the other one can retaliate as well. As in the classical prisoner's dilemma, the cooperative equilibrium is superior to the competitive one, because both firms can save the costs of underutilized productive capacity.

Agent-based models have a lot to say on these issues. However, this review does not report on the huge literature of agent-based models of the prisoner's dilemma, but only its applications to the specific context of clustered firms.

Albino, Carbonara and Giannoccaro pointed out that inter-firm cooperation is an essential component of the competitive advantage of industrial districts [2]. Their agent-based model makes this point by means of a comparison with fictitious "super-agents" at various aggregate levels. Though interesting, this is possibly not the most profitable usage of agent-based technology.

Boero, Castellani and Squazzoni [10] [8] [9] constructed an agent-based model where three kinds of producers must combine their operations in order to yield a product that is commercialized by agents of a fourth kind. The cluster of firms undergoes two transitions through three technological regimes. Each regime is characterized by an optimal combination of production factors to be discovered by the producers. The crucial finding is that the final good can be produced at lower costs if the three component producers are in the same technological regime and at a similar stage in the process of discovery of the optimal combination of production factors. Consequently, random market-like search for the best partner may yield inferior results to long-term partnerships.

Allen and McGlade built an early agent-based model of the fishing fleets of Nova Scotia (Canada) that does not employ object-oriented programming [4] [5]. The model reproduces the interplay of fishing strategies, fishing innovations and environmental response. The highest performance is not reached if all ships imitate one the other's behavior, but rather if they pursue complementary cooperative strategies. The study concludes that in order to exploit a complex system, creative exploration and consensual diversity of strategies may be more effective than selfish short-term adaptive reactions [3].

Development Dynamics

Why do industrial districts form, and why do they disintegrate? Birth and death dynamics are crucial to understanding clusters, and the range of problems is probably larger than the number of connectionist models that have addressed this issue hitherto. In particular, there does not exist any connectionist model dealing with the death of industrial districts in countries of early industrialization and the corresponding birth of other districts in newly industrializing countries.

Giaccaria built the only model where an industrial district is modelled by means of a neural network [22]. A set of small firms compete with a large integrated firm for the production of one single good in variable quantities and prices. The small firms, the large integrated firm, a computational agent and consumers are all represented by means of neural networks. Since some of the small firms learn to react in a similar ways, clusters of firms emerge. In particular, Giaccaria investigates the emergence of leader-follower relationships.

Otter, Van der Veen and De Vriend developed an agent-based model where firms and households decide where to locate according to availability of labor, services, natural resources and recreation areas [29]. The model distinguishes between firms operating in heavy industries, in light manufacturing and in services. Both firms and households do not have perfect information but can only observe the agents that are within a visibility range. The authors observed the emergence of clusters of firms and households of various size and composition depending on exogenous parameters as well as the initial configuration.

Padgett, Lee and Collier proposed an hypercycle model of productive systems where goods flow through firms as chemicals through reactors [30]. Eventually, clusters form around production loops, that are reminiscent of Marshallian industrial districts. Interestingly, economies with more than 4 goods require the existence of clusters in order to sustain production.

Page and Tassier developed an agent-based model where local economies are superseeded by chained stores [31]. Chains form because they exploit a niche that is profitable at several locations. Subsequently, wherever they arrive they homogenize the economic structure and beget other chains in other sectors. Thus, the process is cumulative. However, the final configuration is likely to be suboptimal though it is a local optimum in the environment created by the existing chains. Indeed, decay may be the fate of clusters that do not attain world-wide recognition in the globalized economy.

Brenner constructed a cellular automata model of the spread of industrial clusters depending on a number of factors [11]. The model is calibrated on German regions and suggests that industry concentration depends, among else, on the number of spin-offs, on human capital and its spill-overs, on technological synergies and the availability of shared facilities. Brenner and Weigelt calibrated this model on knowledge spill-overs and specific regional features [12].

Innovative Activity

Proximity to partners and competitors provides opportunities for imitation and innovation that constitute a major drive of the success of industrial clusters. Two interesting agent-based models have been developed on this issue.

Gilbert, Pyka and Ahrweiler built an agent-based model of innovation networks [23] [1]. This model wants to capture the observed empirical trend towards more collaborative research efforts in many industries. The authors apply it to biotechnology and other high-tech industries that exhibit clustered collaborative research efforts. Notably, this model applies also to clusters whose components may be geographically distant from one another, which happens e.g. in the software industry.

Zhang built an agent-based model of industrial clusters inspired by the Silicon Valley [36]. Zhang makes the point that firms do not move to industrial clusters, they are born in them. Thus, the main thrust of industrial clusters is that they nurture an entrepreneurial atmosphere. The model creates a dynamics of creation and imitation of firms and generates a distribution of firms size in accord with empirical data.

Policy Making

Finally, agent-based models have been used in order to evaluate the impact of economic policies on industrial districts. Policies may range from the provision of infrastructures to the creation of consortia to setting up a State-owned enterprise. In many instances, policies for industrial districts are joint efforts of Government agencies and private stakeholders.

Squazzoni and Boero, in the first version of the above mentioned model based on inter-firm cooperation, examined the impact of several policies [33] [34]. In particular, they investigated the impact of a consortium that monitors the evolution of markets and technologies or, alternatively, of a research center that develops technologies on its own. According to their model, the impacts of these two institutions are nearly indistinguishable from one another.

Coelho and Schilperoord developed an agent-based decision support system for the management of science and technology parks [16] [17]. This model has been inspired by and has been tested on the Tagus (Portugal) technology park. Firms build networks depending on technological compatibilities and occasions for social meetings, ranging from conferences to occasional encounters in restaurants and cafeterias. Eventually, technological variety and geographical or institutional drives lead to the formation of clusters of tightly networked firms. By experimenting with different occasions for establishing social ties that can be provided by different institutions, a policy-maker is able to run computer experiments that evaluate the outcome of alternative policies.

Applications for Firms

The models reviewed in the previous section have been designed for scientists and policy makers. Agent-based models of inter-firm networks can be useful for firms as well.

In order to be utilized in the daily operations of firms, agent-based models must be very detailed. They must represent the operations that are carried out by the single units within firms and they must be able to coordinate them.

Furthermore, standardization of inter-firm communication protocols is required. The field is still in its infancy, but important steps have been undertaken in the field of textiles <http://www.moda-ml.org> and heavier industries <http://niip.org>.

Software houses are developing proprietary software for consultancy firms, the reliability and depth of which cannot be accessed. The rest of this section is devoted to introduce the only open-source platform for detailed agent-based modelling of real firms. It is the *java*

Enterprise Simulator developed by Pietro Terna at the University of Turin, <http://web.econ.unito.it/terna/jes>.

The *java Enterprise Simulator* (henceforth *jES*) describes the interactions between organizational units that may be production islands or single workers or whole departments or divisions, depending on the level selected for investigation. Furthermore, there may be units that do not belong to any firm, such as contracted workers. Figure 3 illustrates the scene.

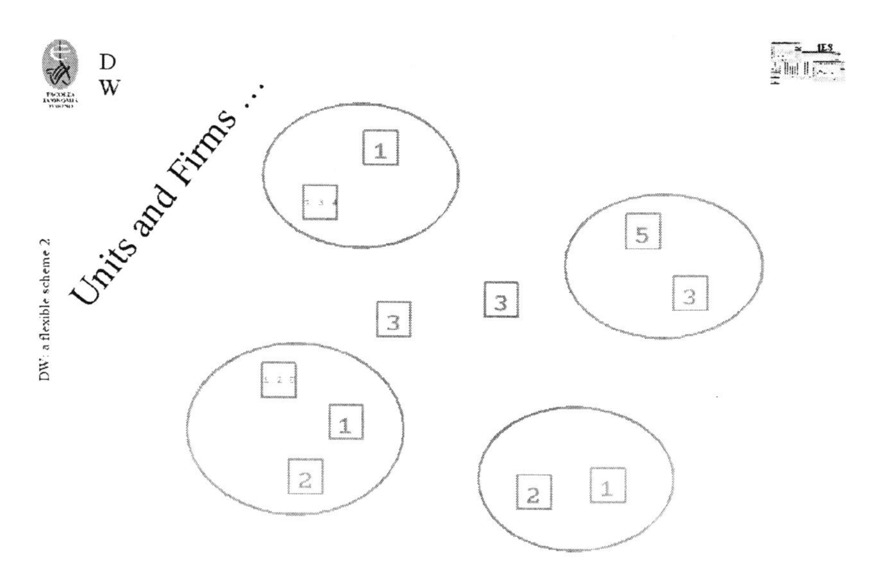

Figure 3. Organizational units and firms in the *java Enterprise Simulator*. By courtesy of Pietro Terna.

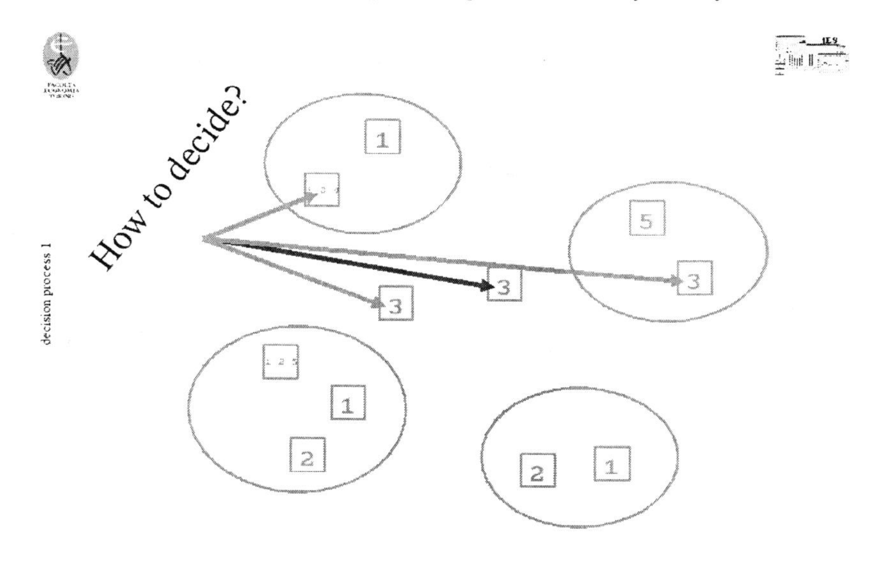

Figure 4. Routing an order that requires step "3" on one of the organizational units that are able to carry it out. By courtesy of Pietro Terna.

The problem is that of routing orders that require a series of steps on units that have different capabilities for each step. Figure 4 illustrates the simplest kind of problem, a situation where step "3" can be accomplished by independent specialized units, by a specialized unit of a firm or by a unit included in a firm which is also able to carry out steps "1" and "4."

In general, problems are more complicated than that. Orders may require specific resources to be procured, or they may entail the possibility of executing one out of several series of steps. Choices may depend on sophisticated algorithms that may require memories of past performances. Outcomes may need to be stored and units themselves may be endowed with warehouses.

The *jES* is able to handle these situations. Orders are modeled as separate objects that are routed by organizational units according to their own behavioral algorithms. Furthermore, a communication matrix specifies which units talk to which other units. This communication structure may represent formal or informal ties as well as collaboration networks within or between firms.

The simulator reconstructs the flows of orders between units and tells decision-makers where the bottlenecks are. Decision-makers may experiment with alternative organizational arrangements and evaluate the costs incurred in each case. For instance, one may evaluate whether it is the case of adding a machine, exchanging internal production with an external partnership or re-arranging the formal hierarchy in order to enforce communication between isolated departments.

Figure 5 illustrates the functioning of the *jES*. Orders implement recipes, which entail instructions regarding what operations should be carried out but no specification concerning which unit will carry them out. This decision is made by the organizational units, assigning e.g. the current step of recipe A (encoded as "101") to unit 2. Depending on the decisions made, the graph on the right of figure 5 illustrates the queues at each unit. Furthermore, detailed outputs regarding costs and proceeds are made available.

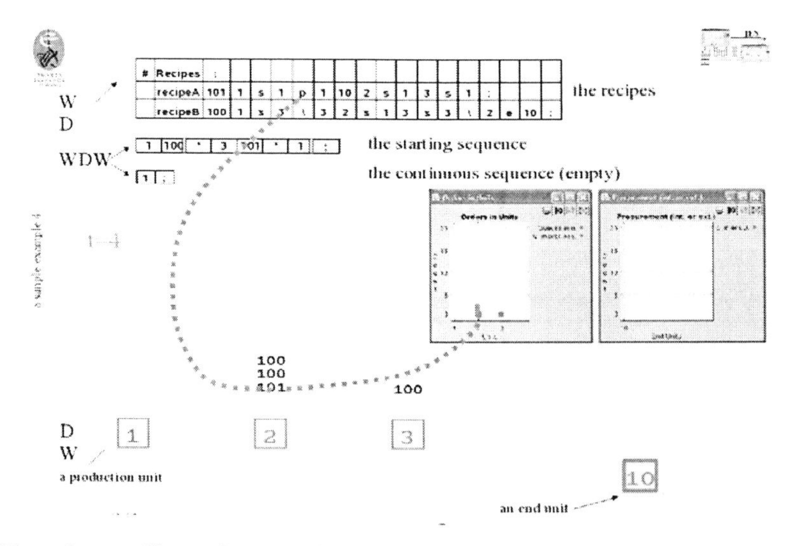

Figure 5. The orders entailing recipes A and B (top) are routed on units 1, 2, 3 (bottom). Eventually, their products arrive at the end unit 10 (bottom right), which may represent a warehouse. The graph on the right illustrates the queues at each unit. By courtesy of Pietro Terna.

It is also possible to explore the evolutionary path of a cluster of firms. Suppose that we are able to specify rules by which firms are started and closed down following an economic performance that depends on their interactions. The simulator *jESevol* allows to reconstruct possible histories of birth, life and death of industrial districts. Figure 6 illustrates a typical simulation step, where stripes denote queues at particular firms and light areas the geographical range where they look for partners.

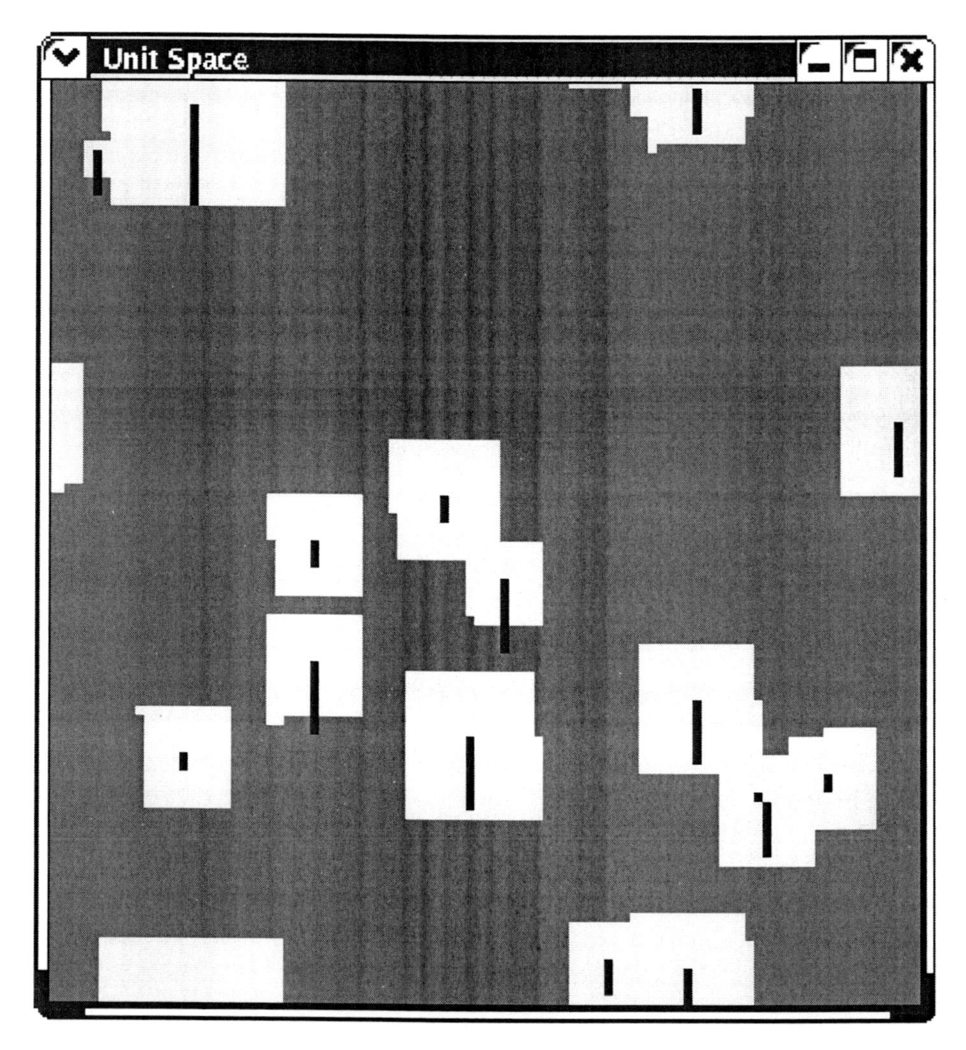

Figure 6. A simulation step of *jESevol*, the evolutionary version of *jES* designed for studying the lifecycle of industrial districts. By courtesy of Pietro Terna.

Detailed agent-based models developed on simulators such as the *jES* provide a bottom-up perspective that complements the top-down approach of models based on differential equations. In fact, bottom-up agent-based models allow to explore the state space that is actually spanned by an organization, possibly discovering configurations that had gone unnoticed from a top-down perspective. The strength of agent-based models of real organizations is that, typically, managers end up with saying, "I would have never thought that *this* could happen!" Indeed, the practical value of agent-based modelling is its ability to produce this sort of emergent properties.

THE CONCLUDING REMARK: TRY IT!

The field of connectionist models of social organisms is burgeoning, it is novel and it is still largely unexplored. In particular, connectionist models of industrial clusters offer an unparalleled tool to understand a fundamental organizational structure of many national productive systems.

Agent-based models are probably the most appropriate connectionist model in this particular field. It is not difficult to become acquainted with this technique, which can be mastered at several levels.

Agent-based models are most easily written in object-oriented languages such as *SmallTalk*, *Objective C* and *Java*. Eventually, a platform may aid the construction of an agent-based model. In general, the more a platform simplifies the construction of a model, the more it constrains it. Therefore, the most user-friendly platform are not appropriate for large empirical agent-based models.

The following list includes the most common non-commercial platforms for agent-based simulation. More comprehensive evaluations of simulation platforms can be found in specialized publications [18] [35]; in particular, a commented list of simulation platforms is available at <http://www.econ.iastate.edu/tesfatsi/acecode.htm>. As a general rule, it is wise to make oneself acquainted with several tools.

Swarm <http://wiki.swarm.org> is the least user-friendly, least constraining platform. It provides the modeller with template structures for building a model, graphical interfaces, random numbers generators and other facilities. Essentially, textitSwarm is a collection of libraries written in *objective C*. *Java* interfaces are available, so models can be either written in *Java* or *objective C*.

JAS (Java Agent-based Simulator) <http://jaslibrary.sourceforge.net> offers the same template structures as *Swarm* making use of *Java* libraries developed for other purposes. Ranks equal to *Swarm* in the trade-off between user-friendliness and programming-freedom, and requires *Java* programming. Potentially, it may capture the interest of the free-software community.

SDML (Strictly Declarative Modelling Language) <http://sdml.cfpm.org> checks the consistency but does not require completeness of logical statements. This might be useful in order to model real-world decision-makers. *SDML* differs in many respect from other platforms, which is its both a weakness and a strength. It requires writing code in its own language, derived from *SmallTalk*.

MADKit (Multi-Agent Development Kit) <http://www.madkit.org> is a platform designed for modelling organizational structures of agents. Agents may be programmed in *Java*, *Jess* or *BeanShell*.

RePAST (Recursive Porus Agent Simulation Toolkit) <http://repast.sourceforge.net> is a *Swarm*-like but more user-friendly platform, explicitly designed for social simulation. Obviously, it is a bit more constraining than *Swarm*. It requires writing in *Java*, *C++* or other languages.

Ascape <http://www.brook.edu/es/dynamics/models/ascape> has been used to make many early social agent-based models, such as *SugarScape*. It requires the basics of *Java* programming, but a number of libraries facilitate the programmer's work. Ovbiously, the usual trade-off between user-friendliness and programming-freedom applies.

NetLogo <http://ccl.northwestern.edu/netlogo>, an offspring of *StarLogo*, is the most user-friendly and most constraining platform. The model builder is required to write pieces of code in a simple procedural language, which these platform combines into an agent-based model. Of course, the drawback of user-friendliness is that the model builder has very little freedom. This platform should not be used for anything beyond very simple models of agents moving on a surface.

PS-I (Political Science – Identity) <http://ps-i.sourceforge.net > is a very user-friendly platform expecially designed to build models in Political Science. Within established Political Science theories, it offers wider possibilities than *NetLogo*.

The most constraining, most user-friendly platforms are generally inappropriate for large empirical models, but they are sufficient to build toy models that may provide interesting insights. However, the reader should be aware that toy agent-based models are being made since several decades. The space of abstract concepts has been largely explored, and those who criticize the connectionist paradigm rightly point to the paucity of empirical and applied models. The next frontier, the challenging task for inventive researchers, consists of getting down to reality.

REFERENCES

[1] Petra Ahrweiler, Andreas Pyka, and Nigel Gilbert. Simulating knowledge dynamics in innovation networks (skin). University of Augsburg, Department of Economics, working paper n.267, 2004.

[2] Vito Albino, Nunzia Carbonara, and Ilaria Giannoccaro. Coordination mechanisms based on cooperation and competition within industrial districts: An agent-based computational approach. *Journal of Artificial Societies and Social Simulation*, 6(4), 2003. <http://jass.soc.surrey.ac.uk/6/4/3.html >.

[3] Peter M. Allen. Evolving complexity in social science. In Gabriel Altmann and Walter A. Koch, editors, *New Paradigms for the Human Sciences*. Walter de Gruyter, Berlin, 1998.

[4] Peter M. Allen and Jacqueline M. McGlade. Dynamics of discovery and exploitation: The scotian shelf fisheries. *Canadian Journal of Fishing and Aquatic Science*, 43:1187–1200, 1986.

[5] Peter M. Allen and Jacqueline M. McGlade. Modelling complex human systems: A fisheries example. *European Journal of Operations Research*, 30:147–167, 1987.

[6] Robert Axelrod and Leigh Tesfatsion. A guide for newcomers to agent-based modeling in the social sciences. In Kenneth L. Judd and Leigh Tesfatsion, editors, *Handbook of Computational Economics, Vol.2: Agent-Based Computational Economics*. North-Holland, Amsterdam, 2005. Forthcoming.

[7] Giacomo Becattini. The marshallian industrial district as a socio-economic notion. In Frank Pyke, Giacomo Becattini, and Werner Sengenberger, editors, *Industrial districts and inter-firm co-operation in Italy*. International Institute for Labour Studies, Geneva, 1990.

[8] Riccardo Boero, Marco Castellani, and Flaminio Squazzoni. Cognitive identity and social reflexivity of the industrial district firms: Going beyond the "complexity effect" with agent-based simulation. In Gabriela Lindemann, Daniel Moldt, and Mario Paolucci, editors, *Regulated Agent-Based Social Systems*. Springer, Berlin, 2004.

[9] Riccardo Boero, Marco Castellani, and Flaminio Squazzoni. Labor market, entrepreneurship and human capital in industrial districts. an agent-based prototype. In Roberto Leombruni and Matteo Richiardi, editors, *Industry and Labor Dynamics: The Agent-Based Computational Approach*. World Scientific, Singapore, 2004.

[10] Riccardo Boero, Marco Castellani, and Flaminio Squazzoni. Micro behavioural attitudes and macro technological adaptation in industrial districts: an agent-based prototype. *Journal of Artificial Societies and Social Simulation*, 7(2), 2004. <http://jass.soc.surrey.ac.uk/7/2/1.html >.

[11] Thomas Brenner. Simulating the evolution of localised industrial clusters –вЂ“ an identification of the basic mechanism. *Journal of Artificial Societies and Social Simulation*, 4(3), 2001. <http://jass.soc.surrey.ac.uk/4/3/4.htm l>.

[12] Thomas Brenner and Niels Weigelt. The evolution of industrial clusters –вЂ“ simulating spatial dynamics. *Advances in Complex Systems*, 4:127–147, 2001.

[13] Sebastiano Brusco, Tommaso Minerva, Irene Poli, and Giovanni Solinas. Un automa cellulare per lo studio del distretto industriale. *Politica Economica*, 18:147–192, 2002.

[14] Myong-Hun Chang and Jr. Joseph E. Harrington. Multimarket competition, consumer search, and the organizational structure of multiunit firms. *Management Science*, 49:541–552, 2003.

[15] Myong-Hun Chang and Jr. Joseph E. Harrington. Organization of innovation in a multiunit firm: Coordinating adaptive search on multiple rugged landascapes. In William Barnett, Christophe Deissenberg, and Gustav Feichtinger, editors, *Economic Complexity: Non-linear Dynamics, Multi-agents Economies, and Learning*. Elsevier, Amsterdam, 2004.

[16] Helder Coelho and Michel Schilperoord. Intersections: A management tool for science and technology parks. In *Proceedings of the XX IASP world conference on science and technology parks*. 2003.

[17] Helder Coelho and Michel Schilperoord. Intersections: experiments and enhancements. In Helder Coelho and Bernard Espinasse, editors, *Proceedings of the 5th workshop on Agent-Based Simulation*. SCS Publishing House, Erlangen, 2004.

[18] Julie Dugdale. An evaluation of seven software simulation tools for use in the social sciences. Technical report, IRIT, COSI project, 2000. Training tool.

[19] Joshua M. Epstein and Robert Axtell. *Growing Artificial Societies: Social Science from the Bottom Up*. The MIT Press, Cambridge (MA), 1996.

[20] Guido Fioretti. Information structure and behaviour of a textile industrial district. *Journal of Artificial Societies and Social Simulation*, 4(4), 2001. <http://jass.soc.surrey.ac.uk/4/4/1.html >.

[21] Masahisa Fujita, Paul Krugman, and Anthony J. Venables. *The Spatial Economy: Cities, Regions and International Trade*, chapter XVI. The MIT Press, Cambridge (MA), 1999.

[22] Paolo Giaccaria. Modellizzazione di un distretto industriale mediante simulazioni fondate su agenti. *Sviluppo Locale*, 4:131–171, 1997.

[23] Nigel Gilbert, Andreas Pyka, and Petra Ahrweiler. Innovation networks –вЂ“ a simulation approach. *Journal of Artificial Societies and Social Simulation*, 4(3), 2001. < http://jass.soc.surrey.ac.uk/4/3/8.html >.

[24] Nigel Gilbert and Pietro Terna. How to build and use agent-based models in social science. *Mind & Society*, 1:57–72, 2000.

[25] Paul Krugman. *Geography and Trade*, chapter II. The MIT Press, Cambridge (MA), 1991.

[26] David A. Lane. Artificial worlds and economics. *Journal of Evolutionary Economics*, 3:88–107, 177–197, 1993.

[27] David A. Lane. Complexity and local interactions: Towards a theory of industrial districts. In Alberto Quadrio Curzio and Marco Fortis, editors, *Complexity and industrial clusters: dynamics and models in theory and practice*. Springer, Berlin, 2002.

[28] Alfred Marshall. *Principles of Economics*, chapter X. MacMillan, London, 1890.

[29] Henri ë tte S. Otter, Anne van der Veen, and Huib J. de Vriend. Abloom: Location behaviour, spatial patterns, and agent-based modelling. *Journal of Artificial Societies and Social Simulation*, 4(4), 2001. < http://jass.soc.surrey.ac.uk/4/4/2.htm l >.

[30] John F. Padgett, Doowan Lee, and Nick Collier. Economic production as chemistry. *Industrial and Corporate Change*, 12:843–877, 2004.

[31] Scott E. Page and Troy Tassier. An ecological model of chains. University of Michigan, Center for Political Studies, working paper, 2003.

[32] Michael Porter. *The Competitive Advantage of Nations*, chapter IV. MacMillan, The MIT Press, 1990.

[33] Flaminio Squazzoni and Riccardo Boero. A computational protyotype of industrial districts. University of Brescia, Department of Social Studies, working paper, 2001.

[34] Flaminio Squazzoni and Riccardo Boero. Economic performance, inter-firm relations and local institutional engineering in a computational prototype of industrial districts. *Journal of Artificial Societies and Social Simulation*, 5(1), 2002. < http://jass.soc.surrey.ac.uk/5/1/1.html >.

[35] Robert Tobias and Carole Hoffmann. Evaluation of free java-libraries for social-scientific agent based simulation. *Journal of Artificial Societies and Social Simulation*, 7(1), 2004. < http://jass.soc.surrey.ac.uk/7/1/6.html >.

[36] Junfu Zhang. Growing silicon valley on a landscape: an agent-based approach to high-tech industrial clusters. *Journal of Evolutionary Economics*, 13:529–548, 2003.

INDEX

A

B

C

D

E

F

G

H

I

S

T

U